# CONCEPTS AND SCHEMATA

# Concepts and Schemata

## An Introduction

ROBERT W. HOWARD

CASSELL

Cassell Educational: Artillery House, Artillery Row, London
SW1P 1RT.

Distributed in North America by Taylor and Francis Inc.,
242 Cherry Street, Philadelphia, PA 19106–1906.

British Library Cataloguing in Publication Data

Howard, Robert W.
   Concepts and schemata : an introduction.
   —(Education)
   1. Concepts
   I. Title   II. Series
   153.2′3     BF311
ISBN 0–304–31370–X

Phototypesetting by Phoenix Photosetting, Chatham
Printed and bound in Great Britain by Mackays of Chatham Ltd.

Last digit is print no: 9 8 7 6 5 4 3 2 1

# Contents

Preface · vii

1 Concepts 1
Introduction 1
Some uses of concepts 6
Some major questions about concepts 13
Plan of this book 16

2 Some more preliminaries 17
Introduction 17
Some basic terms 17
Types of concept 23
Some methods of studying concepts 25

3 Schemata 30
Introduction 30
Some uses of schemata 37
Types of schema 45
Disadvantages of schema use 50
The relationship between concepts and schemata 51

4 Some characteristics of concepts 53
Introduction 53
Some concepts represent basic-level categories 53
A concept's exemplars may vary in typicality 58
Some category boundaries are unclear 62
Some concepts may be understood through metaphors 67

5 The organisation of concepts and schemata in semantic memory 74
Introduction 74
Some characteristics of semantic memory 75
Theories of semantic memory 77

6 Theories of category representation 85
Introduction 85
The nature of representation 86
The classical view 90

The prototype view     93
The exemplar view     100
Which view is correct?     103
Educational implications     106

7 Some ways in which concepts are acquired     107
Introduction     107
Acquisition from instances     108
Acquisition through language     113
Individual differences     116
Why do we acquire the concepts we do?     118

8 Concept and schema development     122
Introduction     122
Concept development in general     124
Concept development in children     130
Theories of cognitive development     132

9 How to teach concepts I: the traditional procedure     136
Introduction     136
Some preliminaries     139
The actual presentation     145
Evaluation of concept learning     147
A sample concept lesson     149
Two modifications of the basic procedure     151

10 How to teach concepts II: some new techniques and implications
    of recent research     155
Introduction     155
Educational implications of some concept characteristics     156
Teaching concepts with metaphors and analogies     163
Concept mapping     169
Ensuring that concepts are well-retained     172

11 Schemata and teaching     175
Introduction     175
Some general applications to teaching     176
Teaching abstract schemata     179
Changing students' existing schemata     185

References     200

Index     211

# Preface

This book provides a general introduction to the field of concepts and schemata, intended mainly for student and practising teachers and for undergraduate psychology students. Its major aims are to give a broad understanding of the two notions, of why they are so important in education and psychology, and (for teachers) a lot of practical advice on how to actually teach them. The few introductory books available in this area in my view do not meet these goals sufficiently to be of much use to students. Though the bulk of work in teaching consists of getting pupils to learn new concepts and schemata and how they relate to each other, there is little material available to really help accomplish this task. In addition, the few practical books available are now out of date. Recent research and theorising in education and cognitive psychology has led to a revolution in understanding of concepts, which has many implications for classroom teaching. This book summarises some major applications and gives two new procedures in addition to the traditional attribute definition method of concept teaching.

Finally, I would like to thank several persons who aided in the production of this book, notably Juliet Wight-Boycott and Debbie Fox at Cassell and four anonymous reviewers who commented on the manuscript.

# Chapter 1

# Concepts

SUMMARY

1.  A concept is a mental representation of a category, which allows a person to sort stimuli into instances and noninstances.
2.  Concepts can be formed by abstracting information from instances.
3.  Concepts have many uses. A major one is to reduce the complexity of the world to manageable proportions. They also enable us to make inferences and solve problems.
4.  How one looks at the world depends on one's concepts, thus they are of fundamental importance in education. Much education involves teaching concepts that people can use to more fully understand the world and deal with it.
5.  Some major questions about concepts under investigation include: why we have the ones we do, how they are learned and how they should be taught, and what information they hold and how they develop.

## INTRODUCTION

This chapter introduces the concept of *concept*. It begins by discussing why we need concepts to survive and gives some examples of concepts. Then follows a discussion of the importance of abstraction in concept learning and a detailed definition of *concept*. Finally, some important uses of concepts are described, followed by a discussion of some important questions about concepts that researchers have asked.

### Why we need concepts

Consider the major problem that a doctor in general practice faces every working day. Hour after hour, a procession of patients, who are suffering from a variety of ailments, comes through the office. The first patient might complain of mild fever, muscle aches and general weakness, a second of insomnia, and a third of headaches. There is an enormous variety of possible symptoms and a vast number of further signs that the doctor's own observations and various laboratory tests will pick up. Symptoms vary greatly in severity and site and laboratory tests have varying degrees of accuracy. So, each patient's troubles are in some sense unique. The problems affecting one patient are different to those of another. Yet, from a mass of information, the doctor has to come to a decision about each case and perhaps prescribe the treatment of it. How is this problem solved? What allows the doctor to make some sense of this wealth of detail and prescribe antibiotics for one case, exercise and a special diet for a second, order an emergency entry to hospital for a third, and dismiss a fourth as a malingerer?

The doctor's problem is a small-scale version of the general problem we all face. The complexities of the world we live in extend beyond the domain of human illness; we are continually bombarded with a bewildering array of sensory impressions. Each impression is unique, just as each patient's troubles are unique. No plant, animal, noise, dwelling, human face, or episode of eating in a restaurant is quite the same as any other. Also, we see the same objects at different angles and distances. Yet, like the doctor, we have to make sense of and bring some order to these situations, otherwise we are unable to behave adaptively, and, like a quack doctor, will behave erratically.

An analogy to science fiction illustrates the importance of adaptive behaviour. Explorers on an alien planet will find that for a period of time, the stimuli in the new environment are unique. The explorers have little idea of what is safe or dangerous other than from rough analogies to their 'Earth' experience (e.g. large animals with sharp teeth are more dangerous than small animals). Therefore, the explorers do not behave adaptively and, consequently, their numbers are reduced. Their survival chances depend on finding some way to make sense of the alien world so that they can act adaptively and find some way of coping with the environmental diversity. These principles apply in the situation where a person moves from one cultural background to a quite different one. The person must somehow make sense of the different actions of the people, who often seem offended by seemingly innocuous remarks and who behave, to the newcomer, in inexplicable ways.

The doctor and other people, too, solve this problem of enormous environmental diversity by forming and using *concepts*. A concept is a mental representation of a category, which allows one to place stimuli in a category on the basis of some similarities between them. Lumping stimuli together by using a concept allows new stimuli encountered to be responded to as class members rather than as unique. Thus, one's past experience in dealing with other category members suggests how to act with this new one. For example, the doctor has a large and well-organised set of disease and person concepts acquired in medical school and in general practice. Each category has an associated set of likely symptoms, a particular cause if known (e.g. a certain virus, bacteria, trauma), a likely time course, and a likelihood of affecting certain types of people (e.g. the elderly, males of Mediterranean descent). Each category also has an associated treatment(s). The category system, then, allows a doctor to simplify the enormous diversity of symptoms and signs. Patients are categorised by using the doctor's concepts, and they are then treated on the basis of their category membership. How to behave adaptively with each patient is then suggested by the category membership. With time and experience, the concept system is further refined. The doctor learns about variations in the symptoms of particular diseases and becomes more adept at categorising patients. He or she also acquires another system of concepts that is used to categorise patients into such classes as the stress-prone, the naturally healthy, the hypochondriacs, and those people who are unlikely to follow his instructions.

Like the doctor we use concepts to deal with the world. We categorise our experience to bring order to it. Otherwise we would have to treat every stimulus encountered as unique. We would always be tied to our immediate situation, being unable to use our past experience in our assessment of the present. The world would be a confused, unanalysed set of stimuli. We might thus treat a lion as a lamb, a shark as a swordfish, and a snake as a worm. Consider how maladaptive a member of society would be if that member lacked any person concepts. There would be no differentiation between an adult and a child, a Nobel Prize winner and an Andean peasant, and a superior and a subordinate. A salesperson who did not categorise customers and tailor both goods shown and salespitches accordingly would soon go out of business.

Here are some further examples of our need for concepts. Consider the concept of *shark*. The category 'shark' includes a variety of individuals, differing in size, colour, degree of ferocity, etc. If while swimming, a person sees a large creature swimming towards him, his concept of that creature is very useful. By categorising the fish as a shark, it can be treated according to its category membership. The person knows that it is possibly dangerous, that it may attack, but that it will not come up on land. So, a course of action is suggested – leaving the sea immediately.

Another example is the concept of *predator*. Consider the following: lion, tiger, spider, polar bear, shark, swordfish, and piranha. They differ in many ways. They differ in size and appearance. Some have scales and fins, and others have hair and legs. They behave differently. Some swim about, others prowl vast land territories, and one waits patiently in a web. They occupy different habitats. Some live on land, two in oceans, and one in the rivers of South America. Yet they can be grouped together in the predator category on the basis of some similarities between them. They all hunt prey and are carnivorous. Having a concept of predator can be very useful, because a wide variety of different species can be treated alike (rather than as unique). They can each be treated as members of the predator category.

An example of a more complex concept is a particular artistic style. After a stroll through an art gallery, one may notice that certain paintings have commonalities of style (Farah and Kosslyn, 1982). In some undefinable way, some paintings seem similar to each other, and one may form a concept of a particular style. New paintings can then be recognised as falling into a particular style category: *Impressionist, Romantic* or *Modernist*. It is often hard to specify just what the similarities are, however. Such style categories also occur in the domains of clothing, sculpture, music, handwriting, poetry and literature (e.g. Hartley and Homa, 1981).

Even animals form and use concepts. The lowly pigeon can acquire such concepts as *person* (Herrnstein and Loveland, 1964), *man-made object* (Lubow, 1974), *oak leaf* (Cerella, 1979), *fish* (Herrnstein and de Villiers, 1980) and *same* and *different* (Malott and Malott, 1970).

## Abstraction

A fundamental aspect of concepts is that they are generally *abstractions* from experience. To abstract is to take out the essentials (or one or more important aspects) of something and to ignore the remainder. Thus, a student may abstract the essential points of a lecture and write them in a half-page of notes or the essence of a poem or novel in a few lines. A skilled mediator may get to the heart of a dispute, sweeping away all the extraneous verbiage, the emotion and the side issues. Abstraction is also a standard device in satire. The satirist gets to the bare essentials of a target situation by stripping it of all pretences, symbols and extraneous words. A related device is to abstract out and greatly exaggerate some aspect of the target. The film *Zelig* satirises our tendency to conform to other individuals and to group norms. The hero literally turns into a member of the particular ethnic group of the person he is talking to. Similarly, an impressionist may satirise a person by abstracting out and exaggerating a few characteristic expressions and gestures.

A concept usually consists of information abstracted from experience, and, therefore, much data about the members may be lost. For example, when forming the concept *predator*, one abstracts out a few similarities, such as 'hunts prey' and 'has sharp teeth', while ignoring a mass of other information, such as habitat, appearance, and behaviour. Figure 1 presents a schematic example. It presents a miniature perceptual world that consists of ten figures. Try grouping them into two categories. One way is to place A, B, F, G and I into one category and the rest in another. One does so by abstracting out the common feature of the first five stimuli – a straight edge. In forming the concept, much information about the figures is lost.

Abstraction to form a concept can be carried out in two major ways (Mervis and Rosch, 1981). The first way is that used in Figure 1 and in the *predator* example above: one takes out one or more common features and uses their presence in new stimuli to categorise them as instances (members of the category). The concept then consists of a set of such common features. The second way is to create some combination of new information not actually present in any particular stimulus. Thus, an idealised concept of *bird* is created by assimilating many typical bird features, such as 'gets about in the daytime', 'flies', 'has a beak and feathers', etc. However, no single real bird may have all these features. To categorise such a given stimulus as a bird or not a bird, the stimulus is compared to the idealised abstraction. In medicine, some disease concepts appear to be idealised abstractions. The doctor may know a long list of possible symptoms that no one patient will have all of. To categorise a given patient as a sufferer, doctors compare their symptoms to the idealisation. If they are sufficiently similar, the diagnosis is made. In this sense too, one can understand the old cliché, 'More X than the X', (e.g. more French than the French). A person's concept of *French person* may consist of a set of features that no real French person has, yet a foreigner may seem more similar to the idealisation.

### The concept of concept

Earlier, 'concept' was defined as a mental representation of a category. The definition can be expanded upon. A category is a class that stimuli are placed in according to some similarities. A concept is something in a person's head that allows him to place stimuli in or out of the category (Anglin, 1977). Thus, the category consists of the stimuli in the outside world and the concept of information in memory. As an illustration, take the category 'dog'. This category includes all real and imaginary dogs in the world, while my own concept *dog* is an idea that allows me to class various animals as dogs. It is important to realise that the two are not the same. A category is distinct from a concept. If I have only ever experienced a beagle, a basset and a poodle, my concept of dog

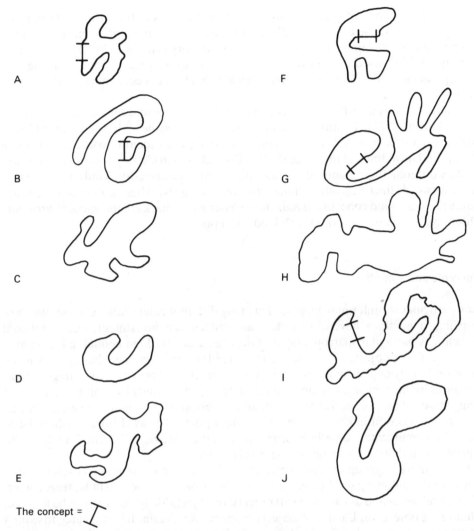

**Figure 1.** A schematic example of abstraction from experience to form a concept. A, B, F, G and I share a common feature and we can abstract this feature and use it to categorise the stimuli. The 'concept' might then consist of a mental image of the straight line feature. Any new stimulus encountered can be placed in or out of the category by seeing if it has the straight line feature.

would not include knowledge of any other dogs, and I might not categorise Great Danes as dogs upon encountering them. The concept also might include much more knowledge than that simply needed to categorise instances (Anglin, 1977). Thus, a person's concept of dog may include much data about their lifespans, habits, evolutionary ancestry, etc. as well as his emotions towards them.

It should be noted that 'concept' is quite a vague term with many different definitions and uses (Flavell, 1970; Sigel, 1983). (The above definition of concept as a mental representation will be used in this book.) Sometimes 'concept' is used synonymously with 'category' and with 'word'. In developmental psychology, 'concept' is sometimes used to refer to a competency or an ability to do some esoteric task. Thus, a child is said to have the concept of 'conservation', 'class inclusion' or 'transitivity' (Farah and Kosslyn, 1982). These concepts really refer to an ability to manipulate information but can be seen as reflecting a representation of a category (Halford, 1982). In daily life, 'concept' is often used to refer to an idea, e.g. 'Today we present some startling new concepts in fashion!', 'This new washing machine is a brilliant concept years ahead of its time'.

Finally, there is a distinction between *identity* concepts and *kind* concepts (Clark, 1983; Anglin, 1977). Identity concepts pertain to the same object seen at different angles, orientations and distances. Thus a person has an identity concept of his dog Rover, his Uncle Jim and the space shuttle 'Columbia'. An identity concept is necessary to place different impressions of the same object into one category. Kind concepts place at least two distinct individual things into one category. Thus, a dog and a cat are instances of the kind concept *animal*, and a spider and a shark are instances of *predator*. This book is mainly concerned with kind concepts.

**Concepts and stimuli**

Any particular stimulus may be placed in many different categories. A house may be a dwelling, a home, a haven, a burden, an obstacle, an investment, and a national treasure. A particular sparrow may be categorised as a bird, an animal, a life form, a danger, a flying object, a nuisance, and a breeder. How we may classify on a given occasion largely depends on our objectives at the time. Hawks may be categorised as nuisances by chicken farmers, but as interesting objects of study by ornithologists, or, if being attacked by one, as dangers. Similarly, a person may categorise in a certain way on a given occasion in order to communicate a point. To say 'I invited a Marxist to dinner' communicates something different than the statement 'I invited a relative to dinner', even though the same person is referred to.

Furthermore, a group of stimuli can usually be categorised in many different ways. Consider the following set: broom, cat, housefly, wineglass, door, nebula, tree, comet. They could be classed as hard and soft objects, or objects likely/not likely to be found in a house, or objects on Earth and objects in space, etc. Again, how we categorise on a given occasion depends on our purposes. Indeed, we often form *ad hoc* concepts to categorise objects for a certain purpose (Barsalou, 1983). Barsalou gives such examples as: *things to take on a camping trip, things to sell at a garage sale*, and *foods not to eat on a diet*. Because ad hoc concepts are formed to achieve a certain goal (e.g. losing weight), they are not as well-established in memory as more familiar concepts, such as *fruit* and *dwelling*.

Finally, categories may or may not be mutually exclusive. Thus, a person can only be male or female, or moving or still. However, a human can be a mammal, an extrovert, a salesperson, and a guitar player.

## SOME USES OF CONCEPTS

Concepts have many important uses. Here are some major ones.

**Making sense of the world**

This use was mentioned at the beginning of this chapter. Concepts enable us to make enough sense of the world to behave adaptively. We split up the infinite complexity of the environment into categories, perceiving the stimuli as category members rather than as unique impressions. Thus, we see sameness instead of boundless diversity. This use is important and requires expansion here.

How we look at the world depends on the concepts we know and use in order to understand it. Different people hold quite different concepts and thus look at aspects of the world in different ways. Consider, for example, a hypothetical uprising by some people in a small South American nation and the ways in which the event could be viewed. A Marxist holds such concepts as *class, exploitation of the workers,* and *revolution*, and may use them to understand the uprising. His interpretation may be that the exploited workers have spontaneously risen up against the oppressive ruling class in an attempt to throw off the imperialist yoke. A right-wing conservative, however, holds and uses a quite different set of concepts and may interpret the same event as a few Communist agitators stirring up the contented population against its lawful, democratic government in order to advance monolithic world Communism. A businessman may simply see the event as a threat to trade. Indeed, Beck (1976) argues that many problems in life are due to certain people holding and understanding the world with very idiosyncratic concepts, e.g. the depression-prone person often sees the world as a hostile, dangerous place, and he feels he has little effect on it. A trivial event, such as a shoelace snapping or mild disapproval from another (which most people would class as unavoidable trivialities), may be regarded as deadly serious and send the person into a deep depression. The susceptibility to depression may vanish when the maladaptive concepts are replaced. Indeed, successful psychotherapy can teach a new set of concepts that induces the person to see the world, his life history, and his difficulties quite differently, which stimulate him to more adaptive behaviour.

It should be stressed that the world can be viewed in many different ways, according to each person's set of concepts. Another example is the domain of illness. Western medicine, until recently, was based on a purely mechanical model. The human body was seen as a machine that sometimes went wrong because of external causes, such as trauma or micro-organisms. Disorders were seen as mechanical problems to be fixed by prescribed procedures. However, this completely mechanistic model is giving way somewhat. It is becoming clear that such factors as social support and mental attitude have much to do with health, which the purely mechanical model cannot explain. A positive mental attitude, for instance, may lessen the probability of contracting cancer, or speed up recovery from certain disorders.

The Western system of disease concepts is not the only way to look at the domain of illness. Traditional Chinese medicine provides a quite different conceptual framework. A major concept is *chi* – a life energy that flows around the body. Physical disorders, it is believed, result from disruption of the flow at various points in the body. Treatment, in part, is based on restoring the natural chi flow. Acupuncture is one method of restoration.

Another example is *land*. To westerners, land is a commodity that can be owned by individuals and that is sold or used. To most individuals, land is important but has no great spiritual significance. Such a concept of land is incomprehensible to the Australian

Aborigine. Land cannot be owned by individuals and it has much spiritual and mystical significance.

Indeed, a new concept that provides a new way of looking at the world can change the course of history, as using it induces people to act differently. Such concepts as *Marxism, Islam, Feminism, divine right of kings, constitutionalism* and *open classroom* induce people to see the world in new ways and adapt their actions accordingly.

For this reason, concepts are of fundamental importance in education. A major goal of most instruction is to teach students a set of new concepts that they can use to better understand and thus better deal with some stimulus domain. For instance, the expert physicist holds a well-developed set of concepts, while the layperson does not. The physicist's understanding of and ability to deal with the physical world is therefore much more substantial. A major goal of physics education is to teach students the physicist's set of concepts and how it should be used. Medical courses aim at teaching students the system of disease concepts and how this system should be used, as well as specific medical skills. Courses in literature teach such concepts as *archetype* and *satire*; in music, they teach concepts such as *leitmotif, sonata form, counterpoint, harmony* and *key*. These concepts enhance the students' appreciation of existing works and help them to produce better works themselves. Therefore, a great deal of classroom and textbook instruction involves teaching major concepts, how they relate to each other, and how to use them. Education is largely a process of teaching students conceptual frameworks that they can use to better understand and deal with the world, and also use to learn more about it. Educators should not simply provide countless loosely related facts and figures to be memorised and soon forgotten (Skemp, 1979; Pines and Leith, 1981).

## Allowing inferences

This function is closely related to the above one. One reason why concepts help people to make sense of the world is because they allow people to make inferences. For example, if an object is categorised as a dog, many inferences about it can be made – it probably barks, it has a heart and lungs, it probably has an owner, and it has a lifespan of ten to twenty years. By categorising a person as an extrovert, one can infer that he is likely to be very sociable and enjoy parties, like excitement and dislike being alone. In medical diagnosis, as previously mentioned, as soon as a patient's disorder is categorised, the doctor is more knowledgeable about the illness. (In practice, there is likely to be some interaction between the processes of categorising a stimulus and making inferences about it, as Smith and Medin (1981) note. Thus, before classing a person as an extrovert, we may note that he likes parties and excitement.) Categorisation also tells us what a stimulus is not, since many categories are mutually exclusive. In other words, a stimulus that is an instance of one cannot be an instance of another. If we class a large object on the horizon as a cloud it tells us that it is not alive, it does not have a heart, and it does not have a motor.

A striking example of the importance of knowing useful concepts in order to make inferences comes from the cargo cultists of New Guinea. During the Second World War, the Allies built many airfields on the island to fly in supplies for the troops. How did the planes and supplies come to arrive? Because of a well-developed concept system, a Westerner knew that the goods had to be manufactured, ordered and delivered. The concepts *manufacture* and *order* allow reasonably accurate predictions about when goods will and will not arrive. But many locals were not aware of these concepts and, therefore, could not make sound predictions. They cut out airstrips in the jungle, built ramshackle huts, donned homemade uniforms copied from those of the soldiers and waited for goods-laden planes to arrive.

The ability to make inferences also allows us to store information economically in memory – preserving cognitive economy. For instance, if we know that furniture is often found in buildings and that armchairs, desks and stools are exemplars of furniture, then we can infer that each of these items is likely to be found in buildings. If we know that mammals have hearts and that cats and chimpanzees are mammals, we can infer that they have hearts. If we know that an instance of *speaker of German* knows many words of the language, knows its grammar and can converse with other instances, we can preserve cognitive economy by recalling that Heidi is a speaker of German. It is not necessary to remember that she can do all of the above independent of being in the category. This cognitive economy also allows people to communicate easily with each other. Rather than stating, 'Heidi knows many German words; Heidi knows German grammar, etc.' a person can say, 'Heidi speaks German'.

Making inferences can have a dark side, however – social stereotyping (Anderson, 1980). In this situation undue inferences, based on a person's group membership, are made. A person's concept of *black* may include such traits as lazy, superstitious and poorly educated. Any black person encountered is ascribed these traits, regardless of any evidence to the contrary. The problem is, of course, that such stereotypes can be quite inaccurate and therefore they should not be applied indiscriminately. Occasionally, however, such stereotyping can be more amusing than sinister. A colleague of mine was once victimised when trying to pick up some letters from a post office at a seaside town. He arrived to collect them clad in a T-shirt, faded jeans and with bare feet. The clerk duly handed over some letters but refused to surrender one because it was for *Doctor* X. Her stereotype of *doctor* did not allow for such an instance as my colleague.

## Allowing concepts and stimuli to be related through taxonomies and partonomies

A taxonomy is a tree-like structure whereby concepts are related to each other by class inclusion. Figure 2 presents two examples. The first is a fragment of the *object* taxonomy. At its top is *object*, a very abstract concept that subsumes many others. Thus, objects can be divided into *living* and *non-living* – divisions that are usually seen as mutually exclusive. These concepts can in turn be divided and divided again. Thus, each concept in a taxonomy subsumes those directly below it. Therefore, *animal* subsumes *reptile* and *penguin*. Any instance of reptile or penguin is an animal and living. Each class is included in those above it and each is thus 'nested' (is part of) in the categories above. Each taxonomy works horizontally as well as vertically. The vertical dimension delineates the increasing level of abstraction, and the horizontal one includes mutually exclusive categories at the same level of abstraction. In Figure 2, the vertical dimension for the *literary work* taxonomy goes from *novel, fiction* and *prose*.

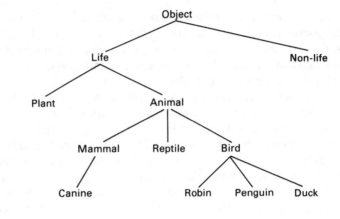

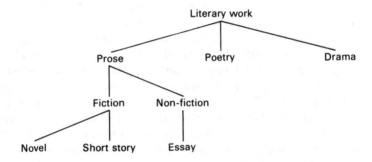

**Figure 2.** Two examples of taxonomies. The most abstract concept is at the top and all directly below it are component concepts.

Knowing the taxonomy allows useful inferences. If we know that robins are living and that terrestrial living objects are based on the DNA molecule, then we can infer that robins are too. Similarly, the relation between concepts is identified. *Plant* and *animal* are related as both are *living; reptile* and *bird* are related as both are types of *animal; essays* and *stories* are both types of *prose*.

In most academic fields such taxonomies are of fundamental importance. They identify and organise the phenomena that the discipline deals with. The concepts within that discipline can be related to each other and predictions can be made. A major goal in a science's early stages is to construct a useful taxonomy so that scientists can make sense of and organise their subject matter. The basic question then is often, 'What is the best way to classify these phenomena?' (Sokal, 1974). Students must be able to master and use the taxonomy.

Figure 3 presents two fragments of scientific taxonomies. The first is from psychiatry. It is used to categorise mental disorders. The practising psychiatrist sees people with a wide range of difficulties, including hallucinations, repetitive rituals and paranoia, and a loss of interest in life. Like the doctor of physical medicine, the psychiatrist must bring some order to the complexities of people's symptoms in order to guide treatment. The psychiatric taxonomy is revised every few years and its validity is debatable. However, it is an attempt to make some sense of a very complex set of phenomena. At its top is *mental disorder*, which is subdivided here into *neurosis* and *psychosis*. The main feature of neurosis is great anxiety, which is coped with by various aberrant methods. Psychosis is much more serious, and is characterised by disorders of thought and/or emotion. Neurosis has many sub-categories. *Obsessive-compulsive* neurosis (characterised by unwanted repetitive rituals and thoughts) is one. Two categories of psychosis and three of *schizophrenia* are shown. Schizophrenia is characterised by thought disorders, withdrawal from other people and hallucinations, and it has many sub-categories. The geology taxonomy is probably more familiar. Again, geology students need to learn the taxonomy and how to use it in order to categorise rocks.

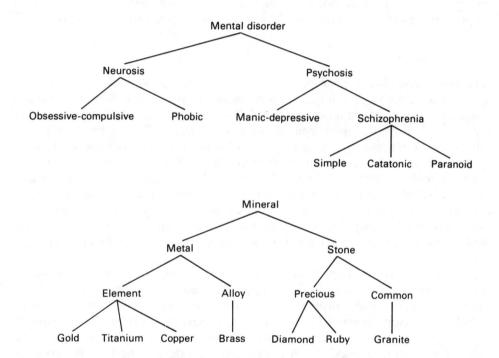

**Figure 3.** Two fragments of scientific taxonomies. The first is from psychiatry and the second from geology.

A related structure is the *partonomy*, which is discussed in more detail in Chapter 3. Concepts in a partonomy are linked by a part-whole relation rather than class inclusion. For example, consider the concepts *eye, nose, lips* and *forehead*. These are all parts or components of *face*. *Face* in turn is part of *body*, which is part of *humanity*. The relation between *face* and *body* is part/whole, which is different from class inclusion. Thus, robin is not part of *bird*, it is an instance of it. On the other hand, *face* is not an instance of *body*, it is part of it.

All the concepts a person knows ultimately connect to each other in a maze of taxonomies, partonomies and other structures. All this knowledge constitutes a person's *cognitive structure*, which is examined in more detail in Chapter 5.

**Forming and understanding propositions**

A proposition is a statement that is composed of two connected concepts saying something about the world and that is true or false. Here are some examples:

Some trees have leaves.
Some fish live in rivers.
Some books are stored in libraries.

Each involves two object concepts (*tree* and *leaf*; *book* and *library*), which are linked by the verb. Much of our knowledge appears to be stored in memory and communicated to others as propositions. Long sentences and larger text segments, such as paragraphs, can be analysed into propositions, and many scientific laws are formulated as propositions. Examples are the law of conservation of energy and Boyle's law.

**Solving problems**

A problem exists when a person has a goal but no obvious way to reach it. Examples are 'getting rich', 'building a bridge', 'sending an astronaut to Mars', 'writing a pleasing symphony' and 'defeating an enemy army'. We use concepts to deal with the myriad problems of daily life, work and of scientific research. Once a problem is well categorised, often one is a long way toward solving it. Consider the example of medicine. Essentially a patient presents the doctor with a set of symptoms and says, 'Here is a problem. Solve it.' The doctor tries to solve it by categorising it, which then suggests a solution. Similarly, an engineer uses concepts such as *material* and *stress* to build a bridge and ensure it stays up, an architect uses concepts such as *building style* and *use* to design a building, and a business manager uses concepts such as *supply and demand, product, cost-effectiveness* and *competition* to solve the problem of staying in business.

   A good way to see the importance of concepts in problem-solving is to compare the concept systems of experts and novices. Experts are usually much more adept solvers. Thus, the expert computer programmer is better able to solve programming problems with clear, concise programs than the novice. The doctor of 20 years' experience is usually better at diagnosis than the new graduate. Why are they better? Studies suggest that experts have better organised concept systems and are better at using them. For example, Chi *et al* (1981) compared the categorisation of physics problems by experts and novices. The novices tended to categorise them by common terms in their wording and other superficial features, while the experts used the principles of physics needed to solve them. Thus, problems 1 and 2 might be put in one category because the law of conservation of energy was needed to solve them, while 5 and 7 would go into another because Newton's third law was needed. Johnson *et al* (1981) found that expert doctors have both a well-organised set of concepts and excellent cross-referencing between the categories. Leinhardt and Smith (1985) found that expert teachers of fractions had a richer and more elaborate set of concepts for the problems of fractions than novice teachers.

   Again, the educational importance of concepts is highlighted. Courses in medicine, computer programming, engineering, management, etc. largely aim at turning out graduates who are able to solve problems in that field, for which they need to learn and use the field's concepts and principles.

**Learning new concepts**

Just as having money allows a person to use it in order to make more, so knowing some concepts enables him to use them to learn more. Ausubel (1968) details some ways to acquire new concepts from old. For instance, an existing concept can be split into two or more concepts: *shirt* into *T-shirt* and *collar shirt*. One can abstract the similarities between *car, bicycle* and *aeroplane* to form *vehicle*. Another way is conceptual combination, which is putting together two or more concepts to create a new one (Osherson and Smith, 1982). Thus *pet* and *fish* can be combined to form *pet fish*. The new category is a sub-set of the other two. Thus, *pet fish* includes some, but not all, fish and some, but not all, pets. Further examples are *socialist state, free university* and *federal politician*. A person's ability to deal with the world is thus enhanced by the acquisition of more concepts. As a child gets older, concepts are learned more and more from existing ones (Ausubel, 1968).

## SOME MAJOR QUESTIONS ABOUT CONCEPTS

Every science has some basic questions to answer. Physicists ask about the fundamental structure of matter, biologists ask how life began, about the mechanisms of evolution and why one cell in a developing organism becomes, say, a neuron and another a skin cell. Astronomers ask about the origin and structure of the universe, about the evolution of stars, and how the planets were formed. Scientists hope that research will ultimately answer such questions and that the answers will build a general theory that can answer any other questions concerning the field that are raised. The theory will consist of a set of interrelated concepts. (The questions scientists ask may change with time, but this issue is not pursued here. See Kuhn 1962 and 1970.)

Psychologists and educators have many questions about concepts to answer. Some questions are very general and their answers can only be speculated upon at present. Some more specific research questions will be described in later chapters. Some important questions about concepts are detailed below.

**Why do we have the concepts we do?**

People from very different cultures are likely to carve up much of the world in much the same way. Berlin (1978), for example, found that quite disparate cultures had fairly similar taxonomies of *plant* and *animal*. Why do we form the concepts we do and not others? What makes us categorise the world in such a way that some uniformity across cultures exists? Why divide up stimuli into *objects* and *events, living* and *non-living things, trees* and *shrubs* and *moving* and *non-moving things*? Why select some bases for categorisation and not others?

Until fairly recently, this question hardly arose (Rosch, 1978). Which concepts we formed were considered completely arbitrary – the product of accident. As we will see, however, recent research suggests otherwise. Those we form may be determined by several factors. Rosch (1978) gives an amusing example of the lack of arbitrariness in our concept systems by the following absurd case of an arbitrary scheme:

On those remote pages it is written that animals are divided into (a) those that belong to the emperor, (b) embalmed ones, (c) those that are trained, (d) suckling pigs, (e) mermaids, (f) fabulous ones, (g) stray dogs, (h) those that are included in this classification, (i) those that tremble as if they were mad, (j) innumerable ones, (k) those drawn with a very fine camel's hair brush, (l) others, (m) those that have just broken a flower vase, (n) those that resemble flies at a distance.

Borges (1966)

What principles make this scheme seem silly and the systems we do have seem sensible?

### Do taxonomies have basic-levels?

A related question is whether a particular level of abstraction on a taxonomy is more useful (more basic) than the others. Is any one level more important, or are they all equally useful. Consider the object taxonomy in Figure 2. Is the *plant/animal* level or the *mammal/reptile/bird* level more useful than the others?

### Do instances of a concept vary in the extent to which they are good exemplars?

Are all instances of a concept equally good? Is a penguin or an ostrich just as good an exemplar of *bird* as a robin or finch? Or, can instances be ordered in terms of the extent to which they are typical instances?
   A related question is whether the boundaries between concepts are clear-cut or not. Is it always clear that a given stimulus is in or out of a certain category? As we will see, many categories seem to have unclear borders. An example is *life*. The border between *life form* and *non-life form* may seem clear-cut but, in fact, it is not. Viruses have some properties of *life* and also some of *non-life*, and biologists are unsure which category to place them in.

### How are concepts acquired and how should they be taught?

How are we able to form concepts so that we can segment the world up and treat different stimuli alike? How do we acquire our concepts? The answer to this question is of great practical value. As we have seen, much of the content of any discipline consists of concepts and the relations between them. Students need to learn the concepts and how they relate to each other in laws, taxonomies and theories and how to use them to solve problems. We can also ask what factors slow down or speed up acquisition and why some individuals learn particular concepts more easily than other people. The practical question 'How should concepts be taught?' breaks down into the following points, listed by Cohen (1983):

1.   How best to present a concept so that the learner can readily understand it.
2.   How to ensure that the learner's concept corresponds to the teacher's. If, for example, a student acquires such concepts as *command economy*, *quark* or *sonata form*, how does the teacher ensure that the student's understanding of a concept is much like the teacher's?

3.   How to make sure that the concept is related to others in a taxonomy, can evolve with experience, is readily used to solve problems and is well-remembered.

## How are categories represented in memory?

Most recent psychological research on concepts has aimed to answer this complex question. To understand it and its importance, the term 'representation' needs to be discussed. The term is vague and is used in different ways (Mandler, 1983; Palmer, 1978). A certain definition will be used in this book. This topic is treated in more detail in Chapter 6.

A representation can, for now, be defined as a relation between two things such that one stands for the other. Thus, a legislator represents his voters' interests, an ambassador his government and a cartoon caricature a person's outstanding features. Thus, there are two things of interest: the one represented (the voters, the government and the person) and the one that represents it (the legislator, the ambassador and the cartoon). The latter captures or models some aspects of the former (Palmer, 1978). Thus a painting represents some aspects of a landscape and a cartoon some aspects of a person. The term 'representation' is also used in another sense. It refers to the thing doing the representing. Thus, the painting and the cartoon are representations of the landscape and the person.

One can look at the relation between the world and the mind as a representation. Our minds model or represent some aspects of the world and we manipulate the representations. Chess players can plan far ahead from a current board position, because they can represent the piece arrangement in memory and work on it to see the results of certain moves. We call that representation 'knowledge' and its manipulation 'thinking'.

Parenthetically, mental representation can be divided into *procedural* and *declarative* knowledge. The distinction is between knowing *how* and knowing *that*. Procedural representation pertains to actions, such as playing tennis or typing. It is greatly resistant to forgetting. We never forget how to ride a bicycle, or how to type. Declarative pertains to facts. We know *that* Buenos Aires is the capital of Argentina or that a robin is a bird. However, such facts can be easily forgotten.

When a person learns to categorise new stimuli as instances of *triangle, bird, command economy* or *reinforcer*, he retains what in memory allows such classification. In what form is the information stored? When a person spends an afternoon at an art gallery and can afterwards identify impressionist paintings, what knowledge has been retained? In other words, what knowledge does a concept hold and in what form is it stored? The question is worth asking, for how concepts are learned and used, and how they evolve and are related to others depend on how they are represented.

## How does conceptual structure develop?

A newborn child has few concepts that humans need to understand and behave adaptively in the world. Yet, over some 16 or 18 years, the child grows from a creature knowing little to a complicated creature who knows numerous concepts, principles, theories and taxonomies. How does this complex structure evolve from such seemingly humble beginnings? How does a child learn the meanings of the many words he knows? Does a young child represent categories like adults, or does the representation format change over time as Jean Piaget and Jerome Bruner have suggested (see Chapter 8)? The question has great practical importance. Firstly, if children do represent categories quite differently, then perhaps teaching should be tailored accordingly. Secondly, an accurate picture of conceptual development will suggest the ages at which important concepts should be taught. A major problem in education is timing. Teaching important concepts before children are ready to learn them can both waste time and resources and can cause much frustration in learners.

A closely related question is how a particular concept or set of concepts evolves with experience in adults (Homa *et al*, 1979; Homa, 1984). Concept learning is never really complete. Concepts continually change, as we saw earlier with the doctor's system. For example, a 17-year-old schoolgirl addicted to Mills and Boon romances is apt to have a somewhat different concept of *marriage* than a 60-year-old veteran of three divorces. A biologist will have a much richer concept of *life* or *tree* than a layperson, and an astronomer has a more developed concept of *the universe* than a student. How does further experience cause concepts to evolve, and how can such evolution be encouraged in students' concepts?

## PLAN OF THIS BOOK

The rest of this book is largely organised around answering these questions. After some preliminaries in Chapter 2, Chapter 3 introduces the closely related notion of *schema*. A schema is a set of related concepts. Chapter 4 then looks at the questions of whether taxonomies have a basic-level, instance typicality and concept borders. Chapter 6 looks at the question of category representation and Chapter 7 at how concepts are learned and why we acquire the ones we do. Chapter 8 looks at concept development and Chapters 9, 10 and, to some extent, 11 look at how concepts should be taught.

## FURTHER READING

Introduction to concepts and concept uses: Anglin (1977), Bolton (1977), Stones (1984), Ausubel (1968).
Questions about concepts: Rosch (1978), Mervis and Rosch (1981).

# Chapter 2

# Some More Preliminaries

SUMMARY

1. Words are labels for concepts and a word's meaning is the attached concept. Thus, a word is distinct from a concept.
2. Generalisation is evidenced by responding similarly to two dissimilar stimuli and discrimination by responding differently to two stimuli. Both are very important in concept learning.
3. A variety of terms that are important in this book are discussed.
4. There are many types of concept, including object and event, concrete and abstract, well-defined and ill-defined, and conjunctive and disjunctive. A concept can be made up of perceptual, functional and/or relational features.
5. Concepts can be ordered along dimensions, such as abstract to perceptual.
6. Concept structure and concept learning can be studied by various methods, ranging from intuitions about language to various experimental procedures.

## INTRODUCTION

This chapter is largely an annotated glossary. It covers some major terms and methods used in the rest of the book. First, some basic terms are discussed and, then, some types of concept and methods of studying concept structure and learning are covered.

## SOME BASIC TERMS

### Concepts, words and word meanings

These three terms are often used synonymously, but some distinctions between them can be made. The following discussion borrows largely from an analysis by Carroll (1964) and Clark (1983) and is pursued further in Chapter 5.

### Concepts*

Chapter 1 defined 'concept' as a person's representation of a category. That representation allows instances to be categorised and contains all the knowledge a

---

* Concepts are italicised throughout this book.

person has about that category. Such a concept is *idiosyncratic*. One person's knowledge of a given category will not be quite the same as someone else's. People have different experiences with exemplars and different ways of integrating new and existing knowledge. The newly qualified doctor's concept of *measles* will differ somewhat from the seasoned general practitioner's, and the new army recruit's concept of *war* will differ from that of the veteran of many campaigns or the German military expert Clausewitz's concept of *war*. Carroll gives the further example of *several*. To some people it refers to two or three, to others five or ten, and yet to others to fifteen or twenty. The number referred to also may vary with context. Similarly, an American's concept of *democracy* will differ greatly from that of someone living in, say, the Soviet Union. Communist nations often refer to themselves as 'democratic' (German Democratic Republic, Democratic Kampuchea), but it is fair to suggest that members of such governments have a different concept of democracy than many Westerners. Similarly, concepts evolve continually, which, again, leads to individual differences.

The differences between various individual's concepts are probably much less marked with concrete ones like *red, table* and *cloud*. Indeed, every culture is likely to have a somewhat similar concept of *star*. However, there will be differences. An astronomer will see a star as an unimaginably distant gas ball, while an ancient Greek might have seen it as a speck splattered on one of the celestial spheres.

*Words*

A word is not a concept. A word is a symbol that labels a concept. Concepts are personal, idiosyncratic and subject to much variation. Words are perceptual invariants, generally spoken and written in much the same way in a particular community. Words are physical entities that speakers of a language learn to perceive and produce. They call concepts to mind, or allow people to communicate concepts to others, e.g. 'Danger!' 'Help!'. Usually the word has an arbitrary relation to the concept it names, with a few exceptions such as 'boom' and 'hiss'. As with a person and his name, the two are distinct. One may know a person's name, yet know virtually nothing about him.

The difference between concepts and words can be clarified by noting that the same concept can be named by many different words. For example, *person* may be named 'human', 'homo sapien', and 'member of the human race'. *Ending* can be named 'termination', 'finish' and 'close', not to mention foreign-language terms such as 'finis'. In addition, many concepts have no names. While a culture tends to name important concepts, many are left unlabelled. An art critic may have an un-named concept of an artistic style, a salesperson may have an un-named concept of a type of customer who responds best to a certain pitch, and magazine editors may have an un-named concept of a type of humour their readers like. Indeed, as discussed in Chapter 8, the pre-verbal child knows many concepts. Education involves not just learning new concepts but also attaching names to ones already known.

Similarly, the same word can name many different concepts. Thus, the word 'club' can refer to an organisation one joins, a suit in a pack of cards and a weapon used to threaten rivals. The word 'form' can refer to a printed sheet, the general shape of some object, a verb synonymous with 'to make up', and the current performance level of a competitor. Often we can only determine the concept a word names by its context.

Some more examples may make the distinction clearer. The well-known novelist Arthur Koestler put it well, 'My concept of a "gene" or of a "seductress" or of

"President Eisenhower" is certainly not the same as it was ten years ago, though the verbal label attached to each of these concepts has remained the same.' 'Meat' used to refer to any food at all. Just a few decades ago, 'progress' (applied to a society) to most Westerners referred to advances in technology and the erection of more factories, buildings and highways. Indeed, at primary school in the 1960s, I was often shown films depicting a new road being constructed through a wooded area. Trees were felled, people were forced to relocate and there was much more traffic, noise and pollution. This sort of construction was presented as a fine exemplar of progress. However, by about 1970, many took 'progress' to mean quite the opposite – advances in technology created more problems than they solved.

### Word meanings
There is no general agreement on the meaning of 'word meaning'. Workers in different disciplines (and within them) have different notions of what the term means (Clark and Clark, 1977; Macnamara, 1982). Most agree that a word *has* a meaning and, therefore, a word and a meaning are different things (Engelkamp, 1983). In psychology, 'meaning' is often taken to refer to the concept associated with a word (Carey, 1982; Macnamara, 1982), and to avoid complexities beyond the purposes of this book that definition is used throughout.

### The value of naming concepts
Naming concepts is very useful and some further uses are described in Chapter 7. Skemp (1971) lists some reasons why. First, as mentioned earlier, naming a concept allows one to communicate it to others. Second, names may promote concept learning. A child who hears the name 'fraction' or 'propaganda' in the presence of various stimuli may try to work out their similarities and form a new concept.

## Discrimination and generalisation

Both these phenomena are important in concept learning. After defining them, their value is described.

### Discrimination
To discriminate between two stimuli is to tell them apart and to respond differently to them. A child who calls one figure a triangle and another a square is discriminating between them. Such discrimination is essential for survival. Animals must discriminate between safe and dangerous places, ripe and unripe fruit, and between parents and other members of the species (Riley, 1968). People must discriminate between red traffic lights and green ones, socially acceptable times and places for certain acts and unacceptable times and places, and between superiors and subordinates. Failure to do so often has severe consequences.

### Generalisation
Generalisation can be seen as the inverse of discrimination. To generalise is to respond in a similar way to two or more discriminably different stimuli. A child who learns to fear and avoid a large dog after a painful bite may generalise the avoidance to other dogs

as well. After learning to drive one car, a person can usually generalise the knowledge to other cars. People do not need to re-learn the task with each new car.

If generalisation did not occur there would be no point in learning anything. As mentioned in Chapter 1, the same stimulus is never exactly repeated, therefore it is necessary to continually generalise. Indeed, lack of generalisation can be a problem in behaviour therapy (Stokes and Baer, 1977). A client may learn some new skills or get rid of a phobia, but the knowledge may not extend outside the therapy room. The skills can seemingly disappear and the phobia re-emerge. Over-generalisation can also occur. Children go through a stage in which they over-generalise the meaning of some words. Classic examples are when babies or young children refer to all men as 'Dada' or all vehicles as cars.

*Importance in concept learning*

To learn a given concept, it is necessary to both discriminate and generalise. People must discriminate between instances and non-instances, common features and irrelevant ones, and between one category and another. Some new concepts may be formed by evaluating the presence/absence of just a single feature. Thus, *equilateral triangle* and *non-equilateral triangle* may be formed from *triangle* by discriminating the presence/absence of three sides of equal length. Generalisation is also important. People must generalise among stimuli to form certain concepts. A child must generalise the similarities between squares, triangles and trapezoids to form the concept of *polygon*. The learner also must generalise from the specific stimuli from which the concept was formed to the new stimuli.

The extent or pattern of over and under-generalisation is an important diagnostic tool in teaching, as explained in Chapter 9. Both over and under-generalisation may tell the teacher just what concept a student has acquired and what further training is needed. A student who sees *primate* as a concept that only includes monkeys needs experience with a wider range of exemplars. A student who believes a *square* to be any four-sided figure needs experience with such non-exemplars as non-square rectangles and parallelograms.

## Exemplars/instances

As mentioned in Chapter 1, these are stimuli that belong to a particular category. Stimuli are instances, because they are perceived as similar in some way. Square and triangle are instances of *geometric figure*, object of *thing*, beagle and poodle are instances of *dog*, measles and mumps of *disease*, and eating out and birth of *event*.

A given category can have any number of instances. Some concepts such as *moon of the planet Mercury* and *pig in space* at present have no real instances (Klausmeier *et al*, 1974). *Earth Moon* has one and *former US President still living* at present has a handful. *Nation* has less than 200 instances, and *molecule, grain of sand, leaf* and *moment* have an enormous number.

A concept's instances can vary greatly in perceived similarity. A concept such as *book* or *person* has instances that, to most people, look much alike. However, *life form* is a much more diverse category, ranging from gorilla, whale and fungus to bacteria. The apparent similarity of such instances depends on the sensory systems of the perceiver.

To human beings, *mammal* seems a quite diverse category, including such varied creatures as mouse, lion, ape, dolphin and whale. Yet, to the humble tick, the category has no diversity at all (Herrnstein and de Villiers, 1980). Ticks can only distinguish non-mammals from mammals by the presence of butyric acid, which mammals exude, so a whale would be just the same to a tick as a shrew or sheep.

Finally, exemplars of a concept can themselves be concepts. Instances of *animal* such as dog and primate are themselves concepts with a variety of instances. Thus, the concept of *dog* includes the beagle, terrier and poodle, which, in turn, have various dogs as exemplars.

## Features/attributes

A concept may consist of a variety of features, which are its parts (Ellis *et al*, 1979). For example, exemplars of *square* have such features as 'four sides of equal length' and 'four internal right angles'. Instances of *bird* have such features as a beak, feathers and the ability of female specimens to lay eggs. One of the features of instances of *predator* is 'hunts prey'. Figure 4 indicates some features of various concepts.

There are many types of feature, three of which are particularly important (Glass *et al*, 1979). The first is *perceptual*. Perceptual features are clearly obvious to our senses. Perceptual features of *bird* include a beak, feathers and the abilities to sing and fly. The second type is *functional*, which reflects the use to which an exemplar can be put (Labov, 1973). A functional feature of *cup* is that it can hold liquids, of *chair*, that it may be sat upon, of *weapon*, that it can be used to attack or defend, and of *dwelling*, that one can be lived in. (There is usually some correlation between functional and perceptual features, however, summarised in the saying, 'form follows function'.) Many abstract concepts seem to be based on functional features. Instances of *vehicle, weapon*, and *furniture* often have just their shared function in common. The third type of feature is *relational*. This type reflects a relationship between two things. Kinship concepts are familiar examples. An *uncle* is someone who has a sibling with a child, an *orphan* is a child whose parents are dead, and an *author* is the writer of a book. Such concepts as *higher* and *perpendicular* are based on a relationship between two things. Many school-taught concepts are based on relational features (Carroll, 1964). Finally, a given concept may be based on just one of the feature types or a combination of the three.

Features also fall into three more important categories. First, features of a given concept may be *defining*. A defining feature is one that an instance must have to be an exemplar. For example, 'has three sides' is a defining feature of *triangle*. Any geometric figure without this feature cannot be a triangle. Similarly, 'hunts prey' is a defining feature of *predator*. The second type is *characteristic* (Rips *et al*, 1973). Many instances of a concept have such a feature, but not all of them do. A stimulus does not have to have a particular characteristic feature to be an instance. For example, 'can fly' is a characteristic feature of *bird*, because most birds can fly, but not all of them do. Salespeople tend to be extroverts, but not all of them are. The distinction between defining and characteristic is not absolute and might be better thought of as a continuum rather than a dichotomy. The final type is *irrelevant*. These features are not relevant in determining if a stimulus is an exemplar or not. Size, for example, is an irrelevant feature in determining whether a figure is a square or a triangle. Native continent and

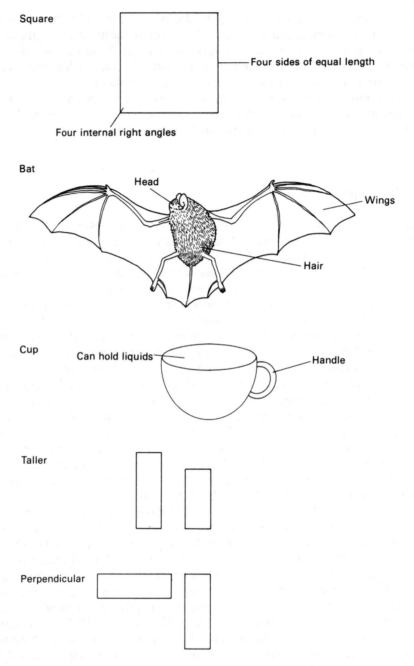

**Figure 4.** Some examples of features of various concepts.

hemisphere are irrelevant features in deciding whether an object is a plant or animal, and colour is irrelevant in deciding if an object is a book.

Finally, features can themselves be considered as concepts. Thus, 'red', 'large', 'extroverted' and 'flies' can be features of some concepts and also concepts themselves.

## Dimensions

Instances of a concept may also vary along different dimensions. Some examples were given above. Exemplars of *mammal* vary in size, appearance, predacity etc. Instances of *occupation* (such as doctor or lawyer) vary in status and in the amount of training required in order to become a member of that occupation. Some dimensions are more salient than others. Status is a very salient dimension of *occupation*, and size and predacity are salient dimensions of *animal* (Smith and Medin, 1981).

## TYPES OF CONCEPT

Concepts can be divided into a number of types. However, there is no universally recognised taxonomy. Perhaps there never will be. Concepts are like people in this sense. People can be categorised in many different ways (tall/short, educated/not educated, interesting/uninteresting, blonde/redhead/other), and how we categorise on a given occasion depends on our purposes. For example, a doctor might categorise patients mainly by their disorder and age, an immigration officer might categorise by nationality, visa status and presence/absence on a wanted list, and an employment counsellor might categorise by occupation. Here are some useful categories of concepts.

### Object and event

Object concepts represent some physical thing at some location in real or imaginary space. Examples are *planet, microbe, tree, car, galaxy, horse, unicorn, troll* and *virus*. Event concepts pertain to time. They represent a particular class or sequence of events. Examples are *hour, holiday, geological age, lifetime, eating out, having a baby* and *running*. Some event categories are represented by *scripts*, because they constitute a more or less fixed sequence of events (see the following chapter). Object concepts have been studied much more than event concepts.

### Eight parts of speech

One can divide words up into eight classes: noun, verb, adjective, adverb, pronoun, preposition, conjunction and article. It can be argued that these words label different types of concept (Carroll, 1964). Thus, nouns name object and event concepts, prepositions label concepts of relative position, etc.

### Concrete and abstract

This distinction is known by several names: simple/complex, non-verbal/verbal and perceptual/abstract (Cohen, 1983). It is perhaps better considered a continuum than a dichotomy. Concrete concepts are very closely tied to our perceptions. They arise from direct experience. Examples are *red, table, tree* and *dog*. Little abstraction is needed to form them and their instances can usually be readily visualised. Abstract concepts are much harder to so pin down, because they are largely divorced from experience. Their component features may be quite obscure and variable to different people. Some examples are *justice, freedom, genius, art, truth, beauty,* and *representation.* What are the defining features of *genius,* for example? Which instances of artistic, literary or scientific work qualify as exemplars and which features determine their category membership? People are likely to disagree on the answers.

Abstract concepts are often built up from complex concepts (Cohen, 1983). An example is *democracy.* A thorough understanding of this concept requires the knowledge of component concepts, such as *government,* the *social contract,* the *rule of law, will of the people,* etc., each of which is itself a complex concept. Indeed, many school-taught concepts are quite abstract, which is one reason why students find some hard to learn. The subject of mathematics, for example, is based on a progressive accumulation of abstract concepts from component concepts. Students who do not grasp an important component concept often get lost as a result (Skemp, 1971).

A complex type of abstract concept is the *proverb,* which defines a category with countless exemplars (Honeck *et al*, 1985). One example given is, 'a net with a hole in it won't catch any fish'. Two instances are 'the sleeping guard did not hear the thieves' and 'the missionary who did not speak the natives' language converted no one'.

Many abstract concepts can only really be acquired through language. Words are needed to both define them and present exemplars (see Chapter 7).

## Well-defined and ill-defined

Well-defined concepts have a clear set of defining features that all instances thereof share. Examples are *square, number* and *molecule.* Ill-defined concepts lack clear-cut defining features. An example is *artistic style,* mentioned in Chapter 1. One may group a set of paintings into a certain category without being able to state any common features of the instances. Many concepts used in everyday life are ill-defined, while many acquired in school are well-defined.

## Artificial and natural

An artificial concept is constructed for a particular use, usually for an experiment. It would be unlikely to be actually used in the real world. Thus, one might have a laboratory concept called *all red circles less than 3 cm in diameter on blue backgrounds* and set subjects in an experiment the task of learning it. Some further examples are in Figures 24 and 25 in Chapter 6. One may experiment with artificial concepts to study the learning of concepts that subjects have no prior experience of or that can be designed to answer some research question.

Natural concepts are existing ones that people in a given culture have constructed and use. Examples are *tree, chair, person, star, hand* and *dog.* Some are more natural than others, however. There is evidence that we are strongly pre-disposed to form some concepts because of our evolutionary history (see Chapter 7), and such concepts seem very natural.

However, the distinction between artificial and natural is, in a sense, tenuous, and is probably best regarded as a continuum from very natural to artificial. The reason is as follows. It has been suggested that many concepts that are natural in one culture may seem quite artificial in another. An African bushman would probably find the urban American's concepts of *table*, *debenture* and *upward mobility* quite strange and artificial. A schoolchild is likely to find the scientist's natural concepts of *ion*, *quark* and *reinforcement schedule* quite artificial. Similarly, a skilled chess player may find such concepts as *passed pawn*, *shattered kingside* and *endgame with opposite-coloured bishops* quite natural, while novices do not.

## Conjunctive and disjunctive

Exemplars of conjunctive concepts have two or more particular features. Consider *green circle*. A stimulus can only be an instance if it is both green *and* a circle. To be an exemplar of *triangle*, a stimulus must have three sides, *and* be a closed figure. Disjunctive concepts are based on *or* rather than *and*. To be an exemplar, a stimulus must only have one of several features. Consider the hypothetical concept *nop*. To be an exemplar of *nop*, a stimulus need only be red *or* have a single right angle *or* be a circle with a radius of at least 6 cm.

Disjunctive concepts seem odd, and indeed are quite scarce in the real world. The usual example is the *strike* in baseball. A given pitch of the ball is a strike if the batter swung and missed, or the ball passed through a certain zone without being hit. Similarly, a *US citizen* is someone born in the United States of America who has not taken out citizenship of another nation, *or* a person who was born elsewhere and was naturalised, *or* a person who was born abroad of American parents (Wicklegren, 1979). A *real number* is an integer, *or* a fraction, *or* a decimal. However, one can argue that any disjunctive concept can be given a conjunctive definition (Wicklegren, 1979). As might be suspected, disjunctive concepts are harder to learn.

## Categorisation of concepts according to stimulus domain

People can also categorise concepts according to the stimulus domain they come from (Cohen, 1983). So, we have person concepts (*extrovert, sister, Bolivian, voter*), scientific concepts (*ion, reptile, gravity, totalitarian state*), legal concepts (*tort, contract, drunk driver*), mathematical concepts (*prime number, limit, square root*), etc. Obviously a given concept can be placed in several domains.

Different domains are likely to differ in the proportion of well-defined and ill-defined concepts and abstract and concrete ones. The social sciences, art and law tend to have many more ill-defined ones than do physics or mathematics. Mathematics has more abstract ones than art.

## SOME METHODS OF STUDYING CONCEPTS

This section briefly describes some major methods of studying concepts and concept learning. Methodology is very important in any science. A field's means of investigating its subject matter limit what can be learned and inferred. Scientists can only answer specific questions when they have the means to investigate them. Questions such as, 'how many angels can sit on the head of a pin?' and 'how many parallel universes are there?' cannot be answered yet, because no known methods of investigation into them exist. Indeed, the history of science is full of cases in which a field languished or progressed at a leisurely pace until a new method led to rapid advances in knowledge. Some recent examples are the electron microscope and gene splicing in biology and space probes in astronomy.

Some major methods of investigating concepts are listed below. The first three listed are used mainly to investigate a person's existing conceptual structure and the last two mentioned are primarily methods of studying concept learning. Some other methods are described in later chapters.

**The interview**

This method is perhaps the simplest. In-depth interviews are carried out in order to determine the nature of people's concepts and bases of categorisation in some domain. The Swiss developmental theorist Jean Piaget interviewed his children over a period of years in order to examine their conceptualisations of the world at various ages. The interview has been much used to investigate various concepts held by students (Sutton, 1980). Nussbaum (1979) interviewed children of various ages in depth in order to determine their concept of the Earth as a cosmic body (see Chapter 3).

**Free-sort task**

In this method subjects are given a set of objects or a list of concepts and are asked to group the stimuli into categories as they see fit, or to group together the stimuli that 'seem the same'. From their groupings inferences about their existing concepts and bases for categorisation can be made. We saw this method in the Chi *et al* study in Chapter 1. Subjects sorted physics problems into categories and it was shown that these experts and novices had quite different bases of categorisation.

**Multi-dimensional scaling**

This is a complex statistical procedure that can cast light on an individual's cognitive structure or knowledge of some domain. The technique represents the perceived similarity between stimuli in terms of physical distance. Subjects are given a series of pairs of stimuli (e.g. horse/dog; kangaroo/bear) and are asked to rate their similarity on a scale. They rate all possible pairs of stimuli in a domain and the ratings are fed into a computer that produces a spatial representation of their similarities. So, the more similar two stimuli are perceived as being, the closer they are located. Figure 5 gives an example. Subjects rated the similarity between pairs of animals and the diagram reflects their perceived similarity. Horse and cow are seen as quite similar and are shown close together, while lion and mouse are perceived as less similar and are shown far apart.

Such a layout can give some clues as to the dimensions a person is using to rate similarity. In the figure the horizontal dimension seems to reflect the animals' size, though there are exceptions. Similarly, multi-dimensional scaling of similarities between nations often produces such dimensions of rating as rich/poor and East/West.

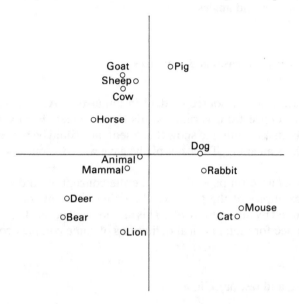

**Figure 5.** The results of a multi-dimensional scaling study of people's perceptions of the similarities between animals. The closer two animals are, the more similar they are perceived as being. From Rips, L. J., Shoben, E. J. and Smith, E. E. Semantic distance and the verification of semantic relations. *Journal of Verbal Learning and Verbal Behaviour*, **12**, Florida: Academic Press, 1973. Reproduced with permission.

## Selective looking and habituation techniques

These methods are often used to investigate categorisation in infants. As might be suspected, pre-verbal children are hard to study and hard to keep interested in various tasks. Therefore, some special methods are needed. The selective looking method involves recording the time an infant spends looking at various stimuli. Children look at what they find interesting and look little at what they find dull. If, for example, we wanted to know whether newborn infants have a concept of *triangle* we could simply present various triangles along with other figures as control stimuli and then record time spent looking at each. If the babies consistently look at the triangles more (or less) than other classes of stimuli, that is some evidence that they have a concept of *triangle*.

The habituation technique makes use of the pervasive capacity we have of getting used to a stimulus that is repeatedly presented. If we play the same record again and again or stay in the same place too long, ultimately boredom sets in. Because infants seem to become easily bored, this factor can be used to determine which concepts they can learn. If we wanted to know whether an infant could learn the concept of *triangle*, we could repeatedly present a variety of triangles until the child hardly looked at them at all. Then we could show some new triangles and control figures to see if the habituation transferred to the new triangles. If so, that is evidence that the child has a concept of triangle. Similarly, we could determine if newborn infants can form an identity concept by repeatedly showing the same stimulus object and then later showing it at different distances and angles.

### Intuitions about words, phrases and sentences

Such intuitions are a major source of data in linguistics. A point is made and then supported with evidence from various words or sentences. For example, American linguist Noam Chomsky wanted to show that a sentence could be perfectly grammatical but have no obvious meaning. The example he gave was, 'Colourless green ideas sleep furiously'.

This method was used on page 19 to make the concept/word distinction, giving as evidence some examples of the same word naming different concepts and the same concept being named by different words. This method will be used again in Chapter 4 as a source of evidence for metaphorical definitions of some complex concepts.

### The basic training and test paradigm

Most studies of concept learning from instances use a basic training and test procedure.* The method has a number of variations that need little explanation here. The experiment is divided into a training and a test phase. In the training phase, subjects are shown instances and try to learn a concept from them. The instances are usually shown one at a time and the subject makes a response and gets feedback. Say, for example, a person is training subjects to acquire the concept of *square*. He could present a variety of different squares interspersed with presentations of non-squares, such as circles and triangles. The subject might only have to press a button when an instance of the concept to be learned is shown, and he gets feedback on whether he is right or wrong. In a variant, two stimuli might be shown at a time (an exemplar and a non-exemplar) and the subject picks that which he believes is the instance. Training continues until a certain number of stimuli have been shown or the subject meets some pre-set criterion of acquisition. The latter could be ten presentations without an error or the ability to state the concept's defining features.

Then comes the test phase. Here stimuli not presented in training are shown to determine if a concept has been learned and, if so, which one it is. Usually no feedback is given, so performance is a function of what was learned in training. Various measures of acquisition include the number of errors, the reaction-time to new stimuli, and the confidence ratings. Thus, a subject might say '5' if he is very confident a new stimulus is an exemplar (or non-exemplar), '4' if less confident, etc.

---

* This method dates back to the study by C. L. Hull, *Quantitative aspects of the evolution of concepts* (1920).

**Reception method**

This method was used a great deal in traditional studies of concept learning, but is less popular nowadays. Generally it was used to study the learning of concrete, well-defined concepts like *red circle* and *three triangles on a blue background* (Bruner *et al*, 1956). The experimenter presents an exemplar or a non-exemplar, one at a time, and the subject says whether each is an exemplar or non-exemplar. The experimenter says if he is right or wrong and shows the next stimulus in the sequence. There is no test phase as such. The stimuli are shown until the subject performs at some pre-set criterion, or until he can state the defining features. The measure used is the number of trials (stimulus presentations) taken to learn the concept.

For example, say the concept is *blue triangle*. The experimenter first presents a figure with four red circles on a yellow background. The subject says it is an exemplar and the experimenter says he is wrong and presents a figure with two blue triangles on a red background. The subject says it is an exemplar and the experimenter says 'Right' and then shows another stimulus. In a variant of the method, an exemplar and a non-exemplar may be shown at the same time and the subject picks the exemplar. Note that a subject has to try to recall the results of previous trials.

**Selection method**

This method is quite similar to the above one, and has been typically used with the same kind of simple, concrete concepts. The main difference is the method of presentation. Rather than having stimuli shown in a fixed sequence, all stimuli in the array are laid out together. The experimenter gives the subject an exemplar and then the subject can select any stimulus in the array and ask if it is an exemplar. The measure is the number of stimuli chosen and a concept is deemed to have been learned when the subject can state the defining features of that concept. This method places much less demand on memory, because stimuli can be neatly sorted into piles and referred to as the subject wishes.

FURTHER READING

Concepts, words and word meanings: Carroll (1964); Macnamara (1982).
Basic terms: Ellis *et al* (1979).
Concept types and methods of studying concepts: Cohen (1983).

# Chapter 3

# Schemata

SUMMARY

1.  A schema is a mental representation of a set of related categories.
2.  A basic problem of life is selecting the right schema to cover a certain situation. Schemata can be elicited in top-down or bottom-up fashion.
3.  Schemata are used in perception, comprehension, memory and learning and so are very important in education. Failure to comprehend may result through not knowing which schema to apply, selecting the wrong one or one different from that intended but still adequate.
4.  Five important types of schema are those for scenes, events, actions, persons and stories.
5.  Using a schema can have drawbacks. A lot of useful data may be filtered out, inadequate schemata are not easily given up, and the wrong schema may be used in a given situation.
6.  The relationship between concepts and schemata is complex and depends on how the two terms are defined. According to the definitions given in this book, concepts are indistinguishable from schemata. Whether a given representation is considered a concept or a schema depends on what you want to do with it.

## INTRODUCTION

What do these vignettes have in common?

It is midnight. The police have been at the scene of the crime for hours but are baffled. So, they call in a detective. He arrives, studies the situation and notes a hair there, a tiny mark on one wall, and an odd arrangement of some objects. 'It's elementary', he says, 'here is what happened and the person responsible is a tall man who has just arrived from Brazil in a cargo ship'.

The intelligence analyst has three facts gathered by field agents and spy satellites. Soccer fields are being built in a certain province of nation X, some materials destined for one port have been diverted elsewhere, and a few staff members have been transferred from one embassy of nation Y to another. From these data he infers that nation Y is upgrading a military base in nation X and plans to invade nation Z from it in three weeks.

A professor gives a two-hour speech on economics. Two audience members are interviewed after the talk. One says he believes that the professor completely shares his own right-wing views and supports his position on free markets, the need for laissez-faire policies, and low taxes. The other says she believes that the professor shares her left-wing views and has said much to support such tenets as state ownership of banks and industries, high progressive income taxes to reduce extremes of wealth, and huge inheritance taxes.

Each vignette illustrates the use of a *schema*. The notion of schema is a very important one and has many implications for education. It can be traced back at least as far as the eighteenth-century philosopher Immanuel Kant, and was brought into psychology by F. C. Bartlett.* Bartlett was somewhat ahead of his time and only in the last decade or so has the concept been widely applied. Schemata are very closely related to concepts and their relationship is discussed at the end of this chapter. First of all the term is defined. It is a somewhat vague notion, which is used in different ways and which has related notions, such as 'frame', that are not discussed here.

## Definition of schema

A schema can be defined as an organised body of knowledge, a mental structure that represents some part of some stimulus domain (Rumelhart and Ortony, 1977; Rumelhart, 1980). Like a concept, a schema is a representation abstracted from experience, which is used to understand the world and deal with it. It consists of a set of expectations about how part of the world is organised; these expectations are applied to categorise various stimuli. This vague definition will make more sense with some examples.

Rumelhart (1980) gives some examples of schemata. Consider first the schema of a *human face*. Like any schema, it consists of several parts or elements that are called 'variables' or 'slots'. The slots include lips, chin, nose, eyes, etc. The face schema prescribes that these parts be organised in a certain way: the eyes are above the nose, the lips are below the nose and the chin is below the lips. If the prescribed arrangement is departed from too drastically – even if all the parts are present – the result would not be a face. Figure 6 illustrates this point. It gives a schematic face and three stimuli. A is a reasonably acceptable face, because the elements of eyes, nose etc. are present and in the places the schema prescribes. But, in C, the elements are all there but are not arranged according to the schema. C is not, therefore, an acceptable face. Now consider B, a Cyclopean face named after the giant in the Ulysses myth. It does not fit the schema exactly, because it has one large eye rather than two eyes. Still, it is an acceptable face, because most of the elements are present and are arranged as would be expected. The conclusion is that a schema's prescribed expectations can be departed from to some extent.

Another example is the schema *buy*. In a pure form, it consists of several slots: a buyer, a seller, money (or some medium of exchange), and the item bought. These slots

---

* F. C. Bartlett, *Remembering: A study in experimental and social psychology*, 1932.

The schema of a human face

A

B

C

**Figure 6.** An example of a schema and two instantiations of it. A and B are reasonably acceptable instantiations of 'face' because they match the schema sufficiently well. C is too discrepant to be an instantiation.

are arranged in a certain way. The buyer gives money to the seller, who then gives the item to the buyer. If these slots are arranged differently in a given situation, then the *buy* schema does not apply to it. So, if person A gives both money and an item to person B and gets nothing in return, such an event would not be an exemplar of *buy*. Or, if person A gives some item and gets nothing in return, the situation is an instance of *give* or *rob* rather than *buy*.

## Some characteristics of schemata

### Schemata have specific instantiations
A schema is an abstraction from experience and a representation. It applies to stimuli in the world in the same way a concept applies to its instances. A schema can thus be *instantiated*. Its slots can be filled in with stimuli. Thus, A and B in Figure 6 are instantiations of the *face* schema. The schema is filled in with actual stimuli. If you had just bought a peach at a fruit shop, the event would be an instantiation of *buy*. You filled the slot for buyer, the shop for seller, and the peach for the item bought. A stranger's face can also instantiate the face schema. The person's specific eyes fill the slots for eyes, his nose the slot for nose, etc. The schema thus acts as a pattern-recognition device.
### The slots
The slots of a given schema can usually be filled with a fairly wide range of stimuli. The nose slot of the face schema can be filled with noses of varying sizes and shapes, and many distances from other parts of a face. The *buy* schema's slot for item sold can be filled with such stimuli as a car, insurance, the services of a plumber or a lawyer, or tuition at

a university. The buyer slot can be filled with countless persons or with organisations such as a bank, an army, or a government. Finally, some slots can be filled in by *default*. Though you cannot actually perceive them in a given situation, your schema tells you that they are there. Say you saw two eyes glaring at you in the dark. You can infer from those eyes and your *face* schema that other parts are likely to be present. There is likely to be a nose, a mouth and a chin, and so values for these parts can be filled in by default. You can also infer that there is a body attached to the face from your *body* schema. Similarly, if you see someone leaving a grocery shop with a bag of groceries, you can fill in what probably just occurred from your *buy* schema. You can infer that the person handed over money for the goods.

Parenthetically, note that instantiations may vary in the extent to which they are good instantiations of the schema (a topic discussed in detail in Chapter 4). Thus, the Cyclopean face in Figure 6 is not as good a face as that in A. Similarly, a beanbag chair would not be as good an instantiation of the *chair* schema as an armchair.

*Schemata are embedded within each other*
Schemata are often organised into partonomies, each schema being part of one and itself composed of schemata. Some examples are shown in Figure 7. Consider the *human body* schema. It consists of such parts as face, arms, legs and trunk. Each can be considered a schema, as described before with *face*. These each bear a part-whole

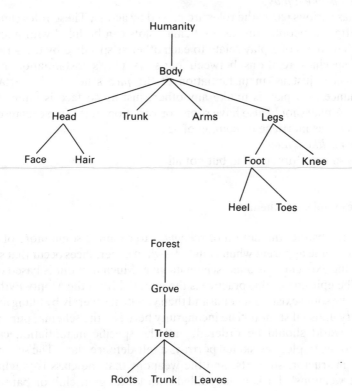

**Figure 7.** Some examples of partonomies. The schemata below each subsumptive schema are part of it rather than an instance of it.

relation to a more inclusive schema. They are part of it, just as a given tree is part of a forest (Markman, 1983).

*Other characteristics*
Two more will be noted. Firstly, a schema is often organised around some theme or idea. Our schema for *eating out* is organised around the theme of being fed, and the schema for *buy* is organised around acquiring some item. Secondly, schemata vary greatly in abstractness, just as concepts do. Some are very specific, such as those for a face or a chair. Others, such as *scientific theory* or *science*, are much more abstract.

## Some analogies

The notion of *schema* can be further illustrated through a cluster of analogies. A schema is like many things, and these analogies should provide a better mental grip on the concept. Some are borrowed from Rumelhart (1980).

1. *A schema is like a sorting device.*
   A sorting device allows us to place some objects in one category and the rest in another, just as a schema allows us to determine that some stimuli are instantiations and others are not.
2. *A schema is like a play.*
   A play has various parts; the roles are played by actors. These roles can be filled by many different people, just as a schema's slots can be filled with many different stimuli. The parts of a play relate to each other as specified by the script, just as a schema specifies relations between parts. A play's instantiation is a specific performance, just as an instantiation of the *face* schema is a certain face. A performance of a play is unlike any other, just as no face is quite the same as another. A play should also have room for variation. It is often organised around a theme, such as marriage or coming of age.
3. *A schema is like a filter.*
   It allows some information in but not all.

## Some more examples of schemata

A good way to abstract the notion of *schema* is to examine some more of one's own. These often become apparent when violated – when experiences occur that significantly depart from the expectations one's schemata give. Much humour is based on violating schemata. The epitome of this practice is the material from the Monty Python troupe. They often take some existing schema and then violate it severely by filling in one or two slots with very unusual stimuli. The incongruity between the schema, our expectations on how the world should be ordered, and the specific instantiation can then be enormous. For example, one sketch portrays a self-defence class. The schema here has slots for the instructor, students, and the weapons that the class is taught to defend against. The weapons' slot is usually filled with knife, gun, club or bare hands – all plausible objects for attack and thus consistent with the schema. But, in the sketch, the instructor insists on teaching defence against attackers wielding pieces of fruit –

bananas, pineapples, and cherries (red and black). In another sketch, a theatre vendor is portrayed. Our schema has hawkers peddling typical slot fillers such as ice cream and chocolate. Yet the vendor sells only seabirds, 'Albatross, stormy petrel on a stick and gannet ripple'. He also vigorously insults his customers, which, again, is not a usual practice of vendors. Another sketch portrays a quiz show in which the contestants' slot is not filled by the usual minor celebrities or ordinary people but by four Communist greats: Karl Marx, Vladimir Lenin, Che Guevara, and Mao Zedong (Tse-Tung). They compete for a lounge suite by answering trivial questions about football cup finals.

A final example is a Monty Python workhorse – the television interview. This schema is highly structured. There are slots for an interviewer, the interviewee/s, the content of the discussion, etc. Usually the interviewee is a celebrity or has recently done something newsworthy, or is publicising a book or film. Discussion is usually very polite and relevant to the audience's interests. The guest is introduced and asked relevant questions, the work being promoted is discussed, and then the guest is politely bade farewell. There is, then, a clear set of expectations about the order of slots and their fillers. In one sketch, however, just about all of them are violated. The interviewer introduces Arthur 'Two-sheds' Jackson, a leading composer publicising his new symphony. The content slot is not filled by talk of music in general or the symphony, the interviewer is, instead, fascinated by the nickname and asks how Jackson got it. It turns out that Jackson once had one shed and was thinking of getting another and since then has been called 'Two-sheds'. The interviewer goes off even further on this tangent, 'Did you write this symphony . . . in the shed?'. The reply is, 'No, it's just an ordinary garden shed'. 'So you wanted this second shed to write in?' asks the interviewer. Jackson gets angry and is then himself chided for straying off the topic of music. The interview ends with 'Two-sheds' being forcibly ejected from the studio and told to get his own programme.

Australian comedian Garry McDonald used to routinely violate the interview schema with real people. He toured the world interviewing various famous persons and asking very silly questions. He strayed off the topic and appeared very nervous and fumbled with his notes. His antics show what can happen when people's schemata are severely violated. Some looked stricken and as if they had no idea what to do, a few just laughed and one (James Garner) stoically sat through it all and at the end wished Garry McDonald luck at the next job he tried.

Let us now return to the vignettes described at the beginning of this chapter and see how each involves a schema. In the first, the detective noted three stimuli: a mark on the wall, the hair and the arrangement of objects. These suggested one or two schemata that might apply to the situation and that allowed him to construct an instantiation. For instance, the mark could have been recognisable as a splatter from a fruit grown only in Brazil, which is only shipped in season and whose first shipment this year had just arrived. The arrangement of objects might have suggest a fight schema, which leads him to infer that a fight of some sort had taken place. Thus, facts suggest schemata, which can then be used to make further inferences.

Police rely on standard schemata all the time. Consider the schemata for murder. Police have a few stock ones such as *jealous husband, beneficiary of a will*, and *revenge-seeker*. Solving a crime is determining which schema applies. They search for clues that suggest a given schema, and the schema then suggests where to look for further information. They can, therefore, construct an instantiation of that particular crime, filling in the culprit slot with a certain person.

Consider the second example. The analyst probably has a schema – built up from past occurrences – for invasions instigated by nation Y. The facts gathered suggest that this schema applies and the schema suggests the timing of the invasion. He may know that citizens of nation X never play soccer but that those of nation Y do, and that the transferees are top spies who are only transferred when an invasion is imminent.

Consider the third vignette. Here two people hold different schemata and only take in information that seems consistent with it. Person A holds a right-wing schema, and filters out all the information from the speech inconsistent with his schema and so believes that the professor shares his views. Person B has an analogous problem.

**Schema selection**

The three vignettes illustrate a fundamental problem of life – the problem of selecting an appropriate schema to guide our actions. Each of us knows millions of schemata and we need to select the right one to use at any given time. When entering a restaurant, we select our *eating out* schema and behave according to its prescriptions. We sit, order a meal and pay for it later. An aircraft crew has a well-rehearsed schema to apply to a given emergency and selects it if required. A student entering a classroom selects his *classroom* schema, which prescribes that he should sit down, get ready with pen and paper, and listen for instructions.

Yet the world is often ambiguous. There may be many different stimuli present and we may miss some key ones suggesting which schema should be selected. We may misinterpret certain stimuli and pick an inappropriate schema. Indeed, an oft-used comedy device is to show people operating on different schemata because of an early error in selection. The resulting clash can occasionally be amusing, and is a staple of just about every situation comedy.

Here are two examples of this problem. First of all, a standard sitcom plot has person A accidentally reading a love letter or diary entry written by person B. The entry waxes lyrical about someone and person A mistakenly believes it is about him. He then operates on this schema, interpreting the various words and actions of B as evidence for his belief. This continues until some incident occurs at the end of the plot that is inconsistent with the schema and the error is realised. Secondly, Taylor and Crocker (1981) cite the example of a play called *She Stoops to Conquer*. The hero is shy and awkward with his upper class fellows but arrogant with those lower on the social scale. On his way to meet his prospective upper class bride he stops at what seems to be an inn. He orders the 'innkeeper' about, is amorous toward the innkeeper's daughter and generally behaves in an overbearing manner. However, the 'inn' turns out to be his future father-in-law's house and the daughter his bride-to-be, which is revealed at the end of the play. We can see how incorrectly selecting his *inn* schema induced him to behave inappropriately.

The problem of schema selection from ambiguous data is well-illustrated by a criminal trial. The jury must construct an appropriate instantiation of certain events from schemata and data, such as physical evidence and the testimony of eyewitnesses and the police. Often the facts suggest that several different schemata could be selected. The prosecution may argue that the facts suggest an instantiation of, say, the *burglary* schema, in which the burglar slot is filled by the defendant. Evidence will be offered from the data. The defence may counter that the burglary schema does not apply at all – the defendant was taking what was rightfully his, or they may say that someone else should fill the burglar slot. To support the interpretation, different facts may be emphasised, some ignored and those offered by the prosecution discredited. Even when the facts are clear (the defendant was caught red-handed in front of ten witnesses), the jury still may be offered different schemata to instantiate. The prosecution may say that he is a cold, calculating, hardened criminal, who should be imprisoned for society's protection. The defence may counter that he is a hapless victim of circumstances. Trying economic circumstances pushed him into this final desperate error of judgment, for which he is now truly repentant. The jury must select a schema to instantiate. It may use the defence's, the prosecution's, or their own schema.

Schema selection is therefore an intrinsic part of problem-solving. Faced with a problem, we need to select a schema that applies to it and suggests what to do in this situation. Thus, the skilled chess player scans the board for familiar patterns that indicate how to proceed. Mayer (1981) suggests that solving algebra story problems is a matter of finding an appropriate schema. Students often have trouble with them because they pick the wrong schema. Experts have many stored patterns, and solving the problem is a matter of selecting the right one. Mayer surveyed exercise problems from 12 textbooks and found about 20 problem categories from 2000 problems surveyed. About 100 schemata were needed to solve them.

Finally, schemata are activated in 'bottom-up' or 'top-down' fashion. The 'top' refers to the mind and the 'bottom' to stimuli from the environment. In bottom-up activation, data suggest an appropriate schema. Thus, the sense impressions from two eyes seen in the dark suggest that the *face* schema should be activated. Entering a restaurant activates the *eating out* schema. In top-down activation, we have a schema in mind and we search the environment for evidence consistent with it. An example is a court trial in which the judge has already made up his mind about what happened and just looks for supporting evidence. Figure 8 gives another example. It is hard to see the familiar object depicted from just the stimuli. When told that a dog is depicted, however, our schema for *dog* then guides the search and allows us to see the pattern. Most cases of schema selection probably involve both bottom-up and top-down activation. Thus, data may suggest a schema, which we can use to hunt for further evidence.

## SOME USES OF SCHEMATA

Schemata have a number of important uses, all closely related to uses of concepts, which were described in Chapter 1.

### Perception

Schemata provide a means of recognising patterns. The mass of data coming through our senses has to be filtered, analysed and interpreted, for which a person needs schemata. At the broadest level, schemata affect the information a person actually takes in (Rumelhart, 1980). A schema may tell one where to look, for instance. In order to determine what someone is feeling, our *person* schema tells us to look at his face. A

**Figure 8.** An example of top-down activation of a schema. From Carraher, R. G. and Thurston, J. B. *Optical illusions and the visual arts*. New York: Reinhold, 1966.

schema of the solar system provided by Newton's laws of motion told astronomers where to look for the undiscovered planet Neptune, and the schema suggested that a tenth planet exists – as yet undiscovered. After a murder, a detective's schemata suggest where to look for further clues.

Schemata filter out data. We can only absorb a limited amount of information and need some way to extract what is most important for our purposes. Pichert and Anderson (1977) demonstrated this effect of a schema. Students read a single passage describing a house from either the perspective of a burglar or of a housebuyer. The perspective taken affected what was recalled from the passage, evidently because it directed attention to different data. A burglar is likely to notice such things as the number of locks there are, what valuables there are inside and the distance of the site from other houses. A buyer may be more concerned with the number of rooms, the size of the living room, etc.

Schemata can, therefore, cause distortions in perception. An illustration is the old cliché that a person's assessment of another is complete within the first 90 seconds of an introduction and that it is very hard to change that assessment afterwards. If that measure is inaccurate, perception is distorted. Bruner and Potter (1964) give another example. Subjects were shown slides of some object that was greatly out of focus. The slides were slowly focused, and at various points each subject had to guess what object was depicted. Those who had to guess still inaccurately identified the object long after subjects who began with clearer slides had got it right. Evidently, they had, at the early stage, become committed to one schema and were loath to give it up.

## Comprehension

There is an apocryphal story about a man who was hired to lecture a learned audience. Although he was presented as a distinguished scholar, he was just an actor who spouted only disorganised nonsense, sprinkled with jargon. Yet, the audience members interviewed after the lecture felt that he knew his field well and that he had given a well-organised talk that made some cogent points. How were they fooled? How did they 'comprehend' the incomprehensible? To discover this we need to look at what 'comprehension' means according to the schema view.

What does it mean to 'understand' something? What does it mean to say that a course, a book, or a movie makes no sense, or that one student understands a lesson while another does not? To understand something is to select a schema that provides a plausible account of it, and thus allows us to assimilate it to something we know (Anderson, 1977; Rumelhart, 1980 and 1984). Here is an example. If someone were walking along and encountered a house floating upside down about ten feet off the ground, this event would not be readily understood, because his existing schemata cannot easily handle it. Therefore, it seems anomalous. Houses do not fly. Because of his schemata he expects them to be firmly rooted on the ground. So how can a seemingly inexplicable event be understood? One can hunt for a schema to explain it. Perhaps one is asleep and dreaming. Perhaps a fantasy film is being shot and the 'house' is really made of cardboard and is being held up by a helicopter. Perhaps one's eyesight is failing and what seems to be a house is really a balloon. Each schema allows the event to be understood. The old television show 'Candid Camera' used to routinely arrange such inexplicable events. In one episode a car drove directly towards a person and then split in two to avoid him. In another, metal spoons were rigged so that the handle came off when dipped in coffee. Some hidden microphones were set up to greatly amplify a person's sounds of munching in a restaurant. The events seemed very strange to the victims, and they often looked duly puzzled. Their bewilderment vanished when they were told they were on 'Candid Camera', because they then had a schema by which such events could be understood.

A good example of the need for a schema to comprehend is the following passage:
The procedure is actually quite simple. First you arrange things into different groups. Of course, one pile may be sufficient depending on how much there is to do. If you have to go somewhere else due to lack of facilities that is the next step, otherwise you are pretty well set. It is important not to overdo things. That is, it is better to do too few things at once than

too many. In the short run, this may not seem important but complications can easily arise. A mistake can be expensive as well. At first the whole procedure will seem complicated. Soon, however, it will become just another facet of life. It is difficult to foresee any end to the necessity for this task in the immediate future, but then one can never tell. After the procedure is completed one arranges the materials into different groups again. Then they can be put in their appropriate places. Eventually they will be used once more and the whole cycle will then have to be repeated. However, that is part of life.

Bransford and Johnson (1973)

The material makes little sense. Although the sentences are perfectly grammatical, many seem unrelated, and the meaning is unclear. However, it does make sense if a schema that will provide a plausible account of it is suggested. Give it the title 'washing clothes' and read through the passage again. We can understand the passage, because we can assimilate it to our own schema for washing clothes. From a subjective viewpoint, it does not greatly matter which schema one uses to comprehend, so long as it gives a plausible account. As Skemp (1979) points out, a thunderstorm can be understood by assimilation to a variety of schemata: modern meteorology, or mythological schemata, such as Zeus hurling thunderbolts or Thor stamping his hammer. To the people who hold such schemata, they all provide an explanation of the storm. However, the meteorological one is a better guide for action.

Looking at the comprehension process in more detail, we will see that several things are involved therein. First is the stimulus that is to be explained – the floating house, the thunderstorm, or the passage on washing clothes. Second is the schema or schemata used to understand the event, which is instantiated – *shooting a film*, *dreaming*, or *washing clothes*. Third is the specific scenario constructed, which is an instantiation of the schema. It is filled in from the specific stimuli, and other world knowledge if necessary. It can be seen as a specific schema with values all filled in. These points can be illustrated with another incomprehensible passage:

If the balloons popped, the sound would not be able to carry since everything would be too far away from the second floor. A closed window would also prevent the sound from carrying since most buildings tend to be well insulated. Since the whole operation depends on a steady flow of electricity, a break in the middle of the wire would also cause problems. Of course the fellow could shout, but the human voice is not loud enough to carry that far. An additional problem is that a string could break in the instrument. Then there could be no accompaniment to the message. It is clear that the best solution would involve less distance. Then there would be fewer potential problems.

Bransford and Johnson (1972)

Again, the material cannot be readily understood because one does not know what schema to select. Now look at Figure 9, and re-read the passage. The schema to instantiate is *courtship*, and the specific instantiation is in the diagram. The figure allows slots for courter, courtee, and courtship method to be filled. However, additional world knowledge is needed to understand the passage – knowledge of guitars, amplifiers, etc.

Returning to the 'performed' lecture described at the beginning of this section on 'Comprehension', it is now possible to suggest how the audience might have 'understood' the lecture. Parts of the talk might have elicited various schemata, which the audience then used to interpret the discussion. By taking in just schema-relevant data, they may have imposed a 'meaning' on the lecture. It is like reading a very difficult textbook for the first time. A few parts may seem vaguely familiar and putting these together in terms of what the reader knows may yield an interpretation much different from that the author intended. Another such example is from Robert Heinlein's novel *Orphans of the Sky*. In his book, a person who lacks much knowledge of physics is reading the textbook *Basic Modern Physics* and interprets passages in terms of schemata he knows. Thus, the law of gravity (two bodies attract each other directly as the product of their masses and inversely as the square of their distance) is understood as follows. The 'bodies' are human and 'mass' is their capacity for love. When two young people are thrown together, they fall in love and when separated they soon get over it.

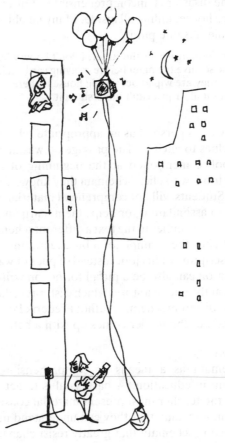

**Figure 9.** A specific schema that makes the material in the balloon passage comprehensible. From Bransford, J. D. and Johnson, M. K. Contextual prerequisites for understanding: some investigations of comprehension and recall. *Journal of Verbal Learning and Verbal Behaviour* **61**, Florida: Academic Press, 1972. Reproduced with permission.

*Reasons for failing to comprehend*
If failure to comprehend is because a schema has not been applied, why are schemata sometimes not used? Rumelhart (1980 and 1984) suggests three reasons. The first is when a person does not know an appropriate schema and cannot readily construct one. An average ten-year-old put into an advanced astrophysics or topology class would understand very little, because he lacks schemata to assimilate the material. Indeed, it takes a lot of time and instruction to instil the appropriate schemata. In the passage on washing clothes above, a person from a culture that had no clothes would find the

material incomprehensible even with a title. Novelist Arthur C. Clarke once said that any sufficiently advanced technology would seem like magic to us, again because we would lack the schemata to understand it.

Such incomprehension often occurs in natural disasters. Many people have a general schema of the world as a reasonably just, stable place. Disasters are often anomalous to this schema, because people's property and the lives of friends and family may be gone in an instant. The *just world* schema cannot handle such events and a common report in the aftermath is that the disaster is 'incomprehensible'. For example, in 1954, a leaky gas main blew up a large house, killing all inside. Many neighbours stood for hours just staring at the gaping hole. As one put it,

> I just stand here all day looking across the street. I don't know why. I can't get over it. To think that they could be so alive the night before, playing cards, talking to us. Then all of a sudden, for no reason, they are wiped out. A big house is there one minute and the next minute nothing is left of it all. I just can't understand it.
>
> Janis (1965)

A second reason is when a person has an appropriate schema, but a given situation does not give enough clues to elicit it. The passage on washing clothes made no sense without a title. The police mentioned at the beginning of this chapter floundered because the clues were too few to elicit schemata they knew. This aspect of schemata is important in teaching. Students will not comprehend material unless the teacher elicits schemata they can use to assimilate it, or helps them learn an appropriate one.

A third reason is when one applies to the text a different schema from that intended by the author. Rumelhart cites the example of a bureaucrat interpreting the passage on washing clothes as a description of his job. Instead of piles of washing, papers are being shuffled about. This reason can also be a pitfall for fiction writers. A standard literary device is to have a twist at the end of a story, which casts preceding events in a new light. The reader has to apply a different schema. Author Frederik Pohl has said that this device is tricky, because sometimes the reader comes up with a better twist than the author.

## Educational implications

This function of schemata as a means of comprehension means that they are fundamentally important in education. A basic goal is to get students to understand material and, to do so, the teacher must present material consistent with the students' schemata, or teach them a schema that they can understand material with. However, students often hold existing schemata that greatly resist change and actually interfere with instruction. Material that cannot be understood with their existing schemata is either ignored, compartmentalised, or learned by rote (see Chapter 11). A good example is a study by Nussbaum (1979). He interviewed children of various ages to determine their schemata of the Earth as a cosmic body. Figure 10 shows the results. Note the quite different schemata and the development. What is especially interesting is how children accommodated various ideas in idiosyncratic ways. In 'a' and 'c' the world is considered flat, but the idea that it is round is accommodated by conceiving of this planet as a flat disc. In later conceptions the Earth is conceived as round, with the sky as a dome overhead and the ground as a cross-section of the planet. Instruction in a lot of geology and in basic geography would be incomprehensible to students who held such schemata, because the information could not be readily assimilated. Also, instruction in, say, plate tectonics or some aspects of gravitation would be incomprehensible to some students because the ideas could not be understood with their schemata. Thus, new ideas were understood in terms of an existing schema and sometimes changed that schema in idiosyncratic ways.

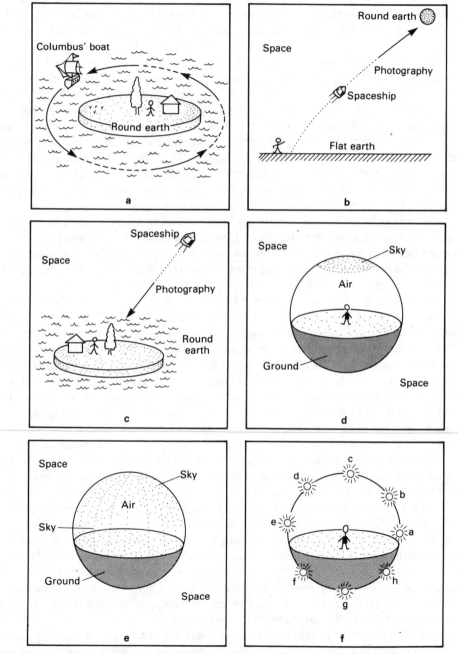

**Figure 10.** A rather striking example of the different schemata people can hold and the need to adapt instruction to them. From Nussbaum, J. Children's conceptions of the Earth as a cosmic body: a cross age study. *Science Education* **63**. Copyright © 1979 John Wiley & Sons, Inc. Reproduced with permission.

**Memory and learning**

Schemata are very important in remembering. Yet, first, we need to distinguish between two types of remembering. *Verbatim* recall is the recall of information learned by rote. Familiar examples are poems and quotations, passages from a book, or the multiplication table. Often little understanding of the material is involved, and it is recalled exactly as it was acquired. *Meaningful* recall is usually recall of the gist or the main ideas, rather than their exact wording. It is often hard to recall the exact wording of a lecture, a joke or anecdote. Instead, a person remembers the main theme.

Schemata affect recall of meaningful material in two major ways (Rumelhart, 1980). Firstly, a schema can affect the form of what we acquire. We tend to remember our instantiated schema of some event rather than the event itself. We take in data relevant to our schema, recall that data and forget the extraneous matter. Thus, an eyewitness to a traffic accident will remember what he thought he saw – his schema of the event – and not the event itself. Secondly, schemata are used to reconstruct the original interpretation of an event from fragments in memory. Rumelhart offers an analogy to perception. If perception is trying to fit a schema to incoming sensory data, then remembering can be seen as trying to fit a schema to interpret data from memory. Here are some studies that support this view. Carmichael *et al* (1932) showed subjects a variety of figures. One, for example, was a pair of circles connected with a line. One group was told that it was a pair of eyeglasses and another that it was a dumb-bell. Later they drew the figures from memory. Those given the eyeglass label tended to draw eyeglasses and those given the dumb-bell label drew dumb-bells. Thus, their schema instantiated at the time of learning affected what they recalled. Spiro (1977) asked subjects to read a story and then gave them a fact either consistent or inconsistent with the tale's implications. When they later recalled the story, recall tended to be distorted to accommodate the new fact. Spiro suggests that errors in recall may be more likely when later material contradicts the schema instantiated at acquisition. A more familiar example is when a person visits a house or sees a film seen many years before. Often the person's memory of these things is different from the reality because, evidently, recall has been distorted to fit schemata.

This finding of memory distortion has had much impact on eyewitness testimony. The verdict in many court cases largely rests on what witnesses say they saw, which the court usually assumes is quite accurate. However, past events are reconstructed with schemata and so recall may be biased. People may believe they saw something, when in fact they only inferred it. Muensterberg (1908), cited by Wessells (1982), gave a unique demonstration of eyewitness unreliability. In a lecture, two students suddenly began to argue. The dispute escalated until one actually pulled out a gun. The professor grabbed his arm, but the gun went off. During the scene's early stages, the professor had quietly peeled and eaten a banana. Fortunately, all had been staged, and when calm was restored, the students wrote down what they had seen. There was much inaccuracy in their reports. Some did not mention the essential events, others reported things that had not happened, and no one mentioned the banana.

Loftus (1979) describes further evidence of eyewitness inaccuracy. A study by Loftus and Palmer (1974) showed that witnesses can be induced to 'remember' events that had not occurred by asking them misleading questions. Subjects saw a film of a car crash. Some were later asked how fast the cars were going when they *smashed* into each other and others how fast when they *hit* each other. Those given the 'smash' wording estimated that the cars had been travelling much faster. Later they were asked if they had seen any broken glass in the film. Again, the 'smash' wording group subjects were more likely to report having seen glass, because broken glass is part of a *high-speed smash* schema.

Finally, schemata can affect how much we recall. Having well-developed schemata for a domain allows one to take in and recall much more information. A good example is chess. Experts have many well-developed schemata for piece formations, acquired from study and countless games, while novices do not. De Groot (1965) showed novices and experts various chess positions for a few seconds and asked them to reproduce each position from memory. The experts were far better at recalling them, usually making few errors. Then random piece placements were tried – positions that would never occur in a real game and that the experts' schemata would be of no use in recalling. The expert/novice difference disappeared. Figure 11 gives a schematic example. Similarly, Chiesi *et al* (1979) compared the recall of experts and novices of baseball knowledge. The experts had well-developed schemata about the game and a great deal of knowledge about goal structures and action sequences abstracted from many games. The subjects read a text that described a fictitious game. The experts recalled many more details. Thorndyke (1977) has pointed out that we have an abstract story schema used to understand stories (see next section). When material is disorganised, so that it does not readily fit the schema, it tends to be poorly recalled.

This function, too, makes schemata important in education. Both learning and recall is much improved if material can be assimilated to a student's existing schemata. Recall is poor if material does not conform to these schemata. Teachers and textbook writers need to tailor material to student's existing schemata so that it can be assimilated to them, or they can teach students schemata that they can assimilate the material to. Everyone has experienced poorly structured material that cannot be related to what they know and that is also very difficult to recall.

## TYPES OF SCHEMA

Schemata can be divided into a number of types, five of which are described here. Mandler (1984) mentions scenes, scripts and stories, to which we can add persons and actions (Hastie, 1981; Taylor and Crocker, 1981).

### Scenes

Scene schemata pertain to the arrangement of objects in space. They encapsulate our knowledge, our expectations that objects should be arranged in certain ways. Examples are the face and body schemata mentioned earlier. We expect their parts to be in certain places. We expect parts of the landscape schemata, such as rivers, mountains, lakes and the sky to be arranged in a certain way (Mandler, 1984). Hills and lakes should be on the ground rather than in mid air. Rivers should flow downhill rather than up, and lake-water should be relatively flat rather than suspended in pillars.

*A.* A random chess position

*B.* A real chess position

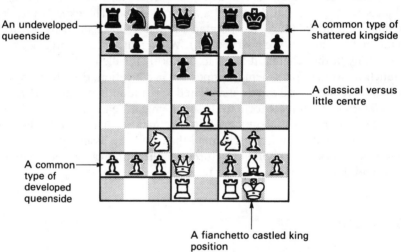

An undeveloped queenside

A common type of shattered kingside

A classical versus little centre

A common type of developed queenside

A fianchetto castled king position

**Figure 11.** An example of how well-developed schemata can improve recall. Position A is a random position that novices and experts would find equally incomprehensible and hard to recall. Position B is a real position. The expert can see familiar patterns of pieces in it, which reduce the amount of information he needs to recall to just a few items. Many patterns have names. The expert's schemata also allow the position to be analysed and suggest courses of action.

A scene schema has vertical and horizontal dimensions. The horizontal dimension encapsulates expectations about object arrangements from left to right, and the vertical dimension encapsulates expectations from the bottom to the top. Scene schemata prescribe greater constraints on the vertical dimension (Mandler, 1984). No doubt gravity is the reason why. Gravity ensures that heavy objects tend to stay on the ground and lighter ones, such as balloons, stay in the air.

Our scene schemata also specify the objects we are likely to see in certain situations (Mandler, 1984). We expect to see stoves and refrigerators in kitchens and sofas and coffee tables in living rooms.

## Events

Scene schemata pertain to space and event schemata relate to time. They encapsulate our abstract knowledge about sequences of events. A simple example is *boiling water*. The events are prescribed. One puts water in a container, applies heat, and the water gets hotter and turns to steam. Another is *acquiring a degree*. A person enrols at a college, studies material, attends classes, passes exams and is eventually awarded the degree. The events occur in more or less a fixed order.

Some event schemata are called *scripts*, after Schank and Abelson (1977), because they prescribe a certain sequence of actions. They cite the prototypical script *eating out in a restaurant*. Some general slots are: being seated, having one's order taken, consuming the food, paying the bill and leaving. The script specifies that each slot occurs in a certain order: first the person enters, then is seated, and then the food arrives. Each slot can be filled with a wide range of stimuli. The waiter slot can be filled by many different people, and the food slot by lobster, steak, etc. Each slot also has sub-slots, and each is organised around some goal. Note, however, that the schema is quite general. Particular restaurants may require a somewhat different sequence of events. In a cafeteria, for example, the client gets the food first, then pays for it, and then is seated. In other places, the customer sits down, orders and then pays immediately.

We all know an enormous number of scripts for a wide variety of social and other situations. Without them we could not behave appropriately or predict the behaviour of others.

## Actions

These can be seen as a type of event schema, which represent only procedural knowledge. Indeed, Piaget's notion of schema seems to be close to the notion of action schema (Flavell, 1963). Bartlett (1932) a long time ago suggested that we have schemata for such routine actions as playing tennis. An example is shooting a basketball into a hoop. The schema consists of slots such as grasping the ball, steadying it for the toss by tensing muscles, judging the distance and force needed for the shot, and then actually throwing the ball. The slots occur in a certain order and can be filled with a variety of actual behaviours. For example, the ball can be grasped in many places, with different grips, etc.

## Persons

We use schemata to understand and predict the behaviour of others (Anderson, 1980; Hastie, 1981). Probably we all develop a general *person* schema, which includes slots for motivations, interests, personality traits etc. When encountering new people, we may instantiate this general schema. A cynic's general schema is likely be to be different from a social worker's.

There are also many more specific person schemata. The first type is for people we know. After repeated experiences with someone, we build up a schema of his traits, likes and dislikes, etc. When he acts contrary to our schema's expectations, we say he is 'not himself' or is 'acting out of character' (Anderson, 1980). The second type is for the person one knows best – oneself. It includes knowledge of strengths and weaknesses, personal traits, and characteristic behaviour in certain situations, based on experiences and the views of others. We use it to understand past and current events and predict future ones. The third type is for various social, ethnic and occupational groups. There might be a schema for librarians and one for bricklayers. The features of the *librarian* schema might be: female, quiet, orderly, etc.; those for the *bricklayer* might include features such as male, strong, a beer drinker, etc.

## Stories

Every culture has stories. They are a staple of books, magazines, television and films, and many conversations largely consist of anecdotes. Stories entertain and often instruct in morals.

Schemata are very important in understanding stories. We construct a specific schema of a given story. An example is from the start of a Jean-Paul Sartre tale cited in Norman (1982), 'They pushed us into a large white room and my eyes began to blink because the light hurt them'. Immediately the reader tries to construct a scenario for the events depicted. One obvious venue is a prison. Perhaps the hero is about to be interrogated. Another is a hospital.

We also have more general story schemata, which are instantiated, and are therefore used to understand specific stories. For example, there is a schema for murder mysteries. It has slots for the killer, the victim, the motive, the detective, the suspects, etc. To understand a detective story, this schema is instantiated with details. The victim slot is filled by a named person, and the suspects slot with other characters. A good suspense writer keeps the reader guessing until the end of the book as to how the killer slot should be filled.

Some interesting recent research has suggested that we have a very abstract story schema that is used to understand stories of all types (Thorndyke, 1977; Thorndyke and Yekovitch, 1980). It develops at an early age. Work in this area is often referred to as the 'story grammar approach', but the research can be regarded as looking at a very abstract schema. It has general slots for setting, main characters, and episodes. One hypothesised schema was proposed by Mandler (1984). It has slots that relate to each other in certain ways. First of all there is a setting, which may introduce the time and place and the main character/s. Secondly, the story has one or more distinct episodes, each of which has a beginning, a development and an ending. Each episode is usually organised around a goal. The hero has an aim, which he tries to achieve, and the ending describes his success or failure. An example is Franz Kafka's novel *The Castle*. The setting is Europe in this century and there is a hero. The book consists of a series of episodes, each of which reflects his aim of entering the castle. Each episode consists of a new method used. The development is his application of the method, and the ending is his failure to achieve it. The episodes are connected just by time. One episode occurs after another and there is no specific causal connection. In another type of story, each episode leads directly to the next. The events in one precipitate the events of the next.

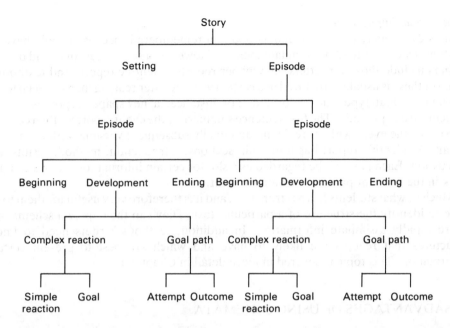

**Figure 12.** A story schema for the two-episode story in Table 1. The details in the story can be assimilated to the schema and thus understood. From Mandler, J. M. *Stories, scripts and scenes: aspects of schema theory.* Hillsdale, N. J.: Erlbaum. Reproduced with permission.

Figure 12 and Table 1 give an example. Figure 12 presents Mandler's schema of a simple two-episode story and Table 1 gives a story. The setting is a zoo at some unspecified time, and the protagonist a zookeeper. The two episodes are not causally linked. Each has a beginning (the lions roaring) that poses problems (e.g. quietening them down). Each episode is then resolved (e.g. when the lions go back to sleep).

**Table 1.** A sample story with two episodes from Mandler (1984). Figure 12 illustrates an abstract schema that is used to understand the story.

> All the animals at the zoo receive very good care. A zookeeper stays up each night to watch over them. One night the lions started making a lot of noise. One by one they started to roar and growl fiercely. The keeper was worried that they were sick or hurt. He wanted to see if something was wrong with them. He carried his bag of medicine into the lions' pen. The keeper fully checked over each one of the lions. He soon discovered that they were not sick at all. They were just trying to keep the other animals up. The zookeeper finally got them back to sleep. Soon things were quiet and the zoo was calm again. Later on the elephants all got into a water fight. They used their trunks to toss water at each other. The keeper was mad because they were making a mess. He wanted them all to be quiet and peaceful again. He ran after the frisky elephants with a big stick. He shouted angrily at them to stop the water fight. They paid no attention to him and just ran faster. They squirted lots of water all over the poor man. They made an awful muddy mess in the elephant yard. The zookeeper worked for three days cleaning it up.

What evidence supports the idea of an abstract story schema? Thorndyke and Yekovich (1980) summarise some lines of evidence. Firstly, people tend to recall only part of a given story, but it is the same part. They recall the themes rather than specific details. Secondly, people tend to restructure very poorly written stories, distort them to bring them in line with their schema. Thus, people who read a scrambled story tend to recall it in a form that fits the schema. Thirdly, the more explicit the temporal, causal and intentional relations between events in the story, the more comprehensible people find it.

*Educational implications*

Stories can usually be readily understood and remembered, because people have an abstract schema to readily assimilate them to. However, a story is just one kind of text. Others include those for letters, newspaper reports, scientific reports and textbooks. Each of these is usually structured in a certain way and after reading many of each text a schema for that type can be formed. For instance, a newspaper report is usually structured as a pyramid. The first sentence summarises the event reported, then comes a version of the event with more detail, and finally subsequent versions with even more detail. A scientific report has four main sections: introduction, method, results and discussion. Each part can be regarded as a slot for certain information and we can just look in the relevant part for the data we want.

Much of what students learn is from text, and it is therefore very useful for them to be able to identify the structure of a particular text. They can then apply a schema and more rapidly assimilate information. In addition, textbook writers need to know structures that readers are likely to have and which are best to present certain information. This topic is covered in more detail in Chapter 11.

## DISADVANTAGES OF USING SCHEMATA

Using a schema is like gambling. Sometimes it pays off but at other times it does not (Taylor and Crocker, 1981). Despite the many uses of schemata, relying on them can have drawbacks. Taylor and Crocker list some major ones.

### A lot of useful information may be lost

Since a schema acts like a filter, much data are kept out. Indeed, it is often useful to ignore data that cannot be assimilated. Most people have experienced reading a difficult text and passing their eyes over large, incomprehensible parts. On a fourth or fifth reading those parts may start to make sense because the reader forms schemata that allow them to be assimilated (Norman, 1982).

Yet, in some situations, the schema can filter too well. An example is the knight 'Don Quixote'. in the tale by Cervantes. His schema of the world was several centuries out of date. He saw windmills as giants and filtered out any contrary data. A person may disregard data that are inconsistent with ethnic stereotypes and, so, an inaccurate view is maintained. A person who sees almost all events on the world stage in terms of the East–West conflict ignores many other influences, such as nationalist and regional conflicts.

### Schemata are often hard to dislodge

A consequence of their function as a filter is that schemata are very often hard to dislodge. Once we feel the world is organised a certain way, we are reluctant to abandon that view. Indeed, the 'de-programmers' who try to change the schemata of cult converts often need days of isolation and constant haranguing to even dent them. Some years ago, two scientists suggested a somewhat different model of the DNA molecule to that of Crick and Watson. The new schema met with a great storm of protest. Classical conditioning. which revolutionised psychology early in this century, was discovered independently of Ivan Pavlov by an American. However, it did not fit scientists' existing schemata and the findings were ignored. While some conservatism is needed to perceive a relatively stable world, it can make for a stale field (Kuhn, 1962 and 1970).

We will see in Chapter 11 that this problem occurs in the classroom. It is especially important in science education, which often aims to replace an intuitive, pre-scientific schema (the world is flat; matter is completely solid) with a scientific one. Students strongly hold onto their existing schemata however, and greatly resist efforts to change them. Discrepant data are either ignored or the data change the schema in idiosyncratic ways, as we saw with the Nussbaum study.

**The wrong schema may be used**

This problem was cited earlier as a reason for lack of comprehension. A good example is a study by Langer and Abelson (1974). Subjects listened to a tape of two men talking. One group was told that the tape was a job interview, and the other that it was a psychiatric interview. The latter group found more evidence of 'pathology'. The schema may have induced them to interpret ambiguous data in pathological terms. Skemp (1979) discusses how early schemata that are acquired to cope with mathematics can hinder later learning. Students learn schemata at an early age that work for a time but prove inadequate for more advanced material.

## THE RELATIONSHIP BETWEEN CONCEPTS AND SCHEMATA

By now, you should be asking if 'schema' is just another name for 'concept'. There are indeed many similarities between them. Both are mental representations used to categorise stimuli as instances or non-instances of some category. Their uses also seem similar. 'Comprehension' and 'perception' seem much like 'making sense of the world'. 'Assigning default values' seems much like 'making inferences', and both concepts and schemata are learned by abstracting information from actual instances. How, then, are they different? Why not just call this book *Concepts*?

Unfortunately, this question is quite complex and it has several answers, which depend on how the two terms are defined and the theory of category representation adopted. One distinction is that a schema is a cluster of related concepts, as mentioned in Chapter 1 (Skemp, 1979). Thus the schema for *face* consists of such component concepts as *eyes, nose* and *chin*, related in a certain way. The *eating out* schema consists of such parts as entering the restaurant and paying the bill. By one definition, the component concepts must be related by space or time for the structure to be a schema (Mandler, 1979). Thus, a class inclusion taxonomy by this definition would not be a schema.

The distinction above has some flaws. Firstly, each component concept of a schema can also be considered a schema by the definition. Thus, *eyes* can be considered a schema consisting of such component concepts as *pupil, iris, eyelid* etc. By the same token, schemata such as *face* and *arm* can be considered concepts when they are part of larger conceptual structures. Thus, *face* can be seen as a component of the *body* schema and is thus a concept. Skemp (1979) gives the example of *vegetable*. It is regarded as a concept consisting of such instances as beans and peas and is a component of the *food* schema. However, it can also be considered a schema, since each instance can be reduced to concepts with instances. Thus, each can be seen as either a single concept or a set of related concepts.

Skemp suggests that a useful distinction is that a given representation can be considered a schema or a concept depending on what you want to do with it. For some purposes, it can be seen as a concept and for others as a schema. This distinction will be used in this book, and sometimes the terms will be used to refer to the same representation, according to which aspect we want to emphasise. Sometimes it is useful to consider *face* or *animal* as concepts with instances and at other times as conceptual structures. As schemata, we can look at them in terms of the characteristics of schemata in general – that they are hard to change and act as filters.

Another answer to the above question is to banish the concept of *concept* and just consider all mental representations of categories as schemata. This approach presupposes acceptance of the prototype theory of category representation, which is discussed in Chapter 6.


## FURTHER READING

Schema definition and uses: Rumelhart (1980 and 1984); Skemp (1971 and 1979).
Types of schema: Mandler (1984); Taylor and Crocker (1981).
The concept/schema relationship: Mandler (1979); Skemp (1979).

# Chapter 4

# Some Characteristics of Concepts

SUMMARY

1. Some taxonomies have a basic-level of abstraction. Concepts on this level are often learned first and are most often used.
2. A concept's instances may vary in the extent to which they are typical instances. Typicality in some cases is due to a concept having a family-resemblance structure.
3. Some category boundaries are clear-cut, but others are vague. Sometimes a clear-cut border is imposed on the boundary between two concepts. Also, category borders are moveable according to our purposes.
4. Some concepts are understood with a metaphor, and some complex concepts such as *mind* are understood with a cluster of metaphors, each of which gives a partial understanding of the notion.

## INTRODUCTION

This chapter describes some important characteristics of concepts, mostly found in recent research. All have implications for concept teaching, some of which will be mentioned here and others in Chapter 10. These characteristics also provide a means of evaluating the theories of category representation described in Chapter 6 and those of semantic memory described in Chapter 5. We can compare the theories in terms of how well they account for the characteristics.

## SOME CONCEPTS REPRESENT BASIC-LEVEL CATEGORIES

Chapter 1 described how a given concept exists at some level of abstraction in one or more taxonomies. Thus, *fish* is part of a taxonomy that stretches up to *animal, life form* and *thing*, and down to, say, *salmon* and *perch*. An exemplar of one concept in a taxonomy may also be an exemplar of many others at different abstraction levels. My dog 'Fido', for example, is not just a dog, but it is also a canine, a mammal, a life form and an object. I could refer to Fido with a very abstract name ('Meet my object Fido') or with a very specific one ('Meet my two-year-old, black and brown, pedigree, spotted, beagle Fido') (Brown, 1958).

But, in everyday life, people do not usually operate on any abstraction level they please. It would sound quite ludicrous, in most circumstances, to hear a person say, 'Here comes a black life form' or, 'I typed a letter on my Swiss-made, portable, manual, green, Hermes 3000 typewriter'. One level seems too abstract and the other too specific. Instead, people tend to talk and think about stimuli at one particular level. We are apt to refer to various animals as dogs, cats, possums and bears, rather than as canines, mammals and life forms. We are apt to refer to household implements as tables and chairs rather than as objects, goods or special cane rocking-chairs. This common, oft-used abstraction level is called the *basic-level* (Rosch *et al*, 1976).

Figure 13 presents two taxonomies with the basic-level marked out. It is the level of car, bus and truck in the *vehicle* taxonomy and of maple, birch and oak in the taxonomy for *tree*. The level above the basic is the *superordinate*. In fact, there are several abstraction levels above the superordinate, which are also superordinate levels. The level below the basic is the *subordinate*, and again there are more subordinate levels below those shown. Rosch *et al* argue that when people think and talk about trees and vehicles, they use the basic-level most often.

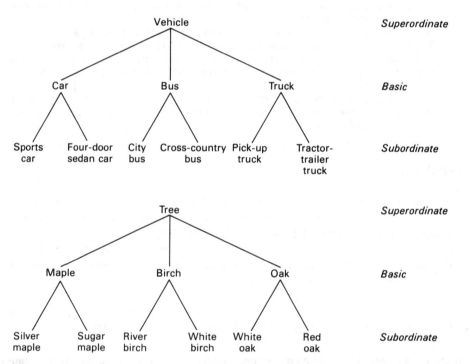

**Figure 13.** Two taxonomies showing superordinate, basic and subordinate levels. Data are from Rosch *et al* (1976).

Basic-levels have been shown on some more esoteric conceptual structures than just *vehicle* and *tree*. Cantor *et al* (1980) found evidence for a basic-level in the psychiatric taxonomy. An informal study by Rosch (1978) suggests a basic-level for event concepts. Students listed the events they had experienced on a certain day and usually picked units of time, such as *made coffee, took a shower* and *went to statistics class*. They did not typically use very broad events or very specific ones such as *picked up the toothpaste tube*. Tversky and Hemenway (1983) showed a basic-level on structures for various environmental scenes. We can divide the world broadly up into indoors and outdoors, but we do not use such terms very often unless being evasive. Rather than saying 'I am going outdoors', we are apt to say 'I am going to school'. The basic-level they found consisted of concepts such as *school, home, beach* and *mountains*. Figure 14 presents their results.

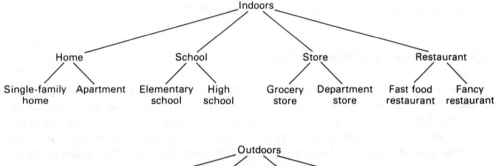

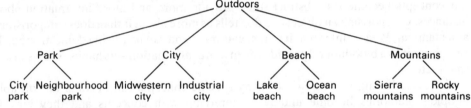

**Figure 14.** The structures for environmental scenes used by Tversky and Hemenway (1983). The study suggested that the middle level (e.g. school, restaurant) on each was the basic-level. From Tversky, B. and Hemenway, K. Categories of environmental scenes. *Cognitive Psychology* **15**, Florida: Academic Press, 1983. Reproduced with permission.

## Properties of basic-level concepts

Basic-level categories are interesting because they have some special properties. First of all, they are usually the first concepts learned on a taxonomy, though Anglin (1977) gives some cases when concepts from other levels are learned first. Parents are likely to teach children *cat* before *animal* or *Siamese cat*, for example.

Secondly, on a taxonomy they are the most abstract concepts whose exemplars have a reasonably similar shape and which can be represented by a visual image. For example, instances of *car* and *truck* look much alike, but do exemplars of *vehicle*? A jet-plane bears little resemblance to rollerskates or a bicycle, or a horse to a space-shuttle. The only common feature to instances of vehicle, as to instances of many superordinate categories, is their shared function. They get people or objects from one place to another. Thus, people can conceive a common shape for basic-level concepts such as *bird, chair* and *table* but not for superordinates such as *animal* and *life form*. The exemplars just look too different.

Thirdly, exemplars of basic-level categories tend to elicit common behaviours, or, to use the vernacular, have 'common motor programmes'. Thus, instances of *chair* tend to produce much the same response – people sit on them – but instances of *furniture* do not. We do not really react to bookends, chair, lamp and coffee-table book in the same specific way.

Finally, objects may first be recognised as instances of a given basic-level category, rather than a more or less abstract one. Rosch *et al* (1976) showed subjects a category name and half a second later a photograph of an object. Each subject had to say whether the object depicted was an instance of the category named. He might, for example, see 'bird' and then later a photograph of a bird. Subjects were quickest to categorise when the word named a basic-level category. Murphy and Smith (1982) replicated this result with artificial categories – specially constructed tool shapes.

### Why pick one level in particular as basic?

Why do we adopt one abstraction level as the basic level and not another? Rosch (1978) argues that the basic-level arises as a compromise between two conflicting requirements. The first is to maximise the amount of information that our concepts provide and the second is to maintain cognitive economy. This should be elaborated. As our concepts become less abstract, they provide more and more information about instances. Categorising an object as a dog tells us more about it than does categorising it as a mammal. We can infer that it barks, eats meat and can be readily domesticated. To categorise it as a bloodhound provides even more information – its habits, keen sense of smell, etc.

However, having and using too many specific concepts can become unworkable. People's memories become unduly cluttered up with concepts and they may be continually making finer discriminations than necessary. The optimal strategy is to maximise the amount of information provided by our concepts, while keeping their number small enough in order that they stay manageable and useful. This trade-off is achieved at the basic-level. Basic-level concepts maximise data provided by using correlations between features in the environment. They make use of 'information-rich bundles of attributes', natural groupings of features that 'cry out to be named'. Instances of particular basic-level categories are thus very obviously different from instances of other basic-level categories.

### The level selected as basic is moveable

Yet the picture is not quite so straightforward. It seems unlikely that everyone will adopt the same level on a given taxonomy as the basic. Since concepts are constructed for practical use, for some persons the cultural basic-level may not be very useful. One such case is with experts. They may adopt a more specific level as their basic-level, because they need to make finer discriminations. The basic-level for *wine*, for example, might be red and white or a slightly more specific level for most people, but a professional wine-taster might need to operate on a much more specific level. While *fish* might be sufficiently abstract and a good basic-level concept for laypersons, a marine biologist or professional fisherman might need a much less abstract level. Rosch *et al* (1976) described an aircraft mechanic whose basic-level was not *aeroplane* as for other subjects in their study, but was more specific. Indeed, Stones (1984) recounts the tale of a teacher who held up a picture of a cow and asked her students to name it. There was no response! Did they not know what it was? She later found out that they were from a farming community and were trying to work out what breed it was! Their basic-level was less abstract than hers.

An analogous phenomenon may occur across cultures. People of different cultures inhabit different environments and therefore need to make different sorts of discriminations. Again, the level they choose as basic may depend on the purposes their environment requires (Dougherty, 1978). Where urban Americans see a tree, the Tzeltal Mayas living in a forest may see an oak. Since the plant taxonomy is more important to forest-dwellers, they need a more specific basic-level. The Eskimos have many categories of snow, just as a professional skier might, because snow is much more important to them and they need to make finer discriminations. Dougherty argues that different cultures may only pay attention to certain features and may greatly exaggerate the correlations between them in order to produce a basic-level.

### Using levels other than the basic

We do, of course, use subordinate and superordinate levels, depending on our purposes. Here are some situations. For example, the statement 'Here comes a black life form' would be appropriate to, say, an extraterrestrial explorer who had no more specific category in which the object could be placed. Similarly, Olson (1970) argues that some contexts require a more specific level than the basic. We could say, 'Look at that flower', if there were only one flower in the scene, but we would need to say 'Look at that rose' if there were several. Another aim is communication. A marine biologist discussing fish with a layperson would be likely to operate on the latter's basic-level rather than his own. Similarly, we might refer to a dog with a superordinate category name to communicate a certain meaning, 'Get that *animal* out of here' (Rosch, 1978). Rosch gives another example of a situation in which a subordinate category name might be appropriate – to satirise a book. She quotes Garis's (1975) parody of a novel that has been accused of being mainly about brand-name snobbery, '. . . lining up my Mongol number 3 pencils on my Goldsmith Brothers Formica imitation-wood desk, I slide into my oversize squirrel-skin L. L. Bean slippers. . . .'

### Educational applications

Since basic-level concepts are the easiest to learn and most used, they should, in most cases, be taught first. Some textbooks recommend starting at the most abstract level of a taxonomy and proceeding downwards (e.g. Ausubel, 1968), but it would seem better to start at the basic-level. Thus, when teaching the *animal* taxonomy, rather than starting from *animal* or *life form* and proceeding downwards, it would be better to start with basic-level concepts, such as *dog* and *cat*, and proceed up and down from them. Research in this area also suggests that superordinate concepts may often be harder to learn, especially with younger children, and they, therefore, may need more extensive teaching.

## A CONCEPT'S EXEMPLARS MAY VARY IN TYPICALITY

Chapter 1 mentioned the question, 'Do exemplars of a concept vary in the extent to which they are good instances?' The answer seems to be 'yes'. As was shown in Chapter 3, instantiations of a schema may vary in the extent to which they are good exemplars. There is much evidence that instances of many concepts can be ranged along a gradient from very typical to atypical. Consider the concept *bird*. Exemplars such as penguin and ostrich seem less typical birds than robin and sparrow. One can readily think of good and poor exemplars of *funny joke, happy person* and *young man* (Wicklegren, 1979). Figure 15 presents some more examples.

Bird

Expression of joy

Third world nation

Chad    Mexico    Malaysia    South Korea

**Figure 15.** Some examples of concepts whose instances vary in typicality.

Just as instances may vary in typicality, so non-instances may vary in the extent to which they are good non-instances (Barsalou, 1983). For example, bat and pterodactyl would be poorer non-instances of *bird* than computer and desk. North Korea is a better non-instance of *democracy* than Paraguay.

### Evidence for typicality

Typicality of a given concept's instances has been shown by a variety of studies. The simplest kind of study uses a rating task. Subjects are given a concept name (e.g. bird, weapon) and a number of exemplars. They then rate the extent to which each is a typical (or good) exemplar. They may use a five-point scale with 5 as very typical and 1 as very atypical. People generally find this task sensible and readily generate ratings. Table 2 presents a representative set of results. The higher the number, the more typical the instance. The table shows that exemplars of the concepts vary considerably in rated typicality. For instance, robin gets a higher rating than goose.

**Table 2.** Typicality ratings for instances of *bird* and *mammal*. The higher the value, the more typical the instance. Data are from Rips *et al.*

| Bird | | Mammal | |
|---|---|---|---|
| *Instance* | *Rating* | *Instance* | *Rating* |
| Robin | 3.00 | Deer | 2.83 |
| Sparrow | 3.00 | Horse | 2.76 |
| Bluejay | 2.92 | Goat | 2.75 |
| Parakeet | 2.83 | Cat | 2.67 |
| Pigeon | 2.83 | Dog | 2.67 |
| Eagle | 2.75 | Lion | 2.67 |
| Cardinal | 2.67 | Cow | 2.58 |
| Hawk | 2.67 | Bear | 2.58 |
| Parrot | 2.58 | Rabbit | 2.58 |
| Chicken | 2.00 | Sheep | 2.58 |
| Duck | 2.00 | Mouse | 2.25 |
| Goose | 2.00 | Pig | 2.17 |

Studies using the above rating task have shown the typicality of the instances from a wide range of concepts. Rosch (1973 and 1975) found typicality effects with *fruit, clothing* and various geometric figures. Armstrong *et al* (1983) found typicality effects with well-defined concepts such as *even number* and *female*. For instance, 4 and 8 were rated as better exemplars of *even number* than 34 and 106, and ballerina was rated as a better exemplar of *female* than policewoman and cowgirl. Pulman (1983, pp. 110–13) found typicality effects with action concepts, such as *look, kill* and *walk*. Assassinate and execute were rated as better instances of *kill* than was sacrifice. Berlin and Kay (1969) showed that people from various cultures agreed that certain wavelengths were good, typical exemplars of colours, such as *blue*.* Other wavelengths were seen as much less typical instances.

Studies using other tasks have demonstrated typicality effects (Mervis and Rosch, 1981). A final source of evidence is from concept learning. Typicality is an important factor. People tend to learn typical exemplars of a concept first and later learn the less typical ones. Indeed, concepts are much easier to learn from typical exemplars. Mervis and Pani (1980) give an amusing example. In one study, children and adults learned artificial concepts from either typical or atypical instances. One child who had to learn from the atypical ones acquired the concept only with some difficulty. But when she had done so, she immediately handed the typical exemplars to the experimenter with the admonition that the task would have been much easier if she had been given them first!

---

* The visual spectrum covers the electromagnetic wavelengths from about 400 to 700 nanometers (nm). Certain wavelengths are perceived as particular colours. Thus, light above about 620 nm is perceived as red.

**Causes of typicality**

Why do exemplars of a given concept differ in typicality? Some theoretical accounts are examined in Chapter 6 but some are mentioned below. There seem to be several causes, which vary with the nature of the concept (Barsalou, 1985). Two reasons are as follows.

*Family resemblance structures*
Instances of some complex natural concepts may only be held together by a set of similarities – a set of family resemblances. Exemplar typicality may result from this internal 'family resemblance' structure. The notion of family resemblance was first applied to concepts by Wittgenstein (1953). First of all it will be explained and then how it applies to concept structure and to typicality will be described.

Figure 16 gives two examples of family resemblance. Consider Section B, ignoring the face in the middle. The family members all look alike, but not in any single way. There is no feature that characterises them all, such as a moustache, or a large nose. Instead one member looks a bit like another, who in turn looks a bit like a third, but in a slightly different way. Thus, some, but not all, have a certain moustache. Some, but not all, have large ears, and some have a beard. The members are thus linked by a set of similarities. One has some features of another, who has some different ones of a third, etc. Now consider Section A, focusing on the five sets of letters and considering each as analogous to a family member. They consist of several features (a, b, c, d, etc.), but there is no single feature that all share. Thus, only 1 and 2 have b, and only 3 and 4 have d. Instead of being linked by a common feature they are linked by similarities. Thus, 1 is somewhat similar to 2 because they share a feature, and 2 is somewhat similar to 3 because they share a feature. So, 1 is a bit like 2, 2 is a bit like 3, and 1 is indirectly linked to 4 and 5 through this network.

Wittgenstein argued that the exemplars of many natural concepts are only held together in this way. Some concepts do not have a common feature that, for example, would correspond to 'hunts prey' for *predator* or 'has four sides' for *square*. His oft-cited example is *game*, which has such exemplars as chess, football, solitaire, poker and space invaders. These instances vary in many ways. Some are entirely mental, such as chess and bridge. Others are mostly physical, such as football, and 'Olympic games', such as boxing and the marathon. Some games, such as blackjack and poker, involve much chance, while others, such as chess, involve little or no chance. What common feature/s do games have which put them all into one category? What are the defining features of *game* which correspond to 'hunts prey' for *predator*?

Certain possibilities can be examined. One is: 'involves competition between two or more players or sides'; this feature characterises chess, poker and bridge, but not solitaire, which has one player. Another possibility is 'provides amusement for the players'. That covers monopoly and solitaire, but not high-level bouts between star tennis players or boxers, who may get no joy from a hard, tense struggle done for a living. That feature also characterises activities not usually classed as games, such as watching television. Another possibility is 'a contest to provide a winner', but this does not cover solitaire or party games such as charades.

Section A

Instances

| 1 | 2 | 3 | 4 | 5 | (Prototype) |
|---|---|---|---|---|---|
| abhi | bcjk | cdlm | deno | efpq | bcde |

Non-instances

| A | B | C |
|---|---|---|
| ahrs | ctyz | dvwx |

Section B

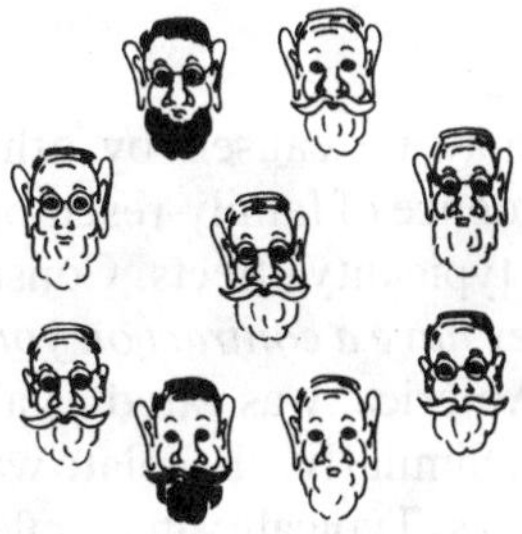

**Figure 16.** Some examples of family-resemblance structures. The prototype for each category (see Chapter 6 for details) has many, or all, of the features that characterise exemplars. It is thus most similar to the instances and least similar to non-instances. Thus, the prototype has few or no features in common with each non-instance, while the exemplars in some cases do. The prototype is therefore more dissimilar to non-instances than to the exemplars. The faces in B are from Armstrong, S. E., Gleitman, L. R. and Gleitman, H. What some concepts might not be. *Cognition* **13**, North Holland Publishing Company, 1983. Reproduced with permission.

Instead, exemplars of *game* are held together by a set of similarities. Chess has some features in common with bridge. It aims to produce a winner, is mental and involves much skill. Bridge has some other features in common with poker – it involves some chance. It has some features in common with soccer – a team, rather than individuals, competes. Soccer has some similarities with baseball – teams compete and both are mostly physical and involve little chance. The conclusion is that any game may be a little like any other, just as one family member may be a little like any other one.

This notion accounts for typicality effects with some concepts. First, note that instances of a concept may vary in the number of such features held in common by pairs of instances. Again, consider Figure 16. In Section A instance 1 has only one feature that characterises some exemplars: b. Instance 2, however, has two features: b and c, and so does 3: c and d. The typicality of instances is correlated with the number of features an instance has. Instances 2, 3 and 4, each with two such features, would be more typical instances than 1 and 5, which only have one. Chess has many shared features of games – it is a contest to produce a winner, often gives amusement, etc. Charades, however, is a less typical instance because it has far fewer shared features. It has no sides, competition, or winner. A robin, therefore, is a typical bird, because it has many features that birds tend to share – it flies, gets around in the daytime, builds a nest, sings, etc. A penguin is atypical because it has many fewer shared features – it does not fly, build a nest, or sing.

Rosch and Mervis (1975) found some evidence for this family-resemblance account of typicality. In one study, they used such concepts as *fruit, weapon* and *furniture*. One group rated the typicality of several instances of each (e.g. for *weapon*, instances such as gun, tank, club, rocket and screwdriver). Then a second group had a short time to write down some features of each instance. For example, they might be given 'bicycle' and have to list features that bicycles have in common. Responses would be 'has two wheels', 'has pedals' and 'you ride on them'. The number of features that a given instance shared with others correlated well with the typicality ratings. Very typical exemplars shared many features with other exemplars and atypical ones shared far fewer.

*Other causes of typicality*
For some concepts, typicality of exemplars may be caused by other factors. For instance, Barsalou (1983 and 1985) found no evidence of family-resemblance structures with *ad hoc* concepts, yet he still obtained clear typicality effects. Consider his concept *ways to escape being killed by the Mafia when they have a contract on you*. 'Change your identity and move to the mountains of South America' was rated as a better instance than 'Change where you are living in Las Vegas'. Similarly, chocolate was rated a better exemplar of *foods not to eat on a diet* than bread was. Typicality may reflect an instance's value on a single dimension. For 'foods . . .' calorie content may be the basis. The typical instances hold more calories. For 'ways to escape . . .', perceived safety may be the basis. The mountains of South America are safer than Las Vegas – from the Mafia, anyway.

## SOME CATEGORY BOUNDARIES ARE UNCLEAR

The existence of typicality effects and poor concept exemplars leads naturally to the following question that was also posed in Chapter 1. Are the boundaries between categories on the same abstraction level definite or vague? Is it always clear whether a given stimulus falls into a particular category? This question might best be answered with an analogy to the borders between nations. The boundary between some countries is quite clear. A river separates Argentina and Uruguay and there is no doubt where the land of one ends and that of the other begins. The border between other nations, however, is uncertain. The one between Indonesia and Papua New Guinea is ill-defined. The terrain is mountainous and jungle-covered, and no one is sure where each country begins. The border between some nations is well-defined, but some people think it is in one place and others see it as somewhere else. For example, Chile and Argentina long disputed possession of some islands near Tierra del Fuego. Chileans saw the border in one place and the Argentinians saw it in another. Finally, some borders may be moveable. Sometimes a given piece of land is in one nation and at another time is in a different country. Over the centuries the borders of Poland have expanded and contracted and sometimes the nation has disappeared entirely.

## Well-defined concepts

The borders between some well-defined concepts are quite clear. It is usually pretty certain whether a given figure is a square, parallelogram, pentagon or rectangle. As long as the defining features are applied rigorously, the border is definite.

## Ill-defined concepts

The borders of many natural concepts are quite fuzzy. Although the categorisation of most exemplars may be quite clear, the atypical ones may pose more of a problem. Ulric Neisser (1967) put it well:

> Ill-defined categories are the rule, not the exception, in daily life. The visual distinctions between dogs and cats, or between beauty and ugliness are ill-defined, just like the conceptual differences between creative science and hack work, or health and neurosis. So are the EEG [electroencephalogram] patterns which indicate a particular stage of sleep, the X-ray shadows which suggest a tumor, the style of painting which identifies a Picasso, or the features which continue to characterise the face of a friend through the years.
>
> Neisser (1967)

### *Evidence for unclear boundaries*

Here are some studies that showed unclear borders. Berlin and Kay (1969), as mentioned earlier, found that subjects readily agreed on focal colours, on best-examples of *red* or *blue*. But they disagreed on the colour categorisation of the wavelengths near the boundaries. Thus, a given wavelength might be called 'red' by one person and some other colour by another.

Labov (1973) examined the border between *cup* and *bowl*. Exemplars of each vary greatly in typicality. A very typical cup might be a teacup with a handle, while a less typical exemplar is perhaps a coffee mug. An atypical cup might be bowl-shaped with no handle. But where is the border between *cup* and *bowl*? To find out, Labov, in one experiment, showed subjects objects like those in Figure 17. They vary according to their height/width ratio. As this width increases, the object seems to become more like a bowl. Subjects were shown objects and had to say whether each was a cup or a bowl. Figure 18 presents the results. As the width increased, fewer subjects called the object shown a cup, suggesting they had different cut-off points. There was no definite border that all subjects agreed upon. Labov also showed that the boundary could be altered by context, again revealing how variable it is. In one context, subjects imagined the object filled with mashed potatoes. As the figure shows, the border then shifted.

McCloskey and Glucksberg (1978) examined the borders between natural concepts, such as *ship, sport, insect* and *kitchen utensil*. Subjects were shown pairs like 'apple–fruit', and they had to say if one member was an instance of the other. There were three types of pairs. In the first type, one member was a highly typical exemplar of the concept named by the other (e.g. carrot–vegetable). In the second, one was a less typical exemplar (e.g. bookends–furniture), and in the third was a clear non-exemplar (e.g. cucumber–furniture). Subjects were tested twice, one month apart. They agreed quite well on the categorisation of the typical and unrelated items and performed much the same in each session with these pairs. The situation, however, was quite different with the less typical pairs. Some subjects categorised them as exemplars and some did not. One might say that a leech was a insect and a stroke was a disease while another did not.

**Figure 17.** Stimuli used by Labov to explore the boundary between cup and bowl. These stimuli represent different kinds of cup. From *New Ways of Analysing Variation in English*. Edited by Charles-James N. Baily and Roger W. Shuy. Washington, D.C. Georgetown University Press. Copyright © 1973 by Georgetown University. Used with permission.

Also, the same person was sometimes inconsistent in both sessions. He might say that bookends was an instance of furniture in one session but not in the other.

### Imposing a boundary on fuzzy category borders

Sometimes we need precise concept definitions and so clear-cut borders on fuzzy categories are imposed (e.g. Zadeh, 1965; Wicklegren, 1979). Experts are particularly likely to impose them. While opposition and government members may dispute whether a specific downturn is a recession, an economist can say so for sure. A recession occurs when gross national product declines in two consecutive quarters. Other precise definitions are that an adult is someone over 18 (or 21) years, and a small business is one with fewer than 50 employees. The definition can be stringent or lax according to people's aims. The Australian Government, for example, defines *unemployed* as anyone actively looking for employment who has worked less than one hour in the past week. The definition is quite strict, because it excludes those who want a job but who have given up searching because of repeated failure and those who earn a little cash each week mowing lawns.

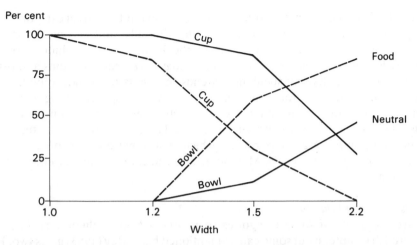

**Figure 18.** Results of an experiment by Labov (1973). As the height/width ratio increases, fewer subjects call the object a cup. The figure also shows how context affects the boundary between cup and bowl. The food context condition alters the boundary. The figure is from *New Ways of Analysing Variation in English*. Edited by Charles-James N. Baily and Roger W. Shuy. Washington, D.C. Georgetown University Press. Copyright © 1973 by Georgetown University. Used with permission.

Particular cultures may impose definite borders. For example, the bounds of *permissible behaviour* are different in England than in Saudi Arabia. In the latter, the category does not include drinking alcohol or partying. *Edible food* may include pork for non-Muslims but would not for Muslims (Sigel, 1983). A society may continually redefine the border of a category over time. For instance, the US Constitution forbids any 'cruel and unusual punishment'. Exactly which punishments go in or out of this category is unclear and is left essentially to each generation of judges to determine. One hundred and fifty years ago, capital punishment was definitely not in the category but in the early 1970s was. The death penalty is now outside the category but in a few years' time might be back in. Perhaps in 20 or 30 years imprisonment and even fines may be included in the constitutional category. Exactly where a border should fall is often greatly controversial (Wessells, 1982). For example, the issues of when human life begins and ends or when material is obscene are much debated.

*Moveable boundaries*
As the above examples suggest, category borders are sometimes quite moveable. Since concepts are constructed for practical use, their limits may need to be expanded or contracted for particular purposes. Skemp (1979), for example, suggests that whether a certain stimulus is included in a given category depends on what people want to do with it. Thus, for some purposes (such as licencing) a moped might be considered a motorcycle and for others (such as insurance and bridge tolls) a bicycle. Similarly, we would narrow the limits of *suitable joke* when speaking to a Rotary Club luncheon group and extend them for the locker room crowd after a football game. A government may extend the border of *drunk driver* (from say 0.08% to 0.05% blood alcohol level) to reduce accident rates, or it may narrow it (to say 0.1%) because of pressure from the liquor trade. The concept *anti-Soviet activity* has very variable bounds.

Lakoff (1973) suggests that we often use *hedges* to extend or retract category borders. A hedge is a qualifying term, such as 'virtually', 'usually' and 'technically speaking'. Thus, the hedge 'par excellence' narrows the limits to just include very typical instances. Robins and sparrows are *birds par excellence* while penguins and ostriches are not. The hedge 'loosely speaking' extends the limits to include stimuli near but outside the usual limits – for example, we can say, 'Loosely speaking a moped is a motorcycle' or, 'Loosely speaking, Homo Erectus was a human being'. The hedge 'technically' may impose a clear cut-off point. Hedges allow us to categorise and re-categorise stimuli for given purposes, which means that our categories can be very flexible, according to our needs. Metaphors also can extend category boundaries (see next section).

*Reasons for fuzzy boundaries*
Why are the limits of some categories so imprecise? Some theoretical reasons are considered in Chapter 6 but some can be mentioned here. Rey (1983) gives two. Firstly, a person simply may not know enough about a category to categorise peripheral instances. For instance, some people do not know any or all of the defining features of *fruit*, so are unsure whether a tomato is one or not, or they may not recognise the defining features of *mammal*, and so have trouble with exemplars such as the whale and dolphin. One has to know that mammals give milk to their young, deliver young alive, and breathe air. The second reason is poorly constructed category systems or ones that simply cannot accommodate certain stimuli. Since all concepts are to some extent arbitrary, this event may not be too uncommon. Some examples are as follows. As mentioned in Chapter 1, viruses defy categorisation as *life* or *non-life*. Although they are composed of DNA and proteins and are able to reproduce by taking over a cell, in some respects they are like crystals, which also reproduce. The strange organism *Euglena* cannot be readily categorised as *plant* or *animal*. While it has some features of *animal* that plants lack (e.g. it moves about), it also manufactures chlorophyll, which makes plants green. Which category does it belong to? The platypus has the bill of a duck, the fur and milk glands of a mammal, and lays eggs like a reptile or bird. When the first specimens were taken to Europe, the animal was widely regarded as a hoax.

## Some educational implications

The characteristics of typicality and fuzzy boundaries have several educational implications. First of all, a suggestion is that concepts are best learned from highly typical exemplars and that these should be presented first. The peripheral instances can be acquired later. It is also useful for students to know that category membership is often a matter of degree and that some stimuli are very hard to categorise. This seems especially important with social science concepts, such as *democracy* (see Chapter 10), where there are good and poor exemplars and many borderline cases. In addition, borderline cases must be taught, so that a student's concept is much like the teacher's. A student's concept of *mammal* is inadequate if he does not know about whales and dolphins and why they are instances. Finally, in teaching some disciplines it is useful to tell students the fuzzy nature of the concepts used (such as those in psychiatry and sociology). Then students will have a better basis for understanding the domain that each discipline deals with.

## SOME CONCEPTS MAY BE UNDERSTOOD THROUGH METAPHORS

Many primitive societies populate their worlds with countless supernatural characters. The trees, rocks, lakes, mountains and deserts are regarded as spirits or as physical objects inhabited by them. The Ancient Greeks, for example, saw streams and fields filled with various nymphs, satyrs and demi-gods, and the sun itself as a chariot ridden across the sky by Apollo. Like people, these spirits had their likes and dislikes, got angry and sad, and had various mortals as favourites. Because inanimate objects such as the sun were conceptualised as being much like people, they could be understood as such and the natural world seemed more comprehensible. The Old Norse could explain thunder and lightning as the result of Thor getting angry and pounding his hammer. The moon moved across the sky because it was being chased by a ferocious wolf bent on devouring it. A volcano erupted because the fire demons inside had been offended.

Conceptualising the world in terms of persons also allowed people to believe they could better deal with it and thus had some control over it. They could bring gifts to the fire demons in the volcano to pacify them, just as one might do so to placate an angry person. Sailors caught in a storm appealed to the sea spirits to smooth the waves, and fishermen appealed to them for a good catch. A farmer could ask the cloud spirits for rain. Thus, their extensive knowledge of people and human relations could be brought to bear on understanding and dealing with a quite different domain, the natural world. Because they lacked more useful schemata provided by modern meteorology, geology and gravitational physics, they constructed schemata from their person knowledge.

The above is an instance of use of *metaphor*, a very important phenomenon in understanding concepts and schemata. Metaphors are frequently used to create new concepts and schemata in order to understand the world. Firstly, *metaphor* is defined and described below in some detail and then some uses of metaphors are detailed, followed by a discussion of their use in constructing concepts.

### Definition of metaphor

One view is that a metaphor is a kind of comparison between two concepts in which some aspects of one are transferred to the other to highlight or help understand parts of it (Ortony, 1980). Though usually literally false, such a comparison makes sense when taken non-literally. Consider the following examples from Ortony:

> My surgeon is a butcher.
> His words were harsh.
> The silence was deafening.
> George is a pig.
> Her research program ran into a bramble patch.

Each involves two concepts of concern (*surgeon* and *butcher, word* and *harshness*). Taken literally each is either false or absurd. My surgeon has not trained or worked as a butcher and George is a human being. Silence cannot deafen. Only intense noise can deafen in this sense.

However, each example makes sense if taken as a metaphor – as a transference of some aspects of one concept to the other. This transference suggests a resemblance between the two – an analogy that causes the statement to make sense. 'My surgeon is a butcher' becomes plausible if a few aspects of butcher, one being 'hacks carelessly', are carried over and applied to surgeon. This example is saying that the surgeon is careless like a butcher. Similarly, some aspects of bramble patch (thick, impenetrable, impedes progress) can be applied to research programme, which suggests that it has met with difficulties. Thus, several things are involved in a metaphor. There are two concepts; the aspects of one are transferred (hacks about, impedes progress) and the remaining ones are not transferred (that bramble patches grow in certain localities and have leaves, etc.). In the example of primitive societies given at the beginning of this section, only some aspects of *person* are transferred.

Sometimes a statement is literally correct and is plausible but still is a metaphor because of the context. Ortony (1980) gives the example, 'The Indians were on the warpath'. In the context of a western the statement would be correct literally, but in other contexts would be a metaphor. Consider some children giving their teacher or babysitter a trying time, or some workers about to strike for improved working conditions. They are not Indians and are not going to war, but some aspects of 'The Indians were on the warpath' transfer to the situation.

Metaphors fall into three main types (Ortony, 1980). The first type is *new ones*, which can be amusing for a time. An example from Bierce (1906) is, 'Envelope: The scabbard of a bill. The husk of a remittance. The bedgown of a love letter'. The second type is *frozen* metaphors, which are repeated so often that they become part of the language (e.g. head of state, catch a cold). The third group is *partially frozen*, falling in between the extremes.

Finally, a metaphor has entailments. It has implications. If one applies a concept from one domain to another, many aspects of the first domain are transferred along with those you wish to emphasise. Consider the metaphor 'time is money', popular in western societies but incomprehensible to people in some Asian and South Pacific cultures. By accepting the metaphor, our concept of *time* changes somewhat because the following entailments are added (Lakoff and Johnson, 1980):

Time is a limited resource.
Time is valuable.
Time can be saved up or it can be wasted.
Time should be hoarded.

Similarly, if we accept the metaphor 'an argument is war', our concept of *argument* changes because many entailments follow:

A view can be attacked or defended.
A view can win or lose.

Indeed, a common political device is to present a new metaphor or simile, which can alter people's understanding of some domain because they also accept its entailments (Lakoff and Johnson, 1980). In 1977, US President Jimmy Carter wanted to convince the population that strong measures were needed to combat the energy crisis. He offered the following metaphor:

The energy crisis is the moral equivalent of war.

Many entailments follow and people's concept of the energy crisis changes. The nation must be mobilised, it must take drastic action, and throw its resources and efforts into dealing with the problem. The crisis needs to be defeated as an enemy should be defeated. Some years later, Ronald Reagan offered a metaphor to change people's understanding of the 'Contra' guerillas fighting in Nicaragua:

The Contras are the moral equivalent of the American founding fathers.

If one accepts the metaphor, many entailments follow and those guerillas are seen to have a much more positive role.

## Some uses of metaphors

The value of metaphors has been debated a great deal. One view that long held sway in education is that metaphors are frivolous and unnecessary. An opposing view, now gathering much support, holds that they are extremely important and have many important uses. Ortony *et al* (1978) list some.

*Communicating in a pleasing way*
Metaphors create new and interesting ways to communicate. People find them pleasing. A teacher can use them to make teaching more interesting and to keep students more involved as they try to work the metaphors out. Indeed, many English expressions were once creative metaphors, which now hover just above absolute zero through over-use.

Metaphors are thus a staple of the novelist and poet. Many novels and plays expound a complex metaphor, thus allowing the author to say his piece in an interesting way. For example, the film *They Shoot Horses Don't They* features a marathon ballroom dance in which couples suffer enormous mental and physical strain striving to outlast each other on the dance floor for a modest cash prize. The marathon is evidently a metaphor for American society, the author using it to say that many Americans push themselves to their limits in the 'rat-race' for little gain compared to the cost involved in doing so.

*Bridging the known and unknown*
Good teachers have long used metaphors to bridge the gap between the known and unknown. A student will have a better mental grip on some abstract, unfamiliar concept, like the structure of the atom, if he relates it to something he already knows. Some aspects of the known are therefore transferred to the unknown. An atom can be better understood when the metaphor 'An atom is a miniature solar system' is applied. Similarly, the immune system can be understood in terms of the more familiar concept of *war*, 'White blood cells are the soldiers of the body, defending against invasion by foreign organisms'. The human memory system can be understood with a library metaphor. 'The memory system is like a library. Storage of books is like storage of information. Memory data also are organised like books in a library, etc.' Thus, many new concepts and schemata may be learned through metaphors (Rumelhart and Norman, 1981).

Ortony (1980) points out that a metaphor can highlight some aspects of an unfamiliar concept and show some previously unseen relationships. He gives this example from a social studies textbook: 'Coffee became king in Brazil'. While coffee beans were not literally enthroned, some aspects of *kingship* applied to coffee illuminate well this aspect of Brazilian history. It suggests that coffee was very important, that it greatly affected the economy and the life of Brazilians and got much respect from them. Coffee's role in the nation's development is thus seen in a new light.

*Uses in science*

Metaphors are very important in science. Scientists are much like the primitive peoples mentioned earlier, struggling to understand the unknown and often using metaphors from familiar knowledge domains to do so. Many scientific theories are metaphors taken from some other domain. Indeed, a field may languish until some new metaphor is applied and some new questions and relationships become apparent. For example, the heart for many centuries was conceptualised as working like a furnace! In the sixteenth and seventeenth centuries the water pump was developed and physiologists soon used it as a metaphor for the action of the heart. In psychology, one dominant metaphor for many years was the operant paradigm, taken essentially from animal training. In it, an animal repeatedly made some response for a meagre reward. The metaphor was applied very widely in several disciplines: to normal and abnormal human behaviour, education, language, thinking and even the perpetuation of an entire culture's rituals. By accepting the metaphor, it is necessary to answer certain questions and study certain things. We can ask what reinforcers are maintaining certain behaviour and how we can alter various response patterns. However, in the 1940s the computer was invented and later on became the dominant metaphor in psychology. The mind was conceptualised as a computer, and the metaphor suggested new relationships, new questions and new things to study. The questions suggested by the old metaphor often just became trivial. Instead, the psychologist could ask how the mind takes in data (as a computer does through peripherals). He could ask how the mind represents data (as a computer does in analog or digital fashion), and how it processes it (serially or in parallel) etc. The new questions become important.

## Drawbacks of metaphors

Using a metaphor can have drawbacks. These can be important in teaching situations, as discussed in Chapter 10. While a metaphor may illuminate many aspects of a domain, it can also hide many others, as they are viewed through a too-smoky lens. Metaphors are often over-zealously applied, and thus a person's conceptualisation of some domain becomes inadequate. One example is the treatment of abnormal behaviour. Until the late nineteenth century, it had been variously regarded as due to spirit possession, malevolent witches, and moral weakness. At about that time, the medical profession took the domain over from the legal authorities, reconceptualising abnormal behaviour by using a physical disease metaphor, 'The mind is an organ which gets diseased'. Various mental disorders were felt to be like physical diseases, such as mumps. People behaving oddly were 'mentally ill'. Their strange acts were symptomatic of the 'underlying pathology' – there were signs and symptoms (just as measles spots are symptomatic of a virus infection), a time course (just as influenza may last one week), a prognosis and a set of treatments.

Many entailments follow from this metaphor: such people must be treated by doctors; their actions are due to illness and they are not responsible for them (just as a measles' sufferer is not responsible for his spots); and, they belong in hospitals. People forget, however, that a metaphor is being used. The mind does not really get sick like an organ does (Szasz, 1974). Yet this is often forgotten and people may look blindly for purely physiological causes of such 'diseases', ignoring the many environmental and societal causes, which schemata from sociology and psychology can illuminate. Similarly, the metaphor, 'the mind is a computer' is sometimes applied too enthusiastically (Lachman and Lachman, 1979). Although the metaphor has been very useful, some researchers neglect the many differences between the two, which can result in an inadequate understanding of the mind. The machine is invented and the mind is a product of evolution. Human knowledge is flexible; the computer's is not, and human logic is often fuzzy, whereas the logic of the computer is fixed. Computers are not programmed for emotion. Unlike human beings, the computer did not evolve to hunt for food, dodge predators and get on with peers.

**Metaphorical definition of concepts**

The argument for the great importance of metaphors in learning new concepts and schemata was pushed even further by Lakoff and Johnson (1980 and 1981). They put forward the intriguing thesis that many of our concepts are based on metaphors, which are used to define the concepts and extend and narrow their boundaries. Here is a brief discussion of Lakoff and Johnson's position. The evidence they cite is from intuitions about language. Little experimental work has been done. Most of the examples below are taken or adapted from Lakoff and Johnson (1980 and 1981).

*Types of concept*
They argue that there are two major types of concept: *experiential* and *metaphorical*. Experiential concepts derive directly from our experience with the world and therefore are quite concrete. There are three kinds of experiential concept. The first type is *spatial*. These are relational concepts, such as *up* and *down*, *out* and *in*, *front* and *back*, and *wide* and *narrow*. The second type is *ontological*. These concepts derive from our experiences with certain objects. Examples are *container, entity, substance* and *person*. Our concept of *person* emerges from our many experiences with people. The third type is *structural*. These seem to be like event schemata, as they organise various experiences and activities. Examples are *eating* and *transferring an object from place to place*.

These experiential concepts are used to construct *metaphorical* ones, just as a molecule is built from atoms. Such construction is done by 'projecting' (a metaphor!) one or more experiential concepts onto them, just as the primitive peoples project their familiar person concepts onto the natural world. An example is *time*. Although most species have some sense of time, the concept is quite complex and children often have great trouble learning the concept and various measures of it, such as month, aeon and geological age (Carroll, 1964). Carroll points out that most of us eventually understand *time* with a spatial metaphor. We use experiential space concepts. We see time as a line with the future stretching out in front and the past behind. Events occupy 'points' along the line and moving from one moment to another is conceptualised as shifting from one point to another. Thus, complex temporal order is understood as simpler spatial order.

Here are some examples of ways in which the three types of experiential concept are used to understand metaphorical ones. Consider first the spatial type. We use the concepts *high* and *low* to help understand a person's health, status and mental state and even the state of a nation's economy:

> He is at the peak of health.
> She is in top shape.
> Jimmy is down in the dumps.
> Their spirits were high.
> The economy has crashed.
> Lazarus rose from the dead.

These metaphors might derive from experience as follows. Sick people are usually lying down, while healthy ones are upright and so we think of *health* as up and *diseased* as down. Similarly, deceased people are usually lying down and so Lazarus 'rises' from *death*.

Consider these ontological concepts. The concept of *vitality* is an abstraction from behaviour, but may be understood by projecting the *substance* concept onto it.

> He overflows with energy.
> I have just run out of energy.
> She is full of life.

*Vitality* is understood as a finite substance, which one can have more or less of, just as one can have different amounts of water in a bottle.

Structural concepts structure one concept in terms of another. Consider the example of *life*. One way we understand it is as a gambling game:

> I will take my chances on this course.
> The odds were always against her getting the contract.
> Play your cards right and you will succeed at life.
> He is a real loser.
> She is a good person to have around when the chips are down.

The concept of *understanding* can be understood with a metaphor to vision, 'Understanding is seeing'.

> I see what you mean.
> It looks different from my point of view.
> The lecture was very clear.
> Try to illuminate the whole picture.

### Defining complex concepts with metaphor clusters

The above cases involve the use of one experiential concept to understand another concept. Many complex concepts may be understood only by projecting a *cluster* of experiential concepts onto them, Lakoff and Johnson argue. Consider the concept of *mind*. What is a mind? No one has ever seen or touched one. The concept is very abstract indeed. So how do we learn it and teach it to children so that we can think about it and talk about it? Lakoff and Johnson suggest we project a number of concepts onto it. Each gives a partial understanding because each applies to some aspects of *mind*. The mind is thus partially understood as a container, a brittle object, and a machine:

*The mind is a container.*
I can't get that tune out of my mind.
He is empty-headed.
I need to clear these thoughts out of my mind.
*The mind is a machine.*
My mind is just not working today.
My mind is running out of steam.
My mental wheels have rusted up since I came on holiday.
*The mind is a brittle object.*
His mind just snapped.
You have to handle her with care.
She is very fragile.

Another example is *idea*. What is an idea? How do we understand the concept and teach it to others? We may use some metaphors:

*An idea is a person.*
A brilliant new theory has been conceived by astronomers.
Mendel is the father of modern genetics.
Relativity was Einstein's brainchild.
*An idea is a product.*
We have produced many good ideas here.
That idea needs further development.
*An idea is a resource.*
He ran out of ideas.
Don't waste your ideas. Exploit them.
*An idea is food.*
I can't swallow that idea.
This book is too complex to digest.
He soon got to the meaty part of the paper.

Lakoff and Johnson's work suggests a useful means of teaching complex concepts: a cluster of metaphors can be provided; each metaphor gives a partial understanding of the concept because it illuminates some aspect of it. *Schema* was defined this way in Chapter 3. Analogies were made to a filter, a play and a sorting device. A more detailed example is discussed in Chapter 10.


FURTHER READING

Basic-level categories: Rosch *et al* (1976); Rosch (1978).
Typicality effects: Rosch (1978); Mervis and Rosch (1981).
Concept boundaries: Mervis and Rosch (1981); Lakoff (1973).
Metaphors: Ortony (1979); Lakoff and Johnson (1980 and 1981).

# Chapter 5

# The Organisation of Concepts and Schemata in Semantic Memory

SUMMARY

1. Semantic memory holds an enormous amount of information, which is organised around concepts. It also holds various procedures for operating on the knowledge contained.
2. Semantic memory has separate but connected word and concept systems.
3. Semantic memory is part of long-term memory. The other part is episodic memory, which holds information about life experiences. Working memory holds information that one is immediately thinking about, for a very short time.
4. Network models of semantic memory represent concepts as nodes, and links between them as labelled lines. The first such model is the teachable language comprehender (TLC), which met with criticisms and evolved into the spreading activation model.
5. ELINOR is a large scale model that can represent knowledge of complex sentences and large chunks of text.
6. The network models give useful notations that can represent on paper which schemata a person knows and the conceptual structures a person wishes to teach.

## INTRODUCTION

A person's knowledge of concepts, schemata, the words that label them and the many relations between them is usually considered to be stored in *semantic memory*. The latter holds most of what one knows; for example, that Neil Armstrong walked on the Moon in 1969, that a tarn is a small mountain lake, and that Montevideo is the capital of Uruguay. It holds all the rules, formulas and algorithms a person knows for manipulating concepts and words (Tulving, 1972; Shoben, 1980). Information is stored in it more or less permanently.

This chapter describes semantic memory in some detail for two main reasons. The first is to give a better perspective on concepts and schemata by emphasising their organisation in semantic memory, how they are used, and how semantic memory relates to other memory systems. The perspective will give a better notion of the meaning and importance of cognitive structure (see Chapter 1). The second reason is that the network models of semantic memory to be described give useful notations for the representation of conceptual structures. They can represent a structure someone wishes to teach, can help determine key concepts in a domain that need special emphasis, and can represent what students already know about some domain. Thus, the representations can be a good starting point for instruction. They will be examined in detail in Chapter 10.


## SOME CHARACTERISTICS OF SEMANTIC MEMORY

**Semantic memory seems to have separate word and concept systems**

Semantic memory is generally considered to have separate but connected word and concept systems. Chapter 2 distinguished between concepts and words, but here is a brief recap. Words are symbols for concepts. Thus, the same word can name many different concepts and the same concept can be named by many different words. A concept, also, can be activated by the sight or sound of an object, or from context. The word system has units that range in size from the individual word to the phrase, sentence and paragraph upwards to large text structures (Wicklegren, 1979). The basic unit of the concept system is the single concept. The next is the proposition, which consists of two linked concepts (e.g. fish live in water). A higher-level unit is the schema, which consists of a number of linked concepts (Wicklegren, 1979). (Note however, that this distinction is not absolute. Any concept can be seen also as a schema.)

An intriguing demonstration of the existence of separate word and concept systems is a study by Brown and McNeill (1966). They examined the 'tip of the tongue' phenomenon – that unhappy state in which one cannot quite recall a certain word. In this state, a concept is activated but its label is not, and it is described as 'mild torment, something like being on the brink of a sneeze'. Brown and McNeill induced 57 cases of the state by reading word definitions to students and asking them to name the word. For example, a student might be given, 'Favouritism shown to relatives' and have to name the word 'nepotism', or 'A fishing boat used in Asia' and have to name the word 'sampan'. Subjects verbalised their thinking when trying to recall the name. They could often guess the word's first letter (e.g. N or S) and the number of syllables, but not the word itself. The study also suggested that the word system is organised by the phonological structure of words and the concept system by the similarity between meanings.

There is other evidence for the existence of separate word and concept systems. As we saw in Chapter 3, we tend to remember not the exact wording of sentences and stories but their gist or meaning.


**Semantic memory holds an enormous amount of information**

The average adult holds an enormous amount of information in semantic memory, and no one knows of any limit to its capacity for more. This store of data allows us to bring our past experience to bear on behaving adaptively in the present, as described in Chapters 1 and 3. It allows us to make inferences, comprehend stories and sentences, solve problems and communicate with others. Even understanding a relatively simple sentence requires a vast store of information that must be retrieved quickly and inferences made from it (e.g. Lachman and Lachman, 1979). Consider the following sentence:

Oysters is a popular restaurant dish in Ecuador.

What information must be retrieved to understand it? Firstly, a person has to know the meanings of the words. He must know that oysters are small animals, what eating is, what food is, and that people enjoy eating and must eat in order to survive. He must know that a restaurant is a place that serves food in exchange for money, and that 'dish' in this context refers to a serving of food rather than a type of plate. He needs to know that Ecuador is a nation in South America, and that a nation is a political entity with a government, laws, currency, territory, etc. In addition, many inferences can be made, and indeed often need to be made to fully comprehend. One can infer that Ecuador is likely to have a coastline and a sizeable fishing industry, for example.

In uttering a sentence, a person also needs to use a lot of information. He needs to assess the audience's current level of knowledge and strike a balance between giving too much and too little information (this is called the *given/new contract*). Too little may mean failure to communicate and too much may send the listener to sleep or induce him to suspect the imparter's sanity. Consider the extravagant detail of this sentence, adapted from an idea by Lachman *et al* (1979).

> In Ecuador, a nation in South America, which is a continent in the western hemisphere bounded by the Pacific and Atlantic Oceans and which is populated by Indians and descendants of Spanish and Portuguese settlers . . .

One must only communicate what is necessary to get the message across and any new information. This principle of striking the right balance is also very important in education (Ausubel, 1968). The teacher must determine what a student knows and teach accordingly by not giving too little detail or too much.

The content of semantic memory will differ greatly across individuals (e.g. Cohen, 1983). Though much information is held in common, the Arctic Eskimo knows many things the American urbanite or Argentine gaucho does not. In addition, an individual's store of data is continually changing. We are always adding data, forgetting some, modifying knowledge to fit existing schemata, and learning new concepts, relations between them, and new words.

## Information in semantic memory is well-organised

One point is clear. The information in semantic memory is very well-organised, cross-referenced and amenable to different arrangements according to one's purposes. Concepts, schemata, propositions and words are not scattered about in some random order. This point can be made clearer by an analogy to a large library that holds millions of books and journals. These items are not scattered randomly throughout the building or even housed in the order in which they came in. If they were, it would be too difficult to find any particular volume. One would have to search through the store until finding the volume wanted – an onerous, lengthy task. Instead, items are so arranged that one can readily locate any particular one. Books and periodicals are usually housed separately and non-fiction books are ordered by subject matter. Thus, books on the same topic can be found on the same shelves. Each book is numbered and represented in a catalogue, which again makes retrieval easy. Books could be organised in ways other than by topic, but these are usually much less useful. They could, for example, be ordered by weight, width, length, in the order they came in or according to how much librarians liked reading each one.

If data in semantic memory were not well organised, it would simply take too long to retrieve any piece of information, just as it would take too long to retrieve a certain book from an unordered stack. If a person is asked to name three fruits, or whether a robin is a bird, or where the Ural Sea is, the answer is usually out in a second or two. Such speedy retrieval would be impossible without good organisation. How long would it take to decide if a robin is a bird if you had to hunt through everything you knew? Even before the answer itself is retrieved, we usually know if the question has a sensible answer (a silly question being, 'What was Julius Caesar's phone number?') and if we know it. Indeed, a strategy quiz-show contestants sometimes use (when the first person to signal answers) is to first decide if they know the answer. If so, they signal and retrieve the information at leisure in the extra seconds allowed.

### Semantic memory is just one of several memory systems

Semantic memory is just one memory system. While no one knows just how many systems exist (see Tulving, 1985), a distinction is usually made between *long-term* and *working memory*. Working memory is like a person's immediate consciousness. It holds what he is currently thinking about. The usual illustration is the act of looking up a telephone number and then dialling. Once the number is dialled, it is rapidly forgotten and replaced by other information. The capacity of working memory is limited and information is very rapidly lost from it. Long-term memory has enormous capacity and stores information more or less permanently.

Long-term memory can be divided into *episodic* and *semantic* (Tulving, 1972). Episodic memory holds autobiographical information – data about the events and episodes of our lives. Thus, a person remembers eating cornflakes for breakfast that morning, attending university for three years, holidaying in Paraguay the previous year, and going to a party the night before. The information is marked by the occasion on which it was learned. Information in semantic memory is stored independently of the context in which it was learned. Thus, we know that robins are birds, but we cannot remember exactly where that proposition was learned. The difference can be further illustrated as follows. Suppose that a person learned the following words in a laboratory experiment: horse, fish, envelope, torque, dish and galaxy. He knows the words and their meanings already. That knowledge is stored in semantic memory. What he learned in the experiment is that he encountered those words in the laboratory at a particular time, and this information is stored in episodic memory. The distinction between the two systems is not absolute and is often considered a continuum between two types of knowledge (see Tulving, 1985).

## THEORIES OF SEMANTIC MEMORY

An important class of models is *network* ones. They aim to describe how information is organised in semantic memory and actually used in order to answer questions such as whether a robin is a bird. We will examine three models here. There are others proposed, but it is beyond our present purposes to consider them (see Smith, 1978 or Wessells, 1982). Some of their tenets are not consistent with statements about concepts made earlier, but the main purpose of this chapter is to emphasise the organisation of concepts in semantic memory and describe the models' notations.

### The teachable language comprehender (TLC)

This early model was the forerunner of the others, which either elaborated it or proposed alternatives in reaction to it. It was put forward by Collins and Quillian (1969) basically as an artificial intelligence program. They wanted to implement semantic knowledge on a computer and ensure that the program could answer questions about semantic relations that were not directly programmed. The model is not very complicated.

*Major principles*
The model postulates that words and concepts exist in separate but connected systems, as described earlier. The concept system consists of *nodes*, each node representing one concept and linked to the word that labels it. Thus, the word 'pack' has links to several concept nodes representing different senses of the word (see Figure 19(A)). One node represents the sense of a group (a pack of wolves) and another signifies a bag (he carried a pack). Some concepts have no names, and therefore do not connect to a node in the word network.

The nodes in the concept system are connected to each other by lines called *pointers*. A simple example is Figure 19(B). The concept node for *robin* connects to the node for *bird* with a pointer labelled 'is a'. 'Is a' simply describes the relation between the two concepts (a robin is a bird) and B constitutes a proposition. There are several other types of relation – 'has a' (a robin has a beak), and 'can' (a robin can sing) are two.

The model assumes that concepts are organised hierarchically. They are organised in logical taxonomies. An example is also shown in Figure 19(C). The most abstract concept shown in the fragment is *life form* and then *animal*. Below those are *bird* and *reptile*, also connected by the 'is a' relation pointer, and then *canary*, connected to *bird* by 'is a'. The network is expansible in all directions – innumerable concepts are connected directly and indirectly to those shown in the fragment. They are connected indirectly because the concepts are connected to each other by several links. Thus, *bird* and *life form* are indirectly connected by 'is a' through several links. On the other hand, *bird* and *robin* are connected by just one link. Another tenet is that the system preserves cognitive economy. There is no redundancy of information storage. A particular feature is stored only at one level of abstraction, with the most abstract concept possible. Thus, 'has feathers' and 'has a beak' would not be stored at the *robin* and *sparrow* nodes. They would be stored only at the *bird* node. Similarly, 'reproduces through DNA replication' would only be stored at the *life form* node and not at any node below it.

*Answering questions*
Simple questions that require making inferences can be answered by the network model. A question could be, 'Is a robin a bird?' The robin and bird nodes are activated

A. Fragments of the word and concept networks

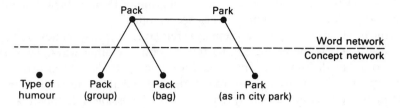

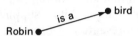

B. A simple proposition consisting of two concepts linked by a pointer

C. A larger fragment of semantic memory. The network is expansible in all directions

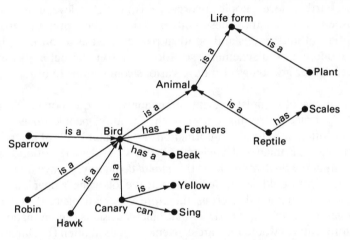

**Figure 19.** The organisation of semantic memory as proposed by the TLC model. A illustrates the separate but connected word and concept networks, and B and C illustrate fragments of the concept network.

by the words and the programme then hunts for a pointer between them. If such a path is found the programme checks to see if the pointer's label is consistent with the question (e.g. that it is 'is a' and not 'has a'). If so, then the question is answered 'yes'. If not, then it is answered 'no'. The model therefore makes a prediction and it can be tested. It should take longer to verify questions that require traversing several links. Verifying 'A robin is a bird' or 'A bird has feathers' should be a quick process, because only one link needs to be traversed. But, to verify 'A robin is an animal' or 'A canary has skin' should take longer, because more than one link must be traversed. Collins and Quillian tested this hypothesis in a reaction-time study with people and it was indeed verified. The more links traversed, the longer the sentence took to confirm.

Finally, it should be noted that the networks in Figure 19 are just representations of semantic memory parts. It cannot be said that there are actually neural systems that correspond to nodes and pointers.

*Problems with the model*

The model was criticised on logical and empirical grounds (Smith, 1978; Lachman and Lachman, 1979). Some major shortcomings are as follows.

Firstly, the model proposes too few semantic relations. The major ones are 'is a', 'has a' and 'can'. Concepts, however, can be related in many other ways. Two relations looked at so far in this book are part inclusion and spatial/temporal order. Others include synonyms, antonyms and contradictories (see Chaffin and Herrmann, 1984). Semantic memory thus has an enormous number of possible relations that are not included in the model.

The maze of relations between concepts may be likened to the organisation of people in a nation. People relate to each other in many different ways, as friends, workmates, siblings, the relationships between parent-child, supplier-consumer, employer-employee, political representative-represented, etc. Some individuals have many connections to other people, while some have far fewer, just as the concepts *plant* and *person* would for most people, connect to many other concepts, while *quark* would connect to only a few. Furthermore, people are organised into higher-level units, just as concepts are organised into schemata. These units include families, pressure groups, sporting clubs, counties, ethnic groups and political parties. Just as a concept can be part of numerous taxonomies and schemata, so, too, a person can belong to many different groups. Such larger groupings also have various connections to other groups and to individuals.

Secondly, the assumption of complete cognitive economy was questioned. While a computer with limited storage space might need such a feature, people do not need complete economy. We often need to store information at particular levels of abstraction to make speedy decisions (Lachman and Lachman, 1979). Consider the notion that 'is dangerous' is stored only at the *predator* node on the *animal* taxonomy. A caveman seeing a charging sabre-toothed tiger would then have to compute the following: a tiger is a feline, a feline is a predator, and a predator is dangerous, therefore a tiger is dangerous. It is much wiser to store 'is dangerous' at the tiger node so that quick decisions can be made. It is likely then that we store features where they are convenient or used often (Lachman and Lachman, 1979). Further, Rosch (1978) argues that such property values are often stored at the basic-level rather than at more abstract ones.

Thirdly, the idea that concepts are logically organised was questioned. Most people probably organise many concepts in a less logical fashion. Two other criticisms are empirical. The model cannot readily explain typicality effects. It should take the same time to verify the statements 'A penguin is a bird' as 'A robin is a bird', but it does not. Also, the experiment that found an effect of the number of links traversed on reaction-time taken to verify the statements was criticised for confounding link number with associative frequency. When associative strength differences are eliminated, the link number effect vanishes (Conrad, 1972).

## The spreading activation model

The TLC was so heavily criticised that Collins and Loftus (1975) were persuaded to revise it. Their 'spreading activation' model has some of the TLC's features but includes others to account for typicality, lack of complete cognitive economy, and the criticism of sparseness of relations. The notion of spreading activation has been used to explain various phenomena and has some educational applications discussed by Gagné (1985).

*Major principles*
As in the TLC, there are separate word and concept systems. Each concept is again represented by a node, and the nodes are connected by labelled pointers. Concepts are, however, not organised hierarchically. They are organised by overall semantic similarity. The more similar two concepts are, the closer they are placed together in the network and the shorter the pointer becomes. Thus, most people would perceive that *cat* and *mouse* are closer than *cobra* and *typewriter*.

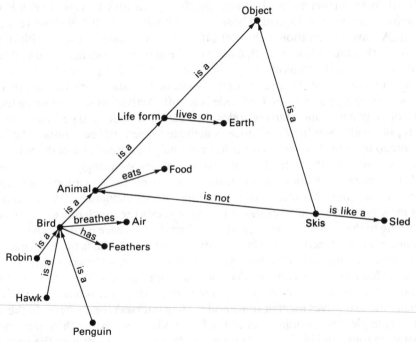

**Figure 20.** A fragment of semantic memory as proposed by the spreading activation model. The closer two concepts are, the more similar they are perceived as being. The figure above is not based on any actual similarity ratings, however.

Figure 20 gives a fragment of the concept system according to this model. It should be noted that concepts are denoted by nodes placed at different locations and they are connected with various sorts of pointer. The shorter the link, the stronger the association between two concepts. Thus, *bird* and *feathers*, which are strongly associated, have a short link, while animal and skis. which have a weaker association, are linked by a longer pointer. Thus, exemplar typicality is represented by line length. Very typical instances of *bird*, such as robin, have a short link, while atypical ones such as penguin have a longer one. The figure also shows a variety of pointer types. The TLC model used 'is a' and a few others, this model uses breathes, eats, lives, is not and any others that we may wish to add. The wide range of possible semantic relations is thereby covered and the 'meaning' of a word is the total number of links its concept node has with other nodes. In essence, the model uses a spatial metaphor to represent the degree to which two specific concepts are related, similarity being represented in terms of distance. Again, it seems unlikely that there are actually neural systems with paths of different length, etc. A final assumption is that an attribute may be stored at any node. There is no need for complete cognitive economy.

Now the rather complex *processing* assumptions can be described. These explain how the system can answer questions of the 'Is a robin a bird?' form. The process is best understood by an analogy given by Lachman and Lachman (1979). Imagine a room full of tuning forks, set at different distances from each other. Each fork corresponds to a concept node and their distance apart corresponds to semantic similarity. If one fork is tapped, it vibrates and sets off adjacent forks, which in turn vibrate to a lesser extent and set off forks further away. Just how much a given fork vibrates depends on its distance from the one first tapped. Those close to it vibrate most and those very far off not at all. A wave of vibration is thus set off, which eventually subsides with time.

Just as a fork is tapped and set off, a node can be activated, but activated in different ways. It can be set off by thinking about the concept, by hearing or reading its name, or by seeing a real exemplar. Once activated, a wave of activation spreads from that node to others along the links. Say the *bird* node is set off. Activation spreads along the 'is a' links to robin, penguin and sparrow nodes, to the animal node, and perhaps from there to the reptile node. Say the *horse* node is activated when we see a horse. Activation would spread from there to nodes for colt, mare, neighs, animal and perhaps life form. The nodes closest to the activated one are set off most strongly, and the wave of activation eventually subsides with time. It also takes time for activation to spread from one node to another. No one knows how much time. Anderson (1976) argues for 50–100 msec per link while Wicklegren (1976) suggests the much quicker 1 msec.

Returning to the 'robin is a bird' question, when the sentence is heard, the robin and animal nodes are each activated. The activation wave then spreads out from each node along its links. In the case of words with several meanings (bank, form), the node activated is determined by context. As each wave spreads it leaves a tag, or label, at each node it traverses. This allows the system to note which paths have been accessed. Eventually the two waves meet at some node. They intersect somewhere. In the 'robin is a bird' example, they would meet at the bird node. The system then examines the links between robin and bird and determines if they are consistent with the verb in the question. A variety of sorts of evidence is summed up to then verify or disconfirm the question (see Collins and Loftus, 1975).

*Evidence for the model*
The model has some empirical support. Collins and Loftus reported some reaction-time studies consistent with it. Another is the *semantic priming* phenomenon. It occurs when subjects are given letter strings and have to quickly decide whether they are words or not. A representative study was carried out by Meyer and Schaneveldt (1971). They showed subjects two letter strings at a time, one being placed above the other. Here are some examples:

| a. | b. | c. | d. |
|----|----|----|----|
| Nurse | Bread | Wine | Tydalf |
| Decanter | Butter | Plame | Zoltn |

Some pairs consist of two real words, others, a word and a non-word, and some, two non-words. The subjects had to quickly determine if both strings in each pair were words. Interest focused on a comparison between two types of pair. Some pairs consisted of two closely related words (bread–butter) and some consisted of two unrelated ones (nurse–decanter). Subjects were quicker to verify the related words as both being words than the unrelated ones. Thus, reading the first word *primes* retrieval of the meaning of the second one in some way. This finding is consistent with the spreading activation model, because we can assume that reading the words activates the corresponding concept nodes. When the pair consisted of related words, activation of the first node rapidly spread to the second, since it had only a short distance to go. Yet, with unrelated words, activation is less likely to have time to spread to the next one.

*Problems with the model*
One major criticism made is that the model is quite complicated and many assumptions are made in it. The parsimony requirement (that scientific theories should be as simple as possible) is not met. Some of its assumptions also seem *ad hoc*.

## Elinor

This network model is a quite complex one that can represent large units of discourse (Norman and Rumelhart, 1975). Like the preceding two models, it represents concepts by nodes and their relations by labelled pointers. It has a number of assumptions that

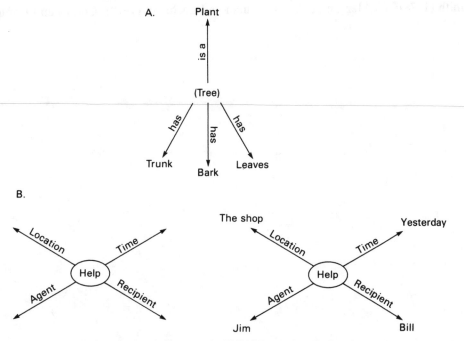

**Figure 21.** Two examples of network fragments in ELINOR notation. B also gives an instantiation of the general schema *help*.

are not greatly relevant to this book. Our concern is to comprehend how ELINOR can represent object and event conceptual structures.

Figure 21 presents two examples of ELINOR representations – *A* and *B*. *A* gives a network for the object concept *tree*. The concept is represented by the word 'tree', but it is analogous to the concept node in the above models. There are a number of labelled pointers from the concept to other nodes. Thus, a tree is a plant, has a trunk, has bark, etc. Further labelled relations to other concepts can be specified and the network is, again, expansible in all directions. *B* gives a network for the event concept *help*. Again, the concept is shown in the labelled node, and it has pointers to other concepts. These are labelled: location, agent, time and recipient. Thus, the simple network gives a schema that can be instantiated by a given case of *help*. The subject can fill in the slot for location, the time the event occurred, who actually did the helping, and who was helped. More complex event concepts can, again, be represented with more pointers.

**Educational applications of network models**

As previously mentioned, these notation systems can be used to represent knowledge of a domain and to teach abstract schemata, which students can learn to instantiate themselves. Some examples are in Chapters 10 and 11.

FURTHER READING

Smith (1978); Wicklegren (1979); Lachman and Lachman (1979); Collins and Loftus (1975).

# Chapter 6

# Theories of Category Representation

SUMMARY

1.  The term 'representation' is used in two main senses. One is as a relation between two things, such that one stands for the other, and the second is as the thing doing the representing. A representation has a content, which refers to the actual information held, and a format, which refers to the form in which it is held.
2.  Theories of representation covered here pertain just to content, each proposing that a person who learns a concept retains certain information about the corresponding category.
3.  The classical view proposes that a learner represents a category as a set of defining features, which all exemplars share. Categorisation is a matter of determining if a given stimulus has them all.
4.  The prototype view proposes that a learner represents a category by some measure of the instances' central tendency and variation. Stimuli are categorised by reference to the prototype.
5.  The exemplar view proposes that a category is represented by one or more specific exemplars. Stimuli are categorised by reference to them.
6.  None of these theories appears to be a complete account. It seems that a person may represent a category in a certain way according to the category itself, circumstances and age level.

## INTRODUCTION

Chapter 1 posed the important question of category representation, which runs as follows. A person who learns concepts such as *musical style, trapezoid, extrovert*, and *measles* retains some information in memory that, amongst other things, allows him to categorise stimuli as exemplars or non-exemplars. What precisely has been retained that allows such categorisation? This question needs to be answered because, as mentioned, how concepts are learned and used and how they should be taught depend on it.

Various theories that posit various representations have been proposed (e.g. Millward, 1980; Cohen and Murphy, 1984). Many fall into three main groups, which, partly borrowing from Smith and Medin (1981), will be dubbed the 'classical', 'prototype' and 'exemplar' theories. Within these groupings are variations on each and also some theories that combine aspects of each. However, only the theories in a pure form will be described in this book. The three theories are outlined in Table 3, which can be referred to whilst progressing through this complex chapter. The present discussion is mostly based on Smith and Medin's perceptive analysis.

**Table 3.** An outline of the three views of category representation. Each pertains to content rather than format.

---

Classical view
The representation consists of a set of common features that all exemplars share. These are abstracted from exemplars. Any stimulus that has them is an exemplar and any one that lacks one feature or more is not.

*Example: bird* The representation consists of features that all birds share, such as 'has a beak', 'has feathers' and 'lays eggs'.

*Prototype view*
The representation consists of a measure of the central tendency (or average) of a category's instances. It can be a highly typical instance or an idealised exemplar, which has most or many characteristic features of the exemplars.

*Example: bird* The prototype consists of an idealised bird that has many characteristic features of birds such as 'flies', 'nests in trees', 'has feathers', etc. Stimuli are categorised as exemplars by comparing them to the prototype. If they are judged to be similar enough, they are classed as exemplars. The prototype is learned either directly or by abstracting some notion of central tendency from experiencing exemplars.

*Exemplar view*
The concept representation consists of one or more memorised exemplars. There is no abstraction of features at all.

*Example: bird* The representation consists of memorised exemplars of just a robin, or of a robin, a hawk and a seagull. Stimuli are categorised as instances or non-instances by comparing them to the most similar exemplar. If similar enough, the stimulus is judged to be an exemplar.

---

First of all, the notion of *representation* needs to be expanded on. As noted before, the term is quite vague and is used in many different ways. The following discussion borrows from an analysis by Palmer (1978), Glass *et al* (1979) and Mandler (1983). Several points need to be made. These include the difference between the content and format of a representation, and between analog and analytic formats.


## THE NATURE OF REPRESENTATION

One of the most astounding mental feats of all is blindfold chess. Although a chessboard has 64 squares and 32 pieces, some people can play an entire game without actually looking at a board. They somehow remember the changing positions of the pieces, the relations between them, and they find good moves as well. Playing one game 'blindfold' sounds impressive enough, yet a few people can play more than one game at the same time. In fact, the world record for simultaneous blindfold games, set by Miguel Najdorf in 1947, stands at an astronomical 45.

This feat illustrates well the idea of mental representation and the processes that operate on mental representations. The chess player has to mentally represent each board and *operate* on each representation by searching for plans, considering the consequences of various moves and looking for ways to counter his opponent's plans. The example also illustrates two things involved in representation: the thing represented (the actual boards) and the things doing the representing (the ideas in the player's head). It also indicates the two main senses of representation. The first is the relationship between two things, such that one stands for the other (the relation between the actual board and the idea of it). The second sense is the thing doing the representing (the idea in the player's head is a representation).

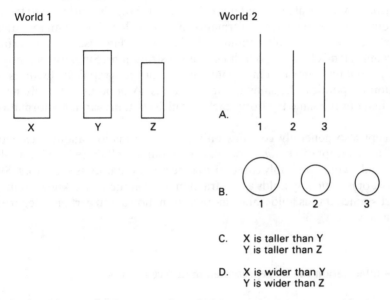

**Figure 22.** A schematic example of representation, which is a relation between a representing world and a represented one. Each set of figures in World 2 represents some part of World 1. Adapted from Palmer (1978).

Figure 22 presents a schematic example of these points. It shows two 'worlds' – a representing world and a represented world. World 1 consists of three rectangles, each of which has different heights and widths. World 2 consists of various figures, which represent the rectangles in World 1. Thus, World 1 is the represented world, analogous to the actual chessboards in the above example. World 2 represents, or models, World 1 in several different ways, and is analogous to the ideas inside the chessplayer's head. Figure 22 can now be used to illustrate the following points.

## A representation may contain some but not all information

The representing world may not model everything in the represented world. In the figure, the parts only represent some information contained in World 1. Consider those in *A*. The three lines only represent the rectangles' heights. They hold no information about width. Thus, number 1 represents the height of the first rectangle (X) by line length, number 2 the height of the second rectangle (Y), and number 3 the height of rectangle Z. In *B*, the same information is represented by circle diameter. Now consider *C*. *C* contains even less data than *A* or *B*. It only holds the information that X is taller than Y, Y is taller than Z and thus X is taller than Z. It does not contain specific measurements of the differences in length. *A* and *B* do hold this information, however. The information a representation contains is called its *content*. The content of *A* and *B* is the same but different from that of *C*.

A more familiar example is a typical representational device – a map. A map of a certain territory represents that territory. A map of Europe, for example, in some way stands for the actual continent, but a particular map only contains some information about Europe. A political map contains information about the nations and the territory each covers. It may also contain information about the locations of major cities, rivers and lakes, but it would usually contain little data about land use and types (farmland, forest, swamp), land elevation, or ethnic group distributions. Similarly, a topographical map may contain information about important geographical features but no information on political divisions or city locations. A good atlas usually has several different maps of the same territory, each of which contains varying information about it.

A concept also generally contains only some information about a category. For example, my concept of *predator* contains some but not all there is to know about the category, and I would probably categorise some non-predators as predators. Similarly, my concept of *person* only holds a tiny fraction of what there is to know about people. An expert's concept thus holds much more information about certain categories then a layperson's.

### The same information can be represented in different ways

Exactly the same information can be held in different ways in a representation. Compare *A* and *B* in Figure 22 again. Each holds the same data about World 1, but does so in different ways. *A* represents it by line length and *B* by circle diameter. The manner in which information is held is its *format*. Content thus pertains to the actual information held and format to the form in which it is held.

Here are some examples. The information in this book is represented as printed words on paper. Thus its format is 'English words on paper'. But, the same data could be held in quite different formats. It could be written in Egyptian hieroglyphics on a wall, stored on magnetic tape as spoken words, or in Morse code as patterns of dots and dashes. Similarly, the concept *house* can be represented in different formats, by using the French word 'maison', a gesture in sign language, or a Morse code sequence. All represent the same information. Similarly, the same format can hold quite different information. Countless different messages can be sent by Morse code, and different books use the same format to hold quite different information.

#### Analog and analytic formats
There are two major types of format: analog and analytic. An analog representation in some way resembles that which it represents. It is in some way similar to it. For example, a mercury thermometer represents temperature in analog fashion on a line scale. As temperature increases, so does the height of the column. An analog computer represents numbers by amount of voltage. The larger the number, the higher the voltage. A photograph is an analog representation of a scene. The representations *A*

and *B* in Figure 22 are analog, because they represent height by a continuously varying distance that resembles height.

An analytic representation bears only an arbitrary relation to that which it represents. It is in no way similar. A familiar example is language. Most words relate to the concepts they represent only by convention, with a few exceptions, such as 'boom' and 'purr' (see Chapter 2). The word 'lion' only represents the concept *lion* because of convention. The same concept could be labelled with an arbitrary term like 'Uborf', or the Russian term, or a sequence of hand signals. A digital computer represents data in an analytic format – as a pattern of on/off states. In Figure 22, the representations in *C* and *D* are analytic. Analytic representations are often called *symbols*. Language is thus a symbol system. Symbolisation is a very powerful tool for thought.

A map illustrates well the distinction between the two format types. It uses both analog and analytic formats. The political divisions and city locations shown are analog, because they resemble the actual represented territory. Similarly, a relief map represents territory elevation in analog format – the height on the map. Yet, some data might be represented in an analytic format. For example, population density might be represented by colour.

### The processes operating on representations

View a representation as roughly analogous to a tangible structure. To do anything to such a structure, we must have *processes*. Thus, a blindfold chess player has to have processes to operate on his board representations in order to find good moves. A digital computer that stores data as on/off states is useless unless those representations can be operated on. We must translate data into on/off state representations, add, multiply and take square roots, and translate the on/off state patterns back into numbers.

Two analogies might clarify the distinction between representation and processes. Posner (1973) offers the analogy to a carpenter. Wood is a relatively fixed, tangible structure. To do anything with wood (e.g. to make furniture) processes such as cutting, chiselling, planing and nailing are necessary. The final result is an altered structure. The second analogy is to a potter. He needs processes such as shaping the clay, smoothing it on a wheel, and firing it in a kiln.

A representation is useless without processes to operate on it. The representations in Figure 22 are useless without the processes of reading the elements, relating them to World 1, etc. A road map is useless unless a motorist can read it and relate it to his destination and follow the routes.

### Category representation

The question of how categories are represented therefore breaks down into questions about content and format. What information has a person retained after acquiring such a concept as *dog* or *democracy* and in what form is that data stored? The three theories to be considered all really just pertain to content, suggesting that people retain certain information about a category which allows instances to be categorised (Farah and Kosslyn, 1982). Little is really known about format. Indeed, the question of format has been much debated with little clear resolution as yet. Anderson (1978) has even argued that it cannot be definitively answered by non-physiological methods. Palmer (1978) maintains that the question is of no great concern to psychology and should be left to the neurophysiologists. This issue is too complex to be discussed here, and this chapter will just consider content. For a discussion of concept format, see Farah and Kosslyn (1982). Format will, however, be considered to some extent in Chapter 8.

We can now turn to the three major theories of content of representation.


## THE CLASSICAL VIEW

This view is by far the oldest, dating back to the Ancient Greeks. Until the last decade or so, it was the dominant theory in psychology and is, as yet, the main theoretical basis for concept teaching in schools. It is relatively simple and elegant and clearly specifies how concepts should be taught. After summarising its main principles, some of its difficulties are discussed.


### Major principles

The view proposes that a category is represented as follows. First, the representation consists of information abstracted from experience. This information consists of a list of one or more defining features – common features that all of the concept's instances share. Thus, the representation of *square* consists of the defining features 'four sides of equal length', 'plane figure', and 'four internal right angles'. The representation of *predator* consists of such defining features as 'hunts prey', etc. A stimulus must have all these features to be an instance. Any stimulus that lacks one or more cannot be an instance. Categorisation is carried out as follows. To determine if a stimulus is an exemplar, a person retrieves the set of defining features from memory and determines if the stimulus has them all. If so, the stimulus is an instance.

Another example is *bird*. The theory proposes that the representation consists of defining features such as 'lays eggs', 'has feathers', 'has a beak', etc. A stimulus must have them all to be a bird and, thus, any animal that has them all is a bird. To determine if, say, a penguin or a bat is a bird, a person must assess whether they have all the defining features.

The classical view is sometimes called the 'rule model' (Millward, 1980). Acquiring a concept can be likened to learning a rule, such as, 'All closed figures with four sides of equal length and four internal right angles are squares', and applying it to classify stimuli.

Briefly, the view proposes that a concept is acquired in the following way. Acquisition is a matter of abstracting the common features from instances (or learning them verbally) and applying them in order to categorise. Thus, *predator* is learned by abstracting common features such as 'hunts prey' and 'is carnivorous', which all of its instances share. *Dog* is acquired by abstracting out 'has four legs', 'has a wet nose', 'barks', etc.

The classical view's implications for concept teaching are therefore quite clear

(Merrill and Tennyson, 1977; Klausmeier and Sipple, 1980). A school-taught concept, such as *ion, sonnet, prime number* and *democracy*, needs to be analysed into defining features by the teacher. The students must learn this set of features and get practice in using them to determine if various stimuli are exemplars. Chapter 9 gives many examples of this approach and here is a brief one. To teach *democracy*, it could be analysed into such defining features as these (although people could debate what its defining features are):

> Has a government responsible to the people through elections
> Has fair elections at regular intervals
> Has approximately equal weighting of each elector's vote.

After students had learned these features, they would be taught to categorise various states as democratic or non-democratic simply by considering whether each had all the features. As discussed in Chapter 10, this procedure may be suitable for teaching some, but not all, concepts.

### Criticisms of the classical view

The theory has been attacked on several fronts. The main criticisms are summarised by many authors (e.g. Anglin, 1977; Rosch, 1978; Smith and Medin, 1981; Medin and Smith, 1984). Some major ones are reproduced below. They are important to note also, because it is necessary to see why teaching procedures based on this view are sometimes inappropriate.

*Many concepts have no obvious defining features*
Some concepts are quite well-defined. It is easy to think of and use defining features for *triangle, mass* and *standard deviation*, but many natural concepts defy such definition. It has proved impossible so far to specify which common features their instances have. This problem was highlighted in Chapter 4, where no common features for instances of the concept *game* could be found, as required by the classical view. Instead, the instances seemed linked in a family-resemblance structure. Even a simpler concept, such as *chair*, is very hard to define (Anglin, 1977). A dictionary might offer 'A seat with four legs and a back for one person'. However, beanbag chairs lack backs and legs, yet are still chairs. It could be defined by function as 'something for one person to sit on', but that definition would include stools, prayer rugs and saddles, which are not chairs. By the same token, if you cut off the beak and plucked out the feathers of a certain bird, would it then not be a bird? The creature then lacks some defining features, but does that mean it is not now a bird?

The situation gets even thornier with complex concepts, such as *genius, intelligence* and *justice*, as discussed in Chapter 2. What are the defining features of *justice*, which allow a given act to be classed as just or unjust? Generations of philosophers have hunted for them with scant success. Perhaps one reason for the problem is that very complex concepts may be defined with metaphor clusters rather than common features, as described in Chapter 4.

This is the problem the school teacher is sometimes faced with. How can complex concepts be taught from this theoretical basis if they are not reducible to defining features?

*The view cannot readily account for typicality and unclear cases*
The view cannot readily explain these phenomena. All instances of a concept should be equally good, since all have the defining features. A penguin or an ostrich should be just as good an exemplar of *bird* as a robin. Similarly, concept boundaries should be clear-cut. If a person knows the defining features and can readily apply them, peripheral instances should be clearly in one category or another.

*Children have trouble abstracting defining features*
This criticism is empirical and derives partly from work by Vygotsky (1962). Its essence is that children are very adept concept learners. Indeed, their vocabulary grows by many words a day at early ages. Yet, they are very poor at abstracting out common features from instances – those invariant features that characterise all in a set of stimuli. Even so, the classical view must say that they are learning so many concepts so easily by abstracting out invariant features. Instead, it seems that they might be using some representation other than defining features. The classical view cannot easily explain how children learn concepts easily while still having difficulty abstracting defining features.

*Characteristic features are sometimes used to categorise*
People may use characteristic features to categorise as well as defining ones. However, the classical view requires that they just use defining ones. A study that showed the use of characteristic features was carried out by Hampton (1979). Subjects listed features of natural concepts, such as *tool* and *fruit*. They then rated the extent to which various instances had the attributes listed. Thus, if 'flies' and 'lives in trees' were listed as features of *bird*, subjects might say that robins had both but that chickens had neither. Later, a second group determined if various stimuli were exemplars of various concepts. The results showed that characteristic features, such as 'flies', affected the time taken to categorise. The more of these features an instance and the concept shared, the faster the categorisation decision. Armstrong *et al* (1983) found a similar result.

*Relations between features*
As well as characteristic features, concepts may contain information about the relations between features. The classical view, however, supposes that the features are just learned in an arbitrary order. Yet, many concepts specify that the features are put together in a certain way. Thus, in my concept of *house*, the elements, or features, (walls, roof, pipes, etc.) are put together in a certain way. If someone rearranged these elements so that all the walls were end to end and the roof and floor were leaning against them, the stimulus would not be a house. Indeed, this kind of argument is made for using the notion of *schema*, because a schema specifies that parts must go together in a certain way. This is why, as mentioned in Chapter 3, the schema notion presupposes a particular theory of category representation, which is discussed in the next section. The classical view can try to bypass this criticism by proposing that the relations between features are considered features themselves (Anglin, 1977). Thus, the relation 'roof on

top' is considered a feature. The problem, then, is that the set of defining features for most concepts gets very large and unwieldy. How would anyone ever learn them?

A related problem is that concepts often contain much more information than just a set of defining features. In addition to knowledge of characteristic features and the relations between them, a concept often contains data about instances and our emotions towards them.

*Implications*

These criticisms suggest that the classical view is at best an incomplete account of category representation. It also may not be a sound theoretical basis for teaching concepts for two main reasons. The first is that many concepts cannot readily be reduced to defining features. The second is that younger students might represent even well-defined categories in other ways. Even when exposed to a teaching procedure aimed at instilling a set of defining features, they may be acquiring something different. If so, then perhaps instruction should be altered accordingly.

## THE PROTOTYPE VIEW

This view was proposed as an alternative to the classical view, especially to account for such factors as typicality and unclear cases. Basically, it proposes that a category is not represented by a set of defining features, but by some measure of central tendency (or average) of a category's instances and some notion of their variation. Unfortunately, the term 'prototype' is somewhat vague and is used in different ways (Smith and Medin, 1981). A prototype representation will be defined here either as a highly typical instance that falls at a category's centre, or as an idealisation. This definition is expanded on below.

The notion of a prototype goes back a long way in psychology but only recently has it been widely applied to category representation. Early proponents of the idea of prototype representation were Attneave (1957), Posner and Keele (1968 and 1970) and later Rosch (1975 and 1978), who extended the notion to natural concepts. First of all the notion is defined in more detail, and then the view is described. Finally, some ways in which the prototype view accounts for the problems of the classical view are examined.

### The notion of prototype

Webster's dictionary defines 'prototype' as a 'forerunner, a model from which others are made'. When a car or an aircraft designer introduces a new model, he usually first builds a working version that is tested out extensively and any problems encountered are fixed by re-designing the model. Later, units are mass-produced from this first model.

The view uses the term 'prototype' in a somewhat analogous way. Basically it proposes that a category is represented by some measure of central tendency of some instances, which, as mentioned, can be a highly typical instance or an idealisation. Stimuli are then categorised as exemplars or non-exemplars by reference to this

**Figure 23.** Some examples of prototypes for various categories.

prototype, just as new units are made by reference to the prototypical car. Figure 23 gives some examples.

Consider first of all an idealised prototype. The prototype is a collection of *characteristic* features of the category; features that instances tend to have but need not have. Here is a major difference between the prototype and the classical view. The latter requires that only defining features are abstracted and used to categorise. Thus, a prototype representation of *bird* might include an idealised bird with such features as 'lays eggs', 'has feathers', 'flies', 'gets around in the daytime', and 'sings'. Not every bird will have all or even many of these features. A specific bird is only likely to have them. If we refer back to Figure 16 on page 61, the middle face is the prototype for the family members, because it has the features that members tend to share: large ears, a moustache and beard. The prototype is thus an idealisation because it combines features that no single member actually has. Similarly, the prototype in Section A is bcde. It is not an actual instance (although it could be). It is an idealisation because it has the features the actual instances tend to share. The final example is the disease *measles*. As mentioned in Chapter 1, a doctor might have an idealised case of the disease – a prototype that combines most or all symptoms that sufferers tend to have. People may be categorised as sufferers by reference to the idealisation.

Finally, the prototype still looks like an actual instance. In Figure 16 both prototypes could be actual instances, as they resemble the instances in some way.

The measure of central tendency can either be a *mean* or a *modal* value. In the cases above, the prototype consists of a modal set of features, a collection of features that instances are likely to have. For some categories, the prototype is a mean value on some dimensions along which the exemplars vary (e.g. height, weight, etc.). Some examples are as follows. Posner and Keele (1968 and 1970) looked at prototype formation for some artificial categories that consisted of dot patterns (see Figure 24). Each category had four instances, which were distortions of a prototype. Thus, the prototype was the average value of the instances on the dimensions along which they varied. In the training phase, subjects learned to sort the 16 patterns shown into four categories. They did not see the actual prototypes at this stage. In a test, they were shown new distortions of the prototypes, each actual prototype, and the 16 training stimuli. Subjects were better at categorising the prototypes than the new stimuli, which suggested they had abstracted prototypes from the training stimuli.

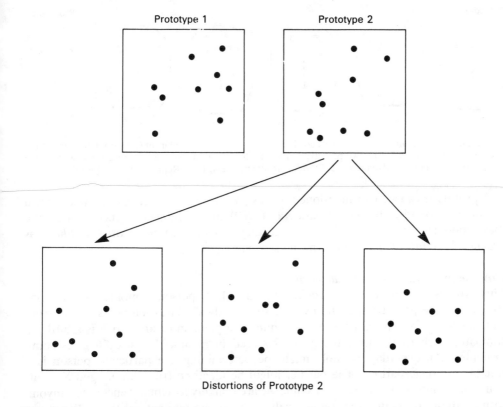

**Figure 24.** Dot patterns like those used by Posner and Keele (1968 and 1970). The patterns are from Posner and Keele (1968) and the figure itself from Glass, A. L., Holyoak, K. J. and Santa, J. L. *Cognition*. Reading, Mass.: Addison-Wesley, 1979. Reproduced with permission.

Reed (1972) also found evidence of subjects averaging values on dimensions to form a prototype. He used schematic faces that differed along several dimensions: length of nose, height of forehead, and distance between the eyes, for example. Some examples are shown in Figure 25. Subjects learned to sort the ten faces in the figure into two categories. Each instance is a distortion of its category's prototype. In a test, they categorised the ten training faces, the prototype of each category (which was not shown in training), and some new faces. They were much better at classifying the prototypes than the new instances, again suggesting they had averaged values of the instance to construct a prototype.

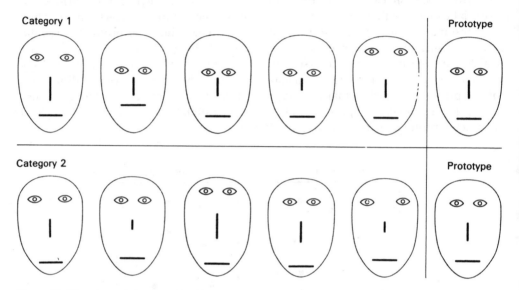

**Figure 25.** The schematic faces used by Reed. The top five faces are exemplars of Category 1 and the bottom five belong to Category 2. The two prototypes are also shown. From Reed, S. K. Pattern recognition and categorisation. Cognitive Psychology **3**, Florida: Academic Press, 1972. Reproduced with permission.

A prototype can also, as mentioned, be a very typical instance. An example is focal *red* or *blue* found in the Berlin and Kay (1969) study. Subjects agreed well on the 'best-examples' of various colours, suggesting that their category of, say, *blue* was organised around such a highly typical exemplar.

*How the prototype is used to categorise*
This process should be examined in more detail. A person compares a particular stimulus to the prototype. If the two are sufficiently similar, then he categorises the stimulus as an exemplar. Thus, to determine if a penguin or an ostrich is a bird, he compares each to the prototypical bird stored in memory. Figure 26 gives some examples. An everyday example might be determining if a particular person is a suitable marriage partner. The partner might be idealised (rich, kind, aged X, well-educated, wants X children, etc.). While we are unlikely to actually encounter anyone with all these traits, different people will have varying numbers of them. We might categorise a person as an exemplar of *suitable marriage partner* if he or she has a certain number of these features.

**Figure 26.** Two examples of prototype matching. Each stimulus is directly compared to the prototype and, if judged sufficiently similar, is categorised as an exemplar.

## Notions related to prototype

The notion of prototype closely resembles some concepts used in other fields and has been around in various guises for some time. Indeed, George Orwell in *Down and out in Paris and London* argues for something like a prototype representation of *tramp*.

> . . . there exists in our minds a sort of ideal or typical tramp – a repulsive, rather dangerous creature, who would die rather than work or wash, and wants nothing but to beg, drink, and rob hen-houses . . . The very word 'tramp' evokes his image.
>
> Orwell (1933, pp. 200–201)

In sociology, a concept related to prototype is called the 'ideal type', which will be looked at in Chapter 10 (page 161). Here are some other related notions.

*Stereotype*
This notion, mentioned in Chapter 1, is much like a prototype, because it may combine most or all features that instances of a given category share. In that sense it is an abstraction. A play or novel may be criticised for 'stereotyped' characters who are too unlike real people.

*Composite*
Journalists sometimes use a 'composite' to define a new category. It is like a prototype of a family-resemblance category. They combine certain features that real instances share to create a combination that illustrates the category well, but no actual instance is likely to have all the features represented. Thus, the concept *modern couple*, by combining features of various real couples, might be defined as follows:

Jim and Sally represent the emerging modern couple. They are both ambitious, hold challenging full-time jobs, and share the household tasks equally. They will not have children until their early thirties and will put them into day care a year or two after their birth. They dine out at least twice a week, favour designer clothes, and hold conservative political views. They shun alcohol and packaged foods, preferring mineral water, raw vegetables, fruit and wholemeal bread.

*Archetype*

Webster's dictionary defines 'archetype' as 'A model or first form, the original pattern from which a thing is made, or to which it corresponds.' It can be an image, a story pattern or a character. Novels, plays and films are usually full of characters and themes derived from basic archetypes. The archetype is thus an ideal that is copied from to create an instantiation, analogous to the way a stimulus is categorised as an instance by comparing it to a prototype.

For example, consider the fictionalised villain. He usually has all the negative traits (greed, cruelty, dressed in black, etc.) without a single redeeming feature. He is, therefore, an ideal. It is unlikely that we would encounter a real person with all those negative characteristics.

Another popular archetype is an American southern sheriff. He is usually middle-aged, overweight, pistol-happy, prone to car chases, and likely to lock people up for little cause. Various exemplars of this archetype have appeared in many recent films.

A more complex archetype is the story pattern – sometimes called the myth or theme. A basic one is good versus evil. Countless works are instantiations of this basic archetype. Other examples are coming of age, redemption after going astray, and boy meets girl (or, as the old joke about early Soviet propaganda films goes, boy meets tractor). A very strong theme, such as the plot of *Romeo and Juliet* or *The Count of Monte Cristo*, may become an archetype, as various writers use it in their own works.

Such archetypes often have a deep effect upon their audiences and literary works usually need to include some instantiations of these archetypes to succeed with their audiences. A film crammed to the brim with instantiations of basic archetypes is *Star Wars*. It uses many routine archetypes, such as good versus evil, a boy coming of age, a villain and a wise mentor. It also uses numerous archetypes from old western movies, instantiated in novel ways. These include the burned-out homestead, the survivor seeking revenge against the perpetrators, a boy who wants to be a gunslinger like his father, his training in use of a weapon, and the saloon full of hard-bitten characters spoiling for a fight. Again, the archetype–instantiation relation can be seen as analogous to that between a prototype and exemplars.

## Some evidence for the prototype view

Some evidence was mentioned above, but there is a lot more. Here are a few studies. Cantor *et al* (1980) found evidence for prototype representations of various psychiatric categories. Hampton (1981) found evidence of prototypes for some very abstract concepts, such as *a science* and *a work of art*. Horowitz *et al* (1982) found evidence of a prototype representation of *lonely person*. They derived a list of 18 characteristic features. Here are seven:

1.  Feels separate from others, different.
2.  Feels isolated, excluded from group activities.
3.  Feels does not know how to make friends.
4.  Feels inferior, that something is wrong with me.
5.  Feels unloved.
6.  Feels depressed.
7.  Is introverted.

No single lonely person is likely to have all 18 features. It is a family-resemblance concept – the person will only have some of these characteristics. A study then showed that subjects use these features to categorise various persons as lonely or not lonely. The subjects read essays describing various characters and then said whether the person depicted was lonely or not. As the number of such features mentioned in an essay increased, so did the likelihood the person would be categorised as lonely.

The above prototypes are abstracted from actual exemplars. Some prototypes may well be innate (Rosch, 1978). Indeed, the Berlin and Kay study suggested that focal colours may be innate prototypes. There may also be innate prototypes for facial expressions. Thus, we may have a prototype *expression of joy* and may determine a given person's emotional state by comparing his expression to such a prototype.

**How the prototype view handles the problems that plagued the classical view**

Generally the prototype view handles the problems that plagued the classical view quite well, largely because it was formulated to do so. These problems and how they are handled are outlined below.

*Lack of defining features*
Defining features are not required at all, since a category representation consists of a set of characteristic features or mean values on several dimensions. A stimulus need only be sufficiently similar to a prototype to be an exemplar. It need not have certain defining features.

*Typicality effects*
These can be explained by assuming that typicality correlates with the number of features an instance shares with the prototype, as the Rosch and Mervis (1975) study suggested. Thus, a typical exemplar of *lonely person* would have many features of the prototype and an atypical one far fewer features. Thus, a highly typical bird would have features such as 'flies', 'eats worms', 'nests in trees' and 'gets around in the daytime'. A less typical one, such as a hawk, would have fewer. The very atypical kiwi has fewer features than a hawk. It cannot fly, gets around at night, and lives in a burrow!

*Unclear cases*
These can be accounted for in several different ways (Smith and Medin, 1981). The first way is when a particular stimulus is about as similar to one prototype as another. The ubiquitous tomato is a good example. It is about as similar to the *fruit* prototype as to the *vegetable* one. Similarly, whales and dolphins may be hard to categorise, because they

resemble the *fish* prototype and the *mammal* one. A second case is when a stimulus has some but not quite enough of the prototype's characteristic features. For instance a person might be categorised as lonely if he possessed four features of the prototype. An unclear case might just have three, and therefore may be considered as a borderline case. The third unclear case is when a specific stimulus is not much like any prototype one knows, and therefore is hard to categorise. A possible example is those unfortunate people who go from doctor to doctor with a set of symptoms that no one can diagnose, for they are not much like any known prototypes.

## THE EXEMPLAR VIEW

This theory is quite new in its current form, though the basic notion in a sense has its roots in the stimulus generalisation paradigm of traditional learning theory (Riley and Lamb, 1979). In the paradigm, a subject was taught a conditioned response in the presence of a certain stimulus and then was tested for generalisation to other stimuli. The basic account has been elaborated on by authors such as Brooks (1978) and Medin and Schaffer (1978). The theory is relatively simple.

### Main principles

A category is not represented as an abstracted set of defining features or as a measure of central tendency. The theory in a pure form proposes no abstraction from stimuli at all. Instead, a learner simply remembers one or more exemplars of a given category without abstracting anything from them. An example is *dog*. Rather than abstracting a set of features from instances, we could represent the category by remembering the beagle next door and the poodle around the corner. Similarly, *bird* might be represented with a specific robin, a specific dove and a specific eagle. Learning a category representation this way is very easy (Farah and Kosslyn, 1982). We only need to remember instances rather than have to analyse them into features.

It should be noted that exemplar representations may involve some abstraction, however (Smith and Medin, 1981). We might represent *dog* with the exemplars beagle and bloodhound. These exemplars are, however, abstractions in that they are not specific objects. Similarly, representing *bird* by a hawk and robin also would involve some abstraction.

*Categorisation with exemplar representations*
Stimuli are categorised as exemplars or non-exemplars by reference to the stored instances. The process is much like prototype-matching. A specific stimulus is simply compared with one or more stored exemplars in memory. If it is similar enough, then it is categorised as an exemplar. For example, if a person's representation of *dog* consisted of a specific beagle and a specific basset and he encountered a greyhound and a cat, these would simply be compared to his stored exemplars. Another way to describe this categorisation process is to call it *analogical reasoning*. A person looks for an analogy – a similarity between a given stimulus and one or more stored exemplars.

## Some examples of exemplar-represented categories

It is not hard to think of categories that appear to be defined by analogy to a salient exemplar. Consider the concept of *a Viet Nam*, which has a few nations as exemplars, such as El Salvador and the Philippines. The concept derives from the French and American experience of backing a corrupt government in a long war of attrition fought against guerilas. The local populations did not support the struggle. Much material, such as arms, poured in, to no avail in the end. The single case of Viet Nam provides an exemplar. Other nations are put into a category by analogy to this exemplar, by an overlap of features. Thus, the US government is warned against increasing involvement in Central America because some nations there might become Viet Nams. The Soviet Union's occupation of Afghanistan is said to be a Viet Nam and the Vietnamese invasion and occupation of neighbouring Kampuchea is sometimes referred to a bit too cleverly as a Viet Nam for Viet Nam. Both Cuba and Iran also provide exemplars for categories of certain sorts of revolution.

Another example is *a thalidomide*. A number of drugs are put into this category by analogy to the drug thalidomide, which was widely marketed in the 1950s and 1960s as a sedative. But, it had not been adequately tested and later was found to induce birth defects when taken by pregnant women. Any inadequately tested drug with such side effects is often referred to as *a thalidomide*. Anyone questioning the long years of testing needed before a promising drug is released is often told, 'We do not want another thalidomide'. Other examples are *a Trojan horse, a Waterloo, a Watergate, a Catch-22, a Pandora's Box, a Scrooge* and *an Einstein*. It also seems likely that many idiosyncratic person-concepts are based on one or two known exemplars. My concept of *compulsive gambler* is largely based on a single, known exemplar, and I determine if certain other persons fall into the category by comparing them to that exemplar.

## When might categories be represented by exemplars?

Brooks (1978) suggests several cases in which categories might be represented by exemplars. The first is when stimuli are very complex and thus defy easy reduction to defining features. Examples are certain artistic styles and musical styles. As mentioned in Chapter 1, it is often very hard to see what exemplars of certain categories have in common. So, rather than trying to derive some rules by which to categorise them, a simpler strategy is to just remember one or two exemplars. Stimuli can then be categorised by reference to them.

Some stimulus domains are indeed very complex, and a strategy that people operating with them seem to use is exemplar representations. Consider film-making and book publishing. There is no clear set of defining features that allows one to categorise before release a given book or film as *a potboiler* or *a smash hit*. Indeed, a film producer once said that one of the ten films on his list would be this year's blockbuster, but added that he had no idea which one it would be. Some features seem to be characteristic of successful films, such as a good director, a large budget and top stars, but they are not defining features. Many films with these features flop and some without them succeed. Also, the public is notoriously fickle. This year's flop might have been last year's success.

We can deal with such a complex domain by using exemplars to define various categories. Thus, a successful film such as *Star Wars* is often followed not just by sequels but also by numerous clones. A book on some esoteric topic that suddenly does very well is often followed by replicas. Similarly, a book publisher in deciding whether to publish a given manuscript may determine if it is *a publishable book* by comparing it to known exemplars. Has he published anything like it recently? How well did it do? How are books like it faring on the market at the moment?

A related case is with children. As mentioned, younger children have great trouble abstracting defining features. Instead, they may simply memorise exemplars and categorise stimuli by reference to them. Indeed, Kossan (1981) asked young children to define *dog*. Rather than reeling off a list of features, a child might say, 'It's like Rover'.

A second case is when people only have a single instance to learn from. The real world is not much like a typical concept-learning experiment or a classroom. We are not usually shown several exemplars and non-exemplars in succession from which to abstract a concept. Often there is just one exemplar, such as one dog, or one painting, or one Cuba. Some more such cases are described in the next section.

**Distinguishing between the exemplar and prototype views**

A prototype is a measure of central tendency of a set of instances and an exemplar representation is not. A prototype is often an abstraction – a set of features not present in any actual individual instance. Even when the prototype is an actual instance, it falls at the centre of a set of exemplars and has many features those exemplars tend to share. An exemplar representation can also include knowledge of a variety of specific exemplars. The views can be distinguished on other grounds as well (Smith and Medin, 1981).

**How the exemplar view handles criticisms of the classical view**

*Lack of clear-cut defining features*
No difficulty is posed here, because the view does not require them. A complex concept such as *game* by this view would be represented by one or more salient exemplars, such as chess and soccer. The instances need not have any features in common.

*Typicality effects*
We can assume that a concept is likely to be represented by its more typical exemplars. Thus, *bird* is likely to be represented by, say, robin and sparrow, rather than penguin and ostrich. Typicality judgments are made by reference to such exemplars and, so, the more similar a given stimulus is to them, the more typical it is rated.

*Unclear cases*
Stimuli that are hard to categorise may arise from several factors, much like those in the prototype case. Firstly, a given stimulus might not be much like any particular stored exemplar. Smith and Medin give the example of seahorse, which may be hard to categorise as a fish or crustacean, because it does not look much like exemplars of either

category. Secondly, a stimulus may be similar to salient exemplars of more than one category. Again, the tomato looks much like salient exemplars of both *fruit*'and *vegetable* and is therefore hard to classify.

### Criticisms of the view

One criticism is that memory capacity would have to be very large indeed to accommodate the huge number of exemplars a person must remember. However, a counter argument is that no one yet knows of any such limit to long-term memory and so this criticism is not strong (Farah and Kosslyn, 1982). A second criticism is that the view gives little clue as to what holds a category together – as to why certain exemplars are perceived as similar (Medin, 1983; Medin and Smith, 1984). Therfore, no obvious constraints are imposed by the view on the concepts that we are likely to form.

## WHICH VIEW IS 'CORRECT'?

The emerging consensus seems to be that no one view is a complete account of category representation (Kemler-Nelson, 1984). Instead, it seems likely that representing a given category in a particular way is best seen as a *strategy*, the use of which depends on the category, the learner, the circumstances, and the concept's intended use. People need to use a variety of such strategies to stay flexible and to adapt to changing circumstances. Indeed, this interpretation has been hinted at above. The following factors may affect the type of representation used.

### Different categories are represented in different ways

Concepts differ greatly in their abstractness, number of exemplars, and complexity of component concepts, and they are based on different kinds of feature. We can thus contrast highly abstract concepts, such as *justice* and *intelligence*, with concrete ones, such as *red* and the dot pattern and schematic face concepts. Some concepts can be readily shown to have defining features (*square, triangle*), often because they are constructed so. Others, such as *game*, seem to be represented as prototypes and others as exemplars. Some, such as the English alphabet, seem to be defined just by enumeration (Glass *et al*, 1979). Though a person can have a concept of a letter, he must still learn the 26 exemplars by rote. There is no prototypical letter or set of defining features that allows him to categorise all letters as such, in the way a definition of *square* will allow one to categorise all squares.

There is some experimental evidence for the notion that different categories are represented in different ways. Kossan (1981) had groups of children learn three types of concept: a type based on defining features, a family-resemblance type with no common features and one composed of exemplars with distinctive features. The subjects tended to abstract defining features from the first type. Thus, they acquired classical-view representations. But, concepts that had exemplars with distinctive features were acquired best with an exemplar strategy. Kemler-Nelson (1984), using artificial categories, found that the task set and the learner influenced the way a category was represented. Some conditions induced a family-resemblance representation rather than one of defining features.

### A category may be represented in multiple ways

An individual may represent a certain category in more than one way. Thus, he might acquire a prototype representation but still store information about specific exemplars. These can be used when needed. Indeed, Elio and Anderson (1981) found evidence that subjects in an experiment were abstracting a prototype but also were still using exemplars to categorise.

Some people may have both a prototype and a classical view representation. So, the latter may be used as a back-up and the former for rough-and-ready classification (Medin and Smith, 1984). A likely such case is in medical diagnosis. Every Western doctor knows that the defining feature of say, *measles*, is infection by a certain virus, but it is impractical, and usually unnecessary, to carry around laboratory equipment to test for the presence of the virus. Instead, a prototype whose features consist of external symptoms is used. If a person has a sufficient number of these, then he can be categorised as a sufferer. If there is uncertainty, the doctor can order a laboratory test to see if the defining feature is present. Another example of the defining features being used as a back-up is from Armstrong *et al* (1983) – the concept of *boy*. The defining features include: male, young and human. A prototype might consist of characteristic features such as short, smooth skin, freckles, noisy and energetic. The prototype can be used for quick categorisation, while the set of defining features is used for difficult cases, or to relate the concept to others.

A study by Landau (1982) suggests that different representations may be used in categorisation. Subjects were shown various pictures of people and had to place the person depicted in each in a kin category, such as *mother, brother* or *grandmother*. Later, they had to explain why they categorised as they did. Several variables were manipulated, such as the presence/absence of children in the picture and various signs of age. Subjects tended to use such characteristic features as age and presence/absence of children for the initial categorisation. Thus, they appeared to use a prototype. When justifying the decision, however, they tended to use the defining features of each.

### Individual differences

Different people may represent the same category in different ways. This point has been stressed in several places already. One such case is with experts, who may have a classical-view representation of important categories in their field, while non-experts rely on prototypes or exemplars. Thus, a biologist may know the defining features of *mammal, fungus* and *tree* while non-experts do not. A doctor knows that the defining features of *measles* and *hepatitis* are infection by a certain virus while non-experts may not. As we see in Chapter 9, a shift may occur from exemplar or prototype representations to classical-view ones with increasing expertise, again because experts often need to use defining features. An analogous case is with children. Because they have trouble extracting defining features, they may rely on prototypes and exemplars, as mentioned earlier.

The notion that different people may represent a certain category in different ways has been around for a long time. Indeed, Klausmeier and his colleagues some years ago suggested as much (e.g. Klausmeier *et al*, 1974; Klausmeier, 1976a). They proposed a scheme that has been very influential in educational psychology. They argued that the same concept can be acquired at different levels. Each level reflects an increasing depth of knowledge about the category. All learners are thought to go through the four levels in sequence when acquiring a given concept, though some concepts can only be acquired at the second and third levels. They also suggest that different processes are involved in learning a concept at each level.

Here is a brief summary of their scheme. The first two levels are the *concrete* and *identity* levels. At the concrete, a person can only recognise that an object currently in view has been encountered before. The identity level corresponds to the learning of identity concepts mentioned in Chapter 1. A person can recognise an object as one previously encountered when perceiving it at different distances or angles, when it is partially covered up, and/or in different states of sensory degradation. Thus, a child can recognise a toy rabbit from the front, back or side, by feeling its shape in the dark, or by seeing it in a photograph. The third level is the *classification*, and it pertains to kind concepts. He can place two or more different stimuli in the same category, two or more different exemplars. Thus, a person recognises a poodle and a beagle as being exemplars of *dog* and a mud-hut and a palace as instances of *dwelling*. Although a person can correctly categorise, he cannot state the concept's defining features (if it has them). Klausmeier is vague as to how people are then able to categorise, merely emphasising that they can do so without being able to say how. Clearly, this level can be seen as consistent with exemplar or prototype representations.

The final level is the *formal* one. Here a person can state the concept's name, can readily categorise stimuli as instances or non-instances and can specify the concept's defining features. This level corresponds to a classical-view representation. Klausmeier also argues, consistent with points made earlier in this book, that some concepts cannot be learned at the formal level because they have no defining features, or if so, only very obscure ones. He also states that many scientists have formal-level representations of important categories in their field and that the level to which a person can acquire a certain concept may depend on age and expertise. To learn complex concepts at the formal level may require much knowledge in a given subject. A person may have to know many subordinate concepts, for example.

**Circumstantial differences**

A certain category may be represented in different ways according to such circumstances as the conditions under which the concept is learned and the use to which it will be put. For some purposes, an exemplar or prototype representation may be all that is needed. Thus, a person may lack the need or the will to analyse stimuli into common features (Brooks, 1978). At an art gallery he may just need to discriminate between a few styles of painting in order to impress a companion. Similarly, a student may simply memorise exemplars of a concept to pass an exam rather than try to learn the defining features. In other circumstances, we may need to remember specific exemplars rather than just a general rule (Brooks, 1978). It is useful to know that the particular dog around the corner is a very fierce one.

Another circumstantial difference is limited time and resources to analyse stimuli (Brooks, 1978). In daily life, many things are going on at the same time and we often cannot devote our full attention to learning defining features. Again, memorising exemplars is an easy alternative.

A final difference is training conditions. The category representation may simply reflect how one learned (or was taught) the concept. Indeed, Medin *et al* (1984) found some evidence for this notion. Subjects learned concepts from just exemplars, from a prototype followed by experience with exemplars, or from a prototype presented at the same time as exemplars. The training condition affected the representation acquired. Those in the exemplars only group tended to categorise new instances by reference to stored exemplars, while the other subjects used both stored exemplars and prototypes.


EDUCATIONAL IMPLICATIONS

The material in this chapter has a number of educational implications. The most obvious one is that the method used to teach a given concept needs to be tailored to the nature of the concept and the learners' age and expertise level. The traditional method of teaching concepts uses analysis into defining features, but this method may not be appropriate for some concepts and for younger learners. This point and others will be expanded on in Chapter 10.


FURTHER READING

Representation: Glass *et al* (Chapter 1, 1979); Palmer (1978).
Theories of category representation: Anglin (1977); Smith and Medin (1981); Medin and Smith (1984); Brooks (1978).

*Chapter 7*

# Some Ways in which Concepts are Acquired

SUMMARY

1. Concepts seem to be learned in a variety of ways, broadly divisible into acquisition from instances or from words. Classroom instruction often involves both means.
2. Concepts can be acquired from instances by abstracting out common features, testing hypotheses about a concept's defining features, acquiring a prototype or memorising exemplars.
3. Concepts can be acquired from words in several ways – from a definition, synonyms, and context. Some complex concepts can only really be learned through language. Language also greatly aids classroom concept teaching, because a teacher can use words to define a concept, list important features and point them out in instances.
4. A variety of variables, such as prior knowledge, personality, intelligence and cognitive style, may affect concept learning.
5. We appear to acquire the concepts we do for a variety of reasons. We learn those that are most useful for making inferences and solving problems and that thus promote adaptation. There also may be innate pre-dispositions to form certain concepts. Increases in knowledge may affect the concepts we acquire and so, too, may culture. A certain society picks out particular bases as important for categorisation and members of that society form concepts around them.

## INTRODUCTION

This chapter looks at some ways in which concepts are actually learned. This topic has been touched on in several places already, notably Chapter 6, which described the acquisition of sets of defining features, prototypes and exemplar representations. These will be described in more detail, along with some other ways in which concepts may be learned. It should be noted here that not a lot is really known about concept learning (Homa, 1984). However, some likely methods will be suggested. Much of the material in this chapter is used and expanded upon in Chapters 9 and 10, which look at how concepts should be taught.

First of all a complex point needs clarification. The term 'concept learning' can be applied to a wide variety of phenomena (Wicklegren, 1979). It can refer to acquisition of an identity concept, a prototype, a set of exemplars, and a set of defining features. It can apply to a person learning to attach a name to a known concept and perhaps refining the concept somewhat. Thus, a child with a concept of *ball* may find out that it is labelled by the word 'ball' and may change his concept to bring it in line with the adult meaning, just as a character in a play was delighted to discover that he had been speaking 'prose' all his life. The term can also refer to the evolution of a concept. Therefore, the position adopted here is that a variety of processes are involved in concept learning.

As mentioned in the last chapter, concepts are acquired in many different circumstances and they vary greatly in complexity. Concept learning can be broadly divided into learning from exemplars and from words (Ausubel, 1968). Concepts are often taught in the classroom from words, with perhaps some actual exemplars as well. Both these ways of learning concepts are surveyed, followed by a brief discussion of some individual differences that might affect concept learning. Then the chapter closes with a discussion of an important question mentioned in Chapter 1, 'Why do we acquire the concepts we do?'

## ACQUISITION FROM INSTANCES

This mode has been the one most studied in laboratories. When one or more stimuli are repeatedly encountered, our minds seem to be attuned to picking out similarities between them and forming concepts around them. Thus, the repeated experience of certain stimuli may lead to an internal representation of them or their similarities. In some cases, the features of certain stimuli are so obvious to our senses that abstraction seems nearly automatic, as mentioned earlier. Exemplars of *star* and *cloud* are so perceptually salient and so different from just about everything else that we can form concepts around them with great ease (Carroll, 1964). In other cases, much effort may be needed. A film producer might do a lot of research and analysis in order to determine some possible features of *next season's hit*. Similarly, many scientific concepts, such as *gravity* and *entropy*, took many years and great effort by scientists to abstract from experience.

Acquiring concepts from exemplars can be very slow and cumbersome (Ausubel, 1968). As a result, it might predominate in young children and to a lesser extent in adults, and might occur with less complex concepts. Indeed, many complex concepts simply would not be learned at all by most people if they had to abstract them from experience; the instances do not occur often enough and, without guidance, could not be acquired (Skemp, 1979). In essence, great thinkers of the past have done the abstraction for us and the concepts are passed onto people through language or special exemplar presentations. Pure abstraction from instances is thus not all that common in the classroom, though it occurs to some extent in Bruner's discovery approach (see page 153).

Here are several major methods of acquisition from instances.

### Abstracting one or more invariant features

As mentioned, exemplars of some concepts share common features and acquiring them is a matter of noticing the defining features and applying them in order to categorise new stimuli. As stated above, sometimes the features are so salient that one notices them and groups the stimuli accordingly. An example is the straight line concept in Figure 1, page 5, where the line feature is a very obvious basis for categorisation. If, for example, we have to group the following stimuli into two categories:

ADX ZVB cdj NBU plw

the upper/lower case feature is so salient that it also immediately comes to mind as a basis for categorisation. An everyday example is perhaps noticing the common attributes of a friend's dating partners. One may notice that they are always tall, or blond, or extrovert. Another example comes from a television commercial. It presents, in sequence, a number of people wearing swimsuits. When each person is shown, a voice says, 'She would use X', or 'I do not think he would use X'. Without much thought, it soon occurred to me that alleged users of X were fashionably slender while non-users were not, and the suspicion began to dawn that X is supposed to make users slim. I thus formed a concept of an *X-user*, which allowed me to categorise new instances. This process can be viewed as a form of discrimination learning. We attend to certain stimuli and use their presence to discriminate exemplars from non-exemplars.

Hull (1920) carried out an early study of the learning of concepts with a single invariant feature. Subjects learned concepts, instances of which were Chinese characters. Instances had a single common feature embedded within them. In one experiment, subjects learned to label each exemplar with a single nonsense syllable (e.g. MVG,VOV). Then they learned a second list of character/nonsense syllable pairs. Characters in the second list had the invariant feature and were acquired much more rapidly than the first, suggesting that subjects were abstracting the feature and using it to acquire the pair associations. Interestingly, they reported having no notion that they were doing so.

Hypothesis-testing also may be involved in learning concepts that have invariant features (Klausmeier *et al*, 1974). Thus, a person may notice what seem to be invariant features and test out the hypothesis that they are indeed invariant ones. This method is described below.

## Hypothesis-testing

A hypothesis is a guess about some aspect of the world, which is then tested against reality. We probably often acquire well-defined concepts by first forming hypotheses about their defining features and then testing these against instances. Hypothesis-testing has indeed been much studied in the laboratory (Levine, 1975; Tumblin and Gholson, 1981), generally being examined with the reception or selection methods (see Chapter 2). It is often called an 'active, information-processing strategy', because the learner is actively generating and testing hypotheses. It can thus be contrasted to evidently more passive methods, such as abstracting a prototype or defining features without thinking much about doing so (Bolton, 1977).

Here is a simple example of how hypothesis-testing might be used to learn a concept in the concept identification paradigm. Say we were shown several stimuli in succession and told that some are exemplars of *nop* and our task is to learn the defining features of the concept. The experimenter will tell you if a given stimulus is or is not a 'nop'. One way to proceed is to devise and test various hypotheses about the defining features of *nop*. We might first hypothesise that a 'nop' is a square, and test it by calling several squares 'nops' and non-squares 'non-nops'. We could continue until we encountered a square that was not a 'nop' or a non-square that was. We could then devise and test another hypothesis. Perhaps a 'nop' is a rectangle. This generation and testing continues until we acquire the defining features. For quite obvious reasons, this procedure is called 'win/stay, lose/shift'.

Studies of hypothesis-testing in the identification procedure have revealed a variety of strategies that people use, which are variations on hypothesis-testing. Bruner *et al* (1956) describe several of these. *Conservative focusing* involves taking a single, positive instance and hypothesising that all its attributes are defining features. Then, the subject systematically tests out each feature in turn by selecting stimuli that only differ in one attribute. For example, say that the positive instance is a card with three blue circles. Its features are three, blue and circle. He then selects a card with, say, three blue squares. If the card is still an exemplar, then circle is not relevant and then three and blue can be tested in the same way. If the card is not an instance, then the attribute of figure type is relevant.

A related strategy is *focus gambling*. The subject tests more than one attribute at a time. Consider again the example of a card with three blue circles. He might test the notion that colour and type of figure are relevant by picking a card with three red triangles or yellow squares. If such a card is still an exemplar, then two attributes can be eliminated as irrelevant at the same time. But, if it is not an instance, either attribute could be relevant and must be tested.

A third strategy is *scanning*. In the above two strategies, a subject tests a hypothesis that includes all attributes on a positive instance. With scanning, he tests only attributes, either one at a time or a few at a time. While in the focusing strategies, the learner hypothesises that all attributes are relevant and eliminates certain ones, with scanning, the subject hypothesises that one attribute is relevant and tests that. Thus, he might say yellow is a relevant attribute or that all triangles are instances, ignoring other attributes, such as size and shape.

Researchers have asked a number of questions about concept learning in this identification paradigm. They ask if acquisition is a long, slow incremental process or if it is very rapid. Some studies have indeed shown abrupt shifts in performance, evidently when a subject hits on the right hypothesis (Levine *et al*, 1967). Another question is on how many hypotheses are tested for each trial. We can also ask about the effects of numerous variables, such as IQ, stress, motivation, prior experience, number and sequence of positive and negative instances, and how well subjects remember the results of tests on previous trials. A more interesting question is where the subject's hypotheses come from. Possible sources include those hypotheses that were relevant in the past, salient attributes such as colour and form, and genetic constraints examined later in this chapter.

*Hypothesis-testing in the real world*
As mentioned, hypothesis-testing is most likely to be used to learn the features of well-defined concepts. However, people may try to learn even ill-defined concepts this way (Martin and Caramazza, 1980). Here are some examples of hypothesis-testing in the real world in order to learn concepts.

Some well-defined, natural concepts are conjunctions of already-known attributes, and acquiring such concepts may be a matter of putting these together. Ellis *et al* (1979) give the example of *compact car*. A learner may already know the concept of *car* and then hear the term 'compact' applied to certain cars in ads and conversations. He might initially hypothesise that a compact car is a type of sportscar and test it against various cars labelled 'compact' in ads. After encountering non-instances, he could hypothesise that the term refers to a small car, and test that out. Another example they give is *legal driver*, which is defined by certain attributes that vary from locality to locality. These include features such as 18 years and older, has not had the licence cancelled, and has passed a test for that type of vehicle. If trying to determine the features of a legal driver in a certain place, we could go through each feature to arrive at the correct conjunction of attributes. While such concepts are much more likely to be learned from books or other people, they illustrate the process of hypothesis-testing.

Many scientific concepts are no doubt learned from hypothesis-testing by scientists at the frontiers of research. They often have to abstract concepts from experience. A recent example is the abstraction of the disease concept AIDS. Its exemplars are people suffering from it. Before 1980, the concept did not exist at all, but in that year, scientists noticed an unusual number of cases of some rare syndromes. Several men had a type of pneumonia typically found only in persons with depressed immune systems, and one young man had Kaposi's sarcoma, a cancer extremely rare outside the elderly. These observations suggested the presence of a new disease category, and later research discovered that Haitians and homosexuals were disproportionally affected. This was analogous to telling a subject in an experiment that he has a concept to learn from several instances. But what common features linked these cases?

Some early hypotheses generated were based on analogy to known diseases. One was that the victims were infected by a new virus. Another was that their immune systems had taken a severe battering because their lifestyles resulted in repeated infections from many micro-organisms. A third hypothesis combined the first two. These and others were extensively tested until it became clear that the defining feature of the syndrome was infection by a previously unknown virus.

Hypothesis-testing is also used by children to learn the names of concepts they already know and perhaps to refine existing ones to correspond to their adult counterparts (Carey, 1982). Thus, a child might have a concept of *ball* that has been formed from experience with various round objects. He might hear the name 'ball' applied in various contexts and hypothesise that 'ball' refers to any round object. He might later mistakenly call an orange a ball and be told that the name does not apply. He might then hypothesise that 'ball' refers to any non-organic round object, and test that hypothesis, and his experience will ultimately converge upon the adult meaning. Similarly, a child might hypothesise that 'island' refers to any large land mass, such as a continent or peninsula, then, later, that an island is a large land mass surrounded by water, and finally that it is any piece of land surrounded by water.

## Abstracting a prototype

Chapter 6 noted that a prototype is a measure of central tendency of a set of instances. It can be a highly typical instance or an abstraction of characteristic features of instances. People are likely to form prototype representations of ill-defined categories. Prototype representations have been demonstrated with categories in many stimulus domains. Those mentioned in Chapter 6 included artificial ones and various person categories. Others include emotions (Fehr *et al*, 1982), environmental scenes (Tversky and Hemenway, 1983) and psychological situations (Cantor *et al*, 1982).

How are such prototypes acquired? Some may be acquired directly, by being presented with the central tendency of some instances. Attneave (1957) and Medin *et al* (1984) found that subjects who were shown a prototype categorised new stimuli with it. A second way is from repeated presentation of a set of instances. When shown a series of dot patterns, schematic faces or even lonely persons, our minds seem to be attuned to picking up the similarities between them and forming a prototype (Anderson, 1980).

Some possible everyday examples are as follows. Consider if a person were to buy an item of which he has little knowledge, such as a car or pair of jogging shoes. After visiting various shops and seeing what specific instances are available, he gets some notion of the average quality, durability, appearance and price of the instances available. Any new instance seen can then be compared to this average to determine if it is a good buy. I get an idea of a prototype essay after marking 15 to 20 of a batch. I could then use the prototype to determine the grades of subsequent exemplars encountered. Attneave (1957) cites the 'Chinese all look alike' syndrome. Someone from the West who has little experience of Chinese faces often finds them hard to tell apart and distinguish from other Orientals such as Thais and Japanese. However, with exposure to many such faces, a prototype or 'average face' may form, which also includes some knowledge of the instances' variation.

A prototype may also be a highly typical instance which reflects the central tendency of a set of instances. Children appear to acquire many concepts from a very typical exemplar and add peripheral instances later (Greenberg and Kuczaj, 1982), as we see in more detail in Chapter 8. Bowerman (1980) describes some examples from observing her two children. One appeared to acquire a prototype by seeing the Moon, generalising from it to many other stimuli. She applied the name 'moon' to the peel side of a half-grapefruit, and pulling off a hangnail, for instance. A prototypical experience of kicking a ball was generalised to the actions of kicking a floor fan and pushing her chest against a wall, since the child used 'kick' to refer to these behaviours. Such over-extensions of a word are often based on perceptual attributes such as shape.

*Variables affecting prototype acquisition*
Many studies using relatively concrete concepts have found that certain variables affect prototype acquisition (Homa, 1984). For instance, the more exemplars shown, the better the abstraction of a prototype and the more accurate the categorisation of new exemplars. Homa and Little (unpublished, cited by Homa, 1984) asked some subjects to categorise various instances of ill-defined categories. One group experienced just three exemplars, another six, and a third group nine. The group shown nine exemplars were able to retain the prototype more easily and were more adept at categorising new instances. Thus, the more exemplars shown, the more generalisation occurs. The practical implication is to present a wide variety of exemplars when teaching a prototype concept.

Another variable is the dispersion, or scatter, of the exemplars. The narrower the range (and, thus, the more similar the instances) the easier the prototype is to form (e.g. Goldman and Homa, 1977; Posner and Keele, 1968 and 1970).

**Acquiring an exemplar representation**

A concept may be acquired from a single instance. A child may acquire the concept *dog* from the family pet, or the concept *bulldozer* from seeing only one vehicle. Categorisation of new stimuli is then carried out by analogy to the stored exemplar. To learn a concept this way, a person only needs to discriminate the instance from other stimuli and remember it. Indeed, some concepts can only be acquired by memorising exemplars, as mentioned in Chapter 6. Examples are the English alphabet and digits from one to nine (Glass *et al*, 1979).

It is in some ways hard to distinguish between acquiring an exemplar representation and learning a prototypical instance – showing that the exemplar and prototype views are not that distinct. However, to maintain consistency with the research literature, acquiring a highly typical exemplar at the centre of a category is referred to here as learning a prototype.

## ACQUISITION THROUGH LANGUAGE

The possession of language greatly aids concept learning. Indeed, as children grow older they acquire concepts more and more through words (Ausubel, 1968; Klausmeier *et al*, 1974). The uses of language here are indeed many (Stones, 1984). First of all, as mentioned earlier, important concepts abstracted by great thinkers can be rapidly communicated to people through words. As the experiences and abilities that lead to such abstraction would be beyond those of most people, such concepts would otherwise not have been learned. Secondly, language can speed up the learning of concepts that probably would have been acquired anyway. A schoolteacher can use words to alert students to the fact that there is a concept to be learned, and can use words to emphasise instances and non-instances and why stimuli are one or the other. Thirdly, some concepts can only really be learned through language since no perceptible exemplars exist (Klausmeier *et al*, 1974). Examples are *eternity, infinity* and *soul*. Others, such as *platypus* and *kangaroo*, can be taught through words even when no actual exemplars are available, as can relational concepts, such as *uncle*. Some disciplines, such as philosophy and history, rely mainly on words to teach concepts, because perceptible instances do not exist or are too difficult to actually present (de Silva, 1979).

A teacher can also use language to emphasise a concept's defining features, which may improve learning. Extensive literature documents research on the 'acquired distinctiveness of cues' phenomenon. An example showing the phenomenon is a study by Deno *et al* (1971). Stimuli were various electrocardiogram (ECG) patterns, which could be categorised as indicative of various disorders such as infarction, ischaemia and injury. Some subjects received extensive pre-training in identifying critical features of a normal ECG pattern, evidently allowing them to form a prototype. These features were described in detail and subjects drew and labelled them. Subjects given this training were much better at categorising new ECG patterns as instances of the three disorders in a subsequent test.

Several ways in which concepts can be learned from words have been mentioned in previous chapters. Chapter 2 described how hearing the same name applied to various stimuli may induce a person to try to form a concept. Chapter 4 described how metaphors may be used to form new concepts and schemata and how hedges may enable one to extend and retract category boundaries. The traditional 'vocabulary training' methods of schoolteachers also teach concepts through words (Johnson and Pearson, 1978; Duffelmeyer, 1985). While some concepts can indeed be acquired from these methods, many concepts need more elaborate training, which includes experience with exemplars and non-exemplars (see Chapter 9). Below, various ways of teaching concepts through words are described.

### Definitions

Some concepts are acquired from an oral or dictionary definition. Indeed, a standard classroom method is to give a definition and one or more exemplars. A dictionary will reveal that a kimono is a loose robe-like garment worn by Japanese men and women, that a palindrome is a word that spells the same backwards and forwards, and a chromosome is a rod or thread-shaped body that exists in a cell nucleus and carries the genes. Language thus allows a person to learn a new concept from his cognitive structure. Skemp (1979) gives the example of 'ketch', defined as a sailing boat with two masts. Holding the concepts of *mast, two* and *sailing boat* allows a person to combine them to acquire the new concept.

Studies indeed suggest that learners can readily acquire concepts from definitions (Johnson and Stratton, 1966) when they know the component concepts. For instance, Anderson and Kulhavy (1972) gave university students definitions of unfamiliar words and then found that they could later categorise exemplars of the concepts the terms named. One definition was, 'Atavistic means reversion to a primitive type'. Students were given multiple choice items and had to pick out the single instance of the concept. For example:

a.   The students complained that his approach to teaching was very old fashioned.
b.   Her main object in attending class was to flirt with every boy who sat next to her.
c.   The photographs of the murder scene were so awful that the district attorney hesitated to use them as evidence.

Anderson and Kulhary (1972)

Students were quite adept at picking out the right answer. Their study also suggested some practical tips for teaching concepts by definition. Firstly, and not too surprisingly, make sure the students can readily understand the definition. Secondly ask them to compose sensible sentences that include the term. Thus for atavistic, ask them to produce an example such as, 'The new regime's policies were atavistic'. That way the students have to think about the word and thus find it difficult to learn just by rote.

It is important to note, however, that a definition is just a small part of the knowledge contained in a concept (Wicklegren, 1979). As mentioned earlier, some concepts are so complex that exemplars must be presented as well so that students have some notion of the boundaries. A student's concept of *kimono* is much more satisfactory after exposure to some actual exemplars as well as just the definition.

### Synonyms

The teacher can provide some synonyms and will hope that the learner can abstract a new word's meaning from them. Thus, he may try to teach the meaning of 'quell' by providing synonyms such as 'subdue', 'allay', 'cause to cease' and 'crush'. Indeed, dictionaries often rely on this method, giving a set of synonyms and hoping the reader will extract a certain word's meaning from them. For example, Webster defines 'high' as: 'lofty, elevated, tall, situated far above the ground'.

**Learning from contexts in which a concept's label appears**

Teachers often recommend wide reading to extend vocabulary. Such reading exposes a person to many new words, and may induce him to look up their meanings or infer them from their context. An example of acquiring a meaning from context is given below, from Werner and Kaplan (1950). Try to work out what a corplum is.

> A corplum may be used for support.
> Corplums may be long or short, thick or thin, strong or weak.
> A wet corplum does not burn.
> You can make a corplum smooth with sandpaper.
> The painter used a corplum to mix his paints.
>
> Werner and Kaplan (1950)

From these contexts, most people infer that a corplum is a stick or a piece of wood.

Though a concept may be acquired from a single context, it is usually best to give several. Just one may not be enough to ensure abstraction. For instance, Gibbons (1940) asked students to try to learn some word meanings from a single sentence such as, 'In the beginning, the teacher travelled from one locality to another to meet the students, thereby bringing into existence the *itinerant* teacher.' 'Itinerant' means 'travelling about', but some students exposed to just this single context thought it meant 'immoral', some 'humble' and a few 'intolerable'.

Werner and Kaplan suggest that a person's ability to acquire word meanings from context improves with age. They found that younger children given several contexts often took a meaning from the first one and stuck with it, trying to apply it to later sentences. They had trouble separating a word from its context. De Silva (1979) found a similar developmental trend when studying abstraction of various historical concepts from context.

A variety of processes may be going on when a person learns a concept from context. Klausmeier *et al* (1974) suggest that hypothesis-testing is one, as it is used to determine defining features. In the corplum example, a person might generate a hypothesis from the first and second sentences and test it out in later ones. Johnson and Pearson (1978) suggest that people also use a variety of cues, such as syntax.

**Verbally-presented exemplars**

A study by Johnson and Stratton (1966) illustrates this method, which involves presenting exemplars in the form of words. They gave subjects a verbal exemplar of certain concepts and asked them to practise applying the right word to exemplars. For instance:

> Rustic: a weathered old barn.
> Controversy: two men of differing opinions discuss the social value of a book.
>
> Johnson and Stratton (1966)

The above are exemplars of the concepts, not definitions or synonyms.

**Which method works best?**

Again, this is an important practical question. Serra (1953) points out that teachers often use each of the above methods and also combinations of them. Thus, a definition might be given along with some synonyms and a classification example.

Johnson and Stratton (1966) compared the four methods' effectiveness. Groups of subjects were given the meanings of words such as 'altercation', 'chide', 'alacrity' and 'opulent' by one of the four methods. Thus, one group learned from only a definition of each (e.g. 'An altercation is a social interaction characterised by heated exchange of opposing arguments'). A 'sentences' group read a short story in which each of the four words learned appeared twice. A 'classification' group read short descriptions of objects and events that were exemplars of each. A 'synonyms' group' was given several synonyms for each word. Finally, a fifth group acquired the concepts from all four methods. Each method alone was about as good as any other, but the 'multiple methods' group did better. The practical implication is to do as many teachers actually do – use a variety of verbal methods to teach any one word meaning.

## INDIVIDUAL DIFFERENCES

People differ in many ways, from physical traits such as height, weight, build and general health, to psychological characteristics. The latter can be divided into affective characteristics (motivation, attitudes, self-confidence), personality characteristics (extroversion, activeness, anxiety) and cognitive characteristics (e.g. intelligence). Indeed, the characteristics of students of similar ages and social classes in a single classroom can be enormously different (Wang and Lindvall, 1984).

Such individual differences may affect concept learning. Some variables have been mentioned already – age, intelligence, expertise and cultural background. These may affect what concepts are actually learned, how categories are represented, and where the borders of categories are set. For example, not everyone has the ability to acquire very complex concepts, such as *quark*. Acquiring a sound concept of *relativity* requires much ability as well as vast background knowledge. Motivation can affect the persistence of the student and the time spent in trying to learn a given concept. When possible, it is important to adapt instruction to such individual differences.

This section examines one cognitive factor that appears to affect concept learning – cognitive style. Differences in prior knowledge and developmental level are dealt with in more detail in later chapters.

**Cognitive style**

A cognitive style is a general way in which a person structures and uses information. Each person prefers certain ways of organising data. A cognitive style is not an ability. The latter is a capacity, or a power to do some task at maximum effort (Messick, 1976). A style is a preferred way in which a person does a task, not his power to actually do it. Research on these styles has suggested that they affect many areas of life. For instance, people tend to choose occupations and courses of study that are consistent with their styles (Messick, 1976).

The following are some cognitive styles that seem to affect concept learning. The discussion is largely adapted from Messick (1976).

*Field-dependence and independence*
During the Second World War, a researcher was intrigued by an odd phenomenon. Some aviators would fly into a cloud and come out upside down without realising it until they actually emerged. Others consistently came out just as they went in . . . bolt upright. The reason seems to be that they differed in the extent to which they were affected by context. Field-dependent (FD) persons are much affected by context – by the field that a stimulus appears in. They have great trouble separating a geometric figure from the complex background that it is embedded in, and in determining if they are upright when seated in a tiltable chair. Field-independent (FI) persons are much better at separating a stimulus from its context. They are more likely to use their own frames of reference. They impose their own structure on material to be learned rather than accepting someone else's.

A few studies suggest that this cognitive style may affect concept learning. Nebelkopf and Dreyer (1973) compared FI and FD subjects in a simple concept-attainment task. The FIs tended to show a sudden change in performance, suggesting that they were using a hypothesis-testing strategy. The FDs typically showed steady changes. The implication is that FIs were more active in this paradigm. Two studies suggest that FIs are better at acquiring conceptual structures, because they try to actively impose an organisation on material. Stasz (1974) asked students to rate the similarity of pairs of ten anthropology concepts, and he then applied a multi-dimensional scaling analysis to the data. The FDs tended to make fewer distinctions between concepts, grouping them rather loosely, while the FIs had tighter concept clusters. Stasz *et al* (1976) looked at changes in the organisation of concepts following instruction in social science. The concepts included *culture, civilisation*, and *cultural evolution*. The conceptual structures of FIs became closer, with instruction, to those of the experts, than did those of FDs. Also, the FDs showed less differentiation – they had more concepts in each cluster and some concepts in more than one cluster.

*Breadth of categorisation*
Persons with a wide breadth of categorisation tend to consistently over-generalise, preferring to form broad categories. Thus, they are prone to errors of over-inclusion. Persons with a narrow breadth are prone to errors of under-inclusion. In practice, therefore, those with a wide breadth may need more discrimination training with non-exemplars when learning a certain concept, and those with a narrow breadth may need training with a wider range of exemplars.

*Conceptual differentiation*
This style is readily observed in free-sort tasks. People high on it tend to use many different bases for categorisation and those low on it many fewer. In essence, they differ in what they will accept as similar (Gardner, 1953). People high on it 'honeycomb stimuli into small compartments' (Gardner, 1953), while those low on it accept many disparate stimuli as the same. Thus, a wide variety of different stimuli would be accepted as exemplars of a certain concept.

*Scanning*
This style refers to the way humans focus attention on stimuli. People high on it have a sharp focus of attention. They are able to easily focus on stimuli and resist distractions. Thus, they are thought to have a wider span of awareness, more vivid experience of stimuli, and to be more concerned with detail.

*Representation format preferences*
Chapter 6 distinguished between analog and analytic modes of representation. One can add *enactive* to these (see Chapter 8), which pertains to representation of procedural knowledge (Bruner, 1966). Though it seems certain that adults use all three formats, a person may have a marked preference for one or another. Thus, a person might prefer to represent categories in analog format. It has been suggested that instruction should be adapted to a learner's preferred format of representation.

*Reflection/impulsiveness*
This style refers to the speed of formulating hypotheses and processing information. Impulsive persons do so quickly without much thought, offering the first hypothesis that comes to mind in a concept identification paradigm. Reflective persons take more time, and may consider a variety of hypotheses before responding.

## WHY DO WE ACQUIRE THE CONCEPTS WE DO?

As mentioned in Chapter 1, the world can be divided up into an infinite number of categories based on an infinite number of features. While wide individual and cultural differences do exist in the categorisation of some areas, in others there is much cross-cultural consistency. The example given in Chapter 1 was the biological world. Why do we acquire some concepts and not others? Why form such concepts as *fish, tree, wine, person* and *furniture* but not usually ones such as *animals that resemble flies at a distance, lake that looks like a tiger, animals that tremble as if they were mad* and *blue flower or joke* (a disjunctive concept). Why do the last four seem silly and the others sensible? The question is worth asking, because it may give some clue as to why some concepts are particularly hard to learn and how they may be made easier. The practical question 'How should we classify?' is also asked in many situations and some light can be shed on this.

Some reasons why we acquire the concepts we do seem quite clear. Firstly, as mentioned earlier, some stimuli are so obvious and different from everything else that people in every culture are likely to form a concept around them. (Much of the information contained in the concept may differ however, as we saw with *star*.) Indeed, as stated in Chapter 4, people are likely to form basic-level concepts because these take advantage of obvious correlations between features in the environment. Instances of different basic-level categories are thus quite obviously different from each other. A second factor is repetition. If the same stimulus, or set of stimuli, is repeatedly encountered, we may be induced to form a concept. A third factor, which constitutes a general principle, is *use*. We are likely to acquire concepts that are most useful to us, because they allow us to make inferences and solve problems and thus promote survival (Schwartz, 1984). We acquire concepts such as *food* and *poison*, *predator* and *non-*

*predator*, and *person* and *animal* because they are much more useful than *blue flower or joke*. Indeed, this factor is why different cultures form different concepts in some domains. The Eskimos have several categories of snow as these are useful in their environment, while several categories of camel are not. The reverse is true for the Arabs. Neither culture until recently needed concepts such as *debenture* and *stock portfolio* while the American investor does.

The principle of use also partly determines why some conceptual structures are acquired and kept instead of others. A library organises its volumes by topic, because that arrangement is more useful than one by publisher or colour. Western doctors maintain the system of disease concepts partly because they see it as more useful in dealing with ill health than faith healing, naturopathy, or traditional Chinese medicine. Similarly, patients for whom the Western system has failed are more likely to try treatments based on other conceptual structures.

However, use is only part of the answer. Here are some further possible reasons why we acquire the concepts we do.

### Evolutionary factors

Much research has suggested the existence of evolutionary constraints on what we can learn. Here are some examples from associative learning. An association is a link between two stimuli, or between a stimulus and a response. Certain species seem to be strongly predisposed toward forming some associations and not others (Seligman, 1970; Schwartz, 1984). For example, it is easy to teach a pigeon to peck a disc for grain because pecking is its normal response to food and the link is 'natural'. However, it is much harder to train one to peck a disc to avoid an electric shock. It is easy to train it to wingflap to avoid shock (wingflapping is a usual response to danger). Indeed, many human fears seem to reflect biological predispositions to form certain associations. Surveys often find that very common fears include being alone, speaking to a group, and darkness. Nowadays, these are much less dangerous than in our evolutionary past. In prehistoric times, maintaining solidarity with one's group was a matter of life and death, and a member of a tribe could not afford to make mistakes in front of that group. As we relied so much on vision, we were severely handicapped at night as well. Nowadays the above are not so lethal but the fears still are common. Yet few people report debilitating phobias of dangerous objects like cigarettes. We lack evolutionary predispositions to associate such stimuli with fear.

Such biological factors appear to predispose us into acquiring some concepts and not others. At a broad level, our senses limit what concepts we can learn. Our vision is so good that different concepts of mammals (*whale, lion, mouse*) are quite obvious. As mentioned in Chapter 2, to the tick they are all the same. The dog has a far better sense of smell than we do, and no doubt has olfactory concepts that we cannot form. Some concepts, such as *red*, also seem to be innate.

It has been argued that evolution affects the hypotheses we are likely to test about certain word meanings. There is a good, logical argument for evolutionary influences, which is as follows. The philosopher Quine (1960) poses the problem of trying to learn a foreign language by interrogating a speaker of it. (Judging from numerous fantasy and science-fiction novels, this task just takes a few weeks, even with an alien species. But, would it be so easy?) Say you point to a rabbit and he says, 'gavagai'. You hypothesise that 'gavagai' means 'rabbit' and test the hypothesis by pointing to other rabbits and non-rabbits. He duly says 'gavagai' when each rabbit is pointed to, but says something else when non-rabbits are indicated. While the hypothesis that 'gavagai' means 'rabbit' seems quite plausible, in fact the term could still label an infinite number of other concepts. It could refer to the disjunctive concept *rabbit or light bulb, undetached rabbit part, a species of rabbit found only in that glen*, or *rabbit part seen by an elder in the presence of a non-speaker of our language*. We could easily spend a lifetime formulating and testing out such hypotheses. So, some unfortunate child trying to learn what various words in his native language mean would never learn at all unless there were constraints on the hypotheses he would be likely to test. His set of hypotheses is thus likely to be severely constrained by evolutionary factors in order that he will rapidly converge on the right meaning (Carey, 1983).

The extreme form of the argument for evolutionary effects was put forward by Plato, who maintained that concepts are innate and experience simply unleashes them. Preece (1984) recently also argued that many concepts are innate and this is why some scientific and mathematical concepts (such as some in set theory) are so hard to learn for many students. Concepts that do not seem to have natural bases are ones that students have to work much harder to learn (Palermo, 1983).

In essence, the principle of use is operating here on an evolutionary scale. Organisms with such constraints had a selective advantage over those that did not. Being able to rapidly form concepts that mesh well with the environment promotes survival (Schwartz, 1984).

### Increases in knowledge

Increases in knowledge of some domain may induce a person to acquire new concepts and base existing ones on different features. We saw in Chapter 1 that experts may have somewhat different category systems than novices because they know more underlying principles. Quine (1977) notes that perceived similarity, the basis for categorisation, changes with increasing knowledge. A child may regard a whale and a dolphin as more similar to fish than to cattle. However, with greater knowledge that child may see the two as more similar to cattle, in that they are all mammals. Similarly, only an expert might place kangaroos, opossums and marsupial mice into the category *marsupial*, because much knowledge is needed to see their similarities. Psychiatry is continually revising its category system as knowledge increases through research and clinical experience. Categories are added, deleted and broken up. A recent, deleted concept is *psychosomatic illness*, a category for physical illnesses caused by mental factors. The concept was deleted because research has shown that the mind affects all physical illnesses in some way.

Another example is a tribe in the Sudan that does not distinguish between misfortunes due to accidents (falls, lightning strikes and floods) and misfortunes due to illness. Thus, a trip on a rock which breaks a leg, lack of rain for crops, and a case of measles are all lumped into one basic-level category. The reason seems to be the tribe's lack of knowledge of the causes of such mishaps. They see any accident as due to just one cause – malevolence from witches. Only increasing knowledge about viruses, bacteria, meteorology, and the lack of effect of witchcraft might induce them to break this category into several.

## Cultural factors

In some stimulus domains, different cultures have quite different category systems. The Western and Chinese systems of medicine are quite different, for example. Different cultures select certain bases for categorisation as the most important through differing values and purposes (Carroll, 1964). These values affect which concepts are formed. For instance, the American Psychiatric Association used to categorise *homosexuality* as a mental disease but no longer does so, partly because much of American society now sees it as an alternative lifestyle. The Catholic Church refused to accept Copernicus's schema of the solar system because of the perceived conflict with religious beliefs. In England and Japan, people are divided into social classes largely on the basis of family ties. In Communist nations, party membership is more important and in the United States and Australia personal wealth is a greater factor in determining social status.

A good example of the importance of cultural factors in categorisation is electoral division. A political unit has to group electors (instances) into electorates of some kind, which then produce a representative. There are many ways of so dividing up electors and which method is used largely depends on cultural values. Some bases are common to many but not all cultures. These include proximity (grouping people near each other into single electorates), giving each voter a roughly equal voice, and trying to keep various electorates reasonably homogenous in ethnicity and social class. Most nations also only allow citizens to vote, but some Commonwealth nations allow citizens of other Commonwealth nations to vote.

There are wide differences, however, which largely reflect cultural values. Race is not a basis for categorisation in most nations, but is so in a few countries. New Zealand sets aside four electorates for the indigenous Maori population, who can vote in one of these or in a regular electorate. South Africa has separate parliaments based on race. Some units give priority to an urban/rural factor. Two Australian states give rural voters much more weight than their urban cousins, some 'outback' districts having less than 10% of the number of voters in city districts. Some states give priority to the equal voice principle, ensuring that every vote counts. Electors vote for a party slate, and each party gets representatives according to its share of the vote. Some nations ban political parties altogether, and some nations, such as the Soviet Union, only allow people to vote for one party.

## FURTHER READING

Concept learning in general: Klausmeier *et al* (1974), Homa (1984).
Language and concept learning: Klausmeier *et al* (1974), Stones (1984).
Vocabulary instruction methods: Johnson and Pearson (1978).
Cognitive style and categorisation: Messick (1976).
Why we acquire the concepts we do: Quine (1977), Rosch (1978).

# Chapter 8

# Concept and Schema Development

SUMMARY

1.  Concepts may develop in several ways. The format of representation may change. An exemplar or prototype may shift to a set of defining features. The bases of categorisation may alter.
2.  A conceptual structure may evolve slowly as new concepts are added, old concepts are deleted, and the pattern of relations between component concepts alters.
3.  Conceptual structures also may alter radically in a short time. Such a radical change is called 'accommodation'.
4.  Children begin to acquire concepts in the first few months of life. Partonomic structures are easier to learn and appear to develop earlier than taxonomic structures.
5.  The onset of language greatly affects conceptual development. Concepts can be learned from words and words can be attached to existing concepts.
6.  Piaget proposed that a child goes through four major invariant stages of cognitive development in which concepts are represented in different formats, and different processes are available to operate on the representations. Bruner proposed that, instead of going through stages, a child's dominant format of representation alters with age. Recent research in the information-processing tradition suggests that the critical factor in development is amount of knowledge and strategies (such as rehearsal, which is a process of repetition) a child has in order to acquire new knowledge. Age differences in performance are analogous to novice/expert differences.

## INTRODUCTION

The notion of *development* is basic to many domains. Courses develop, personalities develop, a nation's economy develops, products develop, and the work of writers and artists develops. The term usually implies a progressive change from a simpler, less adequate level to a more complex, more adequate one.

Concepts and schemata also may develop. They may progressively evolve with experience and thus a person's ability to understand and deal with some domain may improve as well. Chapter 1 gave the example of a doctor's disease concepts (such as *measles* and *mumps*) evolving as he encounters more cases. He learns about the variations in symptoms and their severity, certain factors that aggravate a disorder, and about new treatments. Klausmeier *et al* (1974) give the example of *cutting tool*. A child's initial concept may derive from a few exemplars such as a knife and pair of scissors. Upon encountering instances such as hack-saw, chain-saw, chisel and scythe, the concept may alter to include more variable and characteristic features. In some cases a concept may narrow with experience. A child may initially class all motorised vehicles as instances of *car*, but with experience prune the concept until it becomes more like an adult's. A concept also may radically change with experience. In the Nussbaum (1979) study, children's concept of the Earth as a cosmic body altered radically with age, just as an astronomer's concept of *the universe* is likely to greatly differ from the concept he held before studying the discipline.

The situation is much like our expansion of knowledge about a friend as it develops from casual acquaintanceship to deep friendship. Sometimes our concept of the friend changes progressively as we learn more of his sides, motives, likes and dislikes, and ways of responding to various situations. Sometimes our concept can alter quite radically after a few critical incidents – it undergoes a 'revolution', which is one reason why so many love affairs cool off quickly.

Such conceptual development is very important in education for a number of reasons. Firstly, a teacher needs to know that development of a given concept may be a long, slow process, taking much time and effort. Indeed, teachers are often unaware that students' concepts have a long way to develop and that the students' meanings for words are often quite different from the teacher's (Stones, 1984; Bell and Freyberg, 1985). Thus, when a teacher discusses 'life', 'animals', and 'gravity' he may mean one thing and the students take the terms to mean another. As a result, much verbal instruction may simply be incomprehensible. Secondly, much teaching involves encouraging students' existing concepts to further develop – to become more like those of the expert. Thus, physics instruction may aim to develop students' concepts of *electricity, gravity* and *motion*, astronomy instruction, *star* and *the universe*, literature, *satire* and *the novel*, and music, *symphony*. A student may have an initial concept of *metal, base* or *gravity* that needs to be developed, say by replacing a prototype with a set of defining features. Thirdly, a given discipline's concepts are usually continually changing, as concepts grow richer through more research and theorising by scientists. Some concepts are deleted, others added, and their relations re-ordered. Ensuring that students' concepts are open to such development better prepares them for a changing discipline. Finally, which concepts are taught and the order in which they are introduced needs to be tailored to students' level of cognitive development.

The notion of concept development has been mentioned in a number of places in this book already. Chapter 1 posed the basic questions of how concepts develop and what course conceptual development takes. How is a child able to acquire the complex cognitive structure of the typical adult and at what ages are important concepts learned? Chapter 2 gave examples of a word remaining the same while the concept it referred to developed. Chapter 4 mentioned that basic-level concepts are often the first ones learned and that superordinate and subordinate ones may be learned later from them. Chapter 6 described how children and adults may represent a given category in different ways, and that a representation may evolve from exemplars or a prototype to a set of defining features.

The following more detailed discussion of concept development is divided into two closely related parts, mainly for the sake of clear exposition. The first section examines concept development in general, looking at factors apparently common to both children and adults. The second section looks at development specifically in children, partly making use of material in the first section. The final part of this chapter briefly describes Piaget's influential theory of cognitive development, which has much to say about concept development. Some alternatives to Piaget's view are also mentioned.

It should be noted that not a great deal is known about concept development. There is no clear-cut description that gives the ages at which children are likely to learn particular concepts and conceptual structures. Indeed, Clark (1983) says that few researchers seem willing to undertake such a difficult descriptive task. Not a great deal is known about the causes of conceptual development either. There are numerous theories, but it is beyond our present purposes or wishes to cover them all here (see Sigel, 1983, for a review).

## CONCEPT DEVELOPMENT IN GENERAL

### Development of a single concept

A variety of processes may be involved in development of one concept (Homa *et al*, 1979). Discrimination and generalisation are clearly two. A concept may become narrower as non-instances are encountered or broader and more detailed as more exemplars are encountered and a person generalises to them, as in the *cutting tool* example above. Some conditions that may induce a concept to evolve are outlined below.

*The concept becoming part of a conceptual framework*
A concept may develop further when it becomes part of a wider system (Vygotsky, 1962). Thus, a child who learns the mathematical concept of *base* may find that his concept of the *decimal system* has altered. He can see it as just one type rather than the only one. Similarly, a child who acquires the concept of *economic system* and learns about command and mixed economies may find that his concept of the *capitalist system* has changed. He can see it as just one type with certain advantages and disadvantages. A person's concepts of *mammal* and *bird* change upon learning that they are co-ordinates of *reptile* and that both evolved from reptiles.

*Development of a prototype*
Further experience with new exemplars may alter a prototype. Greenberg and Kuczaj (1982) cite some such conditions. Firstly, as mentioned in Chapters 6 and 7, a prototype forms around the central tendency of a set of instances. If a child's initial experience is of atypical instances, then encountering more typical ones may shift the central tendency. For example, say a child's sole experience of dogs is of some beagles and bassets; the prototype could be a short dog with long ears and short hair. Upon encountering larger and hairier dogs, such as Afghans and Great Danes, his prototypical dog could evolve into a larger and hairier one. Similarly, if a child had only ever encountered such exemplars of *fruit* as raspberries, gooseberries and strawberries, his prototype may change upon encountering apples, oranges and bananas.

## Extension of boundaries

Concept boundaries may be extended (Mervis, 1980). Anglin (1977) suggests that children often exclude more peripheral exemplars of certain categories, and development is partly a matter of learning to include them. Thus, children may not include insects and amoebas as exemplars of *animal*, because they seem too different from the prototype. Similarly, they may exclude dates and prunes as exemplars of *fruit*, and seeds and trees as exemplars of *life form* (Bell and Freyberg, 1985). Even many adults exclude more peripheral exemplars of some concepts. Many laypersons who read certain newspapers seem to represent the category of drug with a prototypical drug based on such exemplars as heroin and cocaine. They often seem to exclude legal drugs, such as alcohol and caffeine.

## Changes in bases for categorisation

The features used as bases for people's concepts may change with experience. As we saw in Chapters 1 and 7, experts may use more abstract bases for categorisation. Piaget (1929) found that a young child saw *life* as a concept based on a few features, one being 'moving', and thus it might categorise fire and clouds as alive. With time, children use more abstract bases in addition to 'moving'. Kempa and Hodgson (1976) found a change in the features used to categorise substances as exemplars of *acid* as pupils acquired more knowledge. Younger students' concepts were based on concrete features such as 'sourness' and 'ability to induce a colour change in litmus paper'. With further education, the basis may shift to the very abstract defining feature of 'replaceability of hydrogen by metals'. Indeed, much of the process of becoming an expert involves learning the abstract features of important concepts. Such a task can be quite difficult, because much background knowledge is needed to understand them. In the *acid* example, a student must understand basic atomic theory to comprehend the feature.

## Changes in representation format and content

The format of a representation may alter, as we see in more detail later in this chapter. A person may initially represent a category with, say, an image, and later shift to an analytic representation.

Another shift is from exemplars to a prototype representation. Thus, a person might initially have a representation of *dog*, based on a few known exemplars, and later shift to a prototype upon encountering more instances. Homa *et al* (1981) found that university students used exemplar representations in the early phases of the study, but with further experience developed a prototype.

An important shift is from a prototype (based on characteristic features) to a set of defining features. Here are some examples. Skemp (1979) gives the example of *daddy*. A child's initial concept might be based on a few characteristic features, such as 'a man who lives in the same house as several children and who acts in certain ways toward them'. With time there may be a shift to defining features as the child discriminates between a biological father and a stepfather and learns that the biological father lives in a different house. Finally, the child may acquire the complex relational defining feature. Vygotsky (1962) gives the example of *aunt*. A child's initial concept may be based on the features 'female' and 'a certain age and disposition'. With experience, the relational defining feature is mastered. As mentioned earlier, such a shift may take much time and can be difficult for younger children, who are not very adept at abstracting defining features or testing hypotheses (Farah and Kosslyn, 1982).

Keil and Batterman (1984) provided some empirical evidence for such a shift. They gave children (aged between 4 and 10 years) brief stories that presented exemplars of concepts such as *lie, island, uncle* and *news*. There were two stories for each concept. One emphasised characteristic features and the other defining ones. Subjects were asked if the stories described valid instances of a concept and were sometimes requested to explain their judgments. Results suggested a shift from reliance on characteristic features to defining ones as the age level increased. Here are some examples. Note the use of characteristic features in the first two (with younger children) and the use of defining features in the second two (with older children).

> *Uncle*
>     Experimenter:  'Could that be an uncle?'
>     Subject:  'No . . . because he is little and two years old.'
> *Museum*
>     Experimenter:  'Could that be a museum?'
>     Subject:  'No, a museum is something with dinosaur bones.'
> *Uncle*
>     Experimenter:  'Is he an uncle?'
>     Subject:  'Yes, because he's still my mother's brother.'
>     Experimenter:  'Can an uncle be any age?'
>     Subject:  'Yes.'
> *Island*
>     Experimenter:  'Could that be an island?'
>     Subject:  'Yes . . . because it's surrounded by water. An island's just a piece of land surrounded by water.
>
>                                                        Keil and Batterman (1984)

Inducing such a shift to defining features is the goal of much concept teaching in schools. A teacher often aims to replace a prototype or exemplar representation with a classical-view representation. Thus, the medical student learns defining feature sets for concepts such as *measles* (the presence of a virus). A child may learn defining features, when they exist, of *animal, life, gravity* and *electricity* and other important concepts.

## Development of a conceptual structure

A conceptual structure such as a taxonomy also may develop. This evolution can occur in a number of ways. Concepts can be added or deleted, existing ones combined or broken up, attributes added to concepts, and new relations between them established. The overall pattern of relations in the structure can alter radically as the learner acquires knowledge of principles behind the structure and learns very abstract relations. Such evolution is very important in education. Students are continually organising and re-organising conceptual structures.

An analogy is to a person's growth in knowledge of a group of new schoolfriends or workmates. First of all, he discriminates between different individuals, learns their names and some relations between them. Thus, he may find out that A is B's sister, C is married to Q, and B,C,D and F play poker together. He adds knowledge of more people and relations between them and, with time, starts to learn higher-order relations, which are analogous to schemata. He may learn that certain groups and factions exist and relate in certain ways to other groups. Finally, the picture built up over a period of time can change dramatically. If, for example, a person discovered that a company for which he worked was really a front for a foreign spy ring that half the employees were involved in, his conceptualisation of the people and the structure of social relations would change drastically, just as the Russian revolution of 1917 resulted in a dramatic change in the pattern of social relations in that nation. The two types of change are described in more detail below.

*Slow progressive evolution*
Much education involves teaching a set of related concepts, knowledge of which slowly increases with further instruction. Figure 27 shows some schematic examples of the evolution of conceptual structures. A and B give slow, steady changes, while C shows a radical change. In B, the Venn diagrams represent the overlap in attributes between concepts. As a person's experience grows, the attributes tend to overlap less until the concepts are entirely distinct.

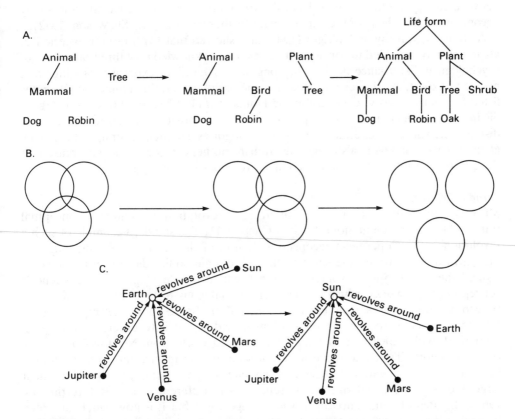

**Figure 27.** Some schematic examples of evolution of conceptual structures. A and B give slow, steady changes while C shows a radical change. In B, the Venn diagrams represent the overlap in attributes between concepts.

A familiar example is the psychiatric taxonomy, which, as mentioned earlier, is revised every few years. As described in Chapter 7, with research, concepts such as *homosexuality* and *psychosomatic illness* have been deleted and some new ones have been added. Research and clinical experience also add new knowledge to existing concepts, such as of new treatments.

Homa *et al* (1981) looked at the development of a set of dot pattern concepts. Each category had a prototype and six instances, which were deviations from it. Subjects learned to categorise the exemplars and at various stages in training rated the similarity of pairs of the instances. A multi-dimensional scaling analysis revealed that the structure of concepts grew tighter (more clearly defined) with experience. Category members were rated as more similar to each other and more different from exemplars in other categories as training progressed.

Champagne *et al* (1981) looked at the development of a geology taxonomy fragment in eighth graders [aged 12 years] with instruction. The students sorted names of geology concepts before and after geology teaching. Figure 28 presents pre and post-training structures for one student. Several changes are shown as this structure evolves; more concepts and relations have been listed after instruction. The student knew more attributes of *igneous*, *metamorphic* and *sedimentary* rocks and made more connections between concepts. Other studies have shown that novices' conceptual structures may become more like those of the experts' with further training (e.g. Shavelson, 1972).

A study by Murphy and Wright (1984) also showed that, with further experience, attributes may be added to concepts. They examined knowledge of three categories of psychological disturbance held by persons of four levels of expertise, ranging from novice to expert. As the level of expertise increased, so did the number of attributes listed for each category. Contrary to the Homa *et al* (1981) study, however, category distinctiveness decreased with expertise. While the novices' categories were quite distinct, showing little overlap, the experts' categories had much overlap. Thus, many attributes of one category also might be listed in another category. The likely reason for the different results is the inherent complexity of person concepts.

*A radical change*
Much classroom instruction aims at inducing a 'revolution' in children's conceptual frameworks, as we see in more detail in Chapter 11. The standard example of such a revolution is the Copernican reconceptualisation of the solar system, showing that the Earth moved around the sun and thus all cosmic bodies did not in fact revolve around the Earth. Such revolutions often occur in the development of a science's conceptual frameworks, which can be seen as analogous to revolutions in children's conceptual frameworks (see Posner *et al*, 1982). Some recent examples are as follows. Einstein's theory of relativity proposed a radically different conceptual framework with which to understand the physical world from Newton's previously accepted theory. Time and space were not separate but inextricably linked, and the belief was that gravitational attraction was due to space being greatly curved near large bodies. Time could run at different rates in different places. Before the late 1960s, the idea of continental drift was a fringe view, but it is now widely accepted by geologists. This theory of plate tectonics gives a radically different schema of the Earth than those theories previously held. According to this theory continents are on moving plates rather than being fixed. Psychology has recently undergone a revolution from behaviourism to cognitivism. In daily life, people may undergo revolutions in their conceptual frameworks after political or religious conversions and successful psychotherapy (see Chapter 1).

Pre-instruction structure

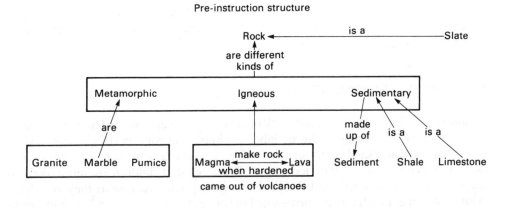

Post-instruction structure

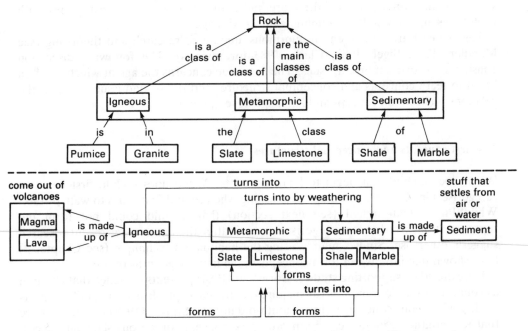

**Figure 28.** An example of evolution of a conceptual structure after instruction. The data are from one student. Note that more concepts and relations have been listed after instruction. From Champagne, A. B. *et al.* Structural representations of students' knowledge before and after science instruction. *Journal of Research in Science Teaching* **18**. Copyright © 1981 John Wiley & Sons, Inc. Reproduced with permission.

Piaget called a major alteration of an existing schema 'accommodation'. A schema changes because it cannot handle certain data. It meets with *anomalies* – facts it cannot account for – and so alters in order that the facts can be handled. Thus, the schema of the Earth as the centre of the universe could not handle various astronomical observations and was eventually replaced by a schema that could handle them. Alternative theories to plate tectonics could not readily explain various geological observations or the distribution of fossils and living species over the continents.

Therefore, they were replaced by a schema that could do so. Accommodation is difficult to achieve and may take much time, however. People generally prefer not to change their schemata (Anderson, 1977).

## CONCEPT DEVELOPMENT IN CHILDREN

A child has the basic developmental task of acquiring concepts needed to make sense of the world and of learning its culture's labels for important concepts (Sigel, 1983). How is this task accomplished? Furthermore, which general developmental trends occur? Some trends have been mentioned earlier. We noted that children are more likely to learn concepts from words and their existing conceptual structure as they get older. Also, children get better at acquiring word meanings from contexts and their power to test hypotheses improves (Spiker and Cantor, 1979). Ausubel (1968) cites the general trend of progression from more diffuse, ill-defined concepts to more specific ones. It was also mentioned that children are more likely to represent categories with prototypes and may shift to defining features with age.

This general area has seen an enormous amount of research and theorising (see Mandler, 1983; Sigel, 1983; Clark, 1983 for reviews). The following discussion considers just two important issues. The first issue concerns the age at which children begin to learn concepts and conceptual structures and the second issue concerns the relationship between concept and language development.

### The first concepts and conceptual structures

When does a child first begin to learn concepts? When does a child first begin to categorise stimuli? This is analogous to asking when a child first starts to walk or talk. While Piaget had argued (see next section) that a child could not form the representations needed for categorisation until after the age of one, recent research suggests otherwise. Studies mainly using the habituation technique (see Chapter 2) have shown that infants can form concepts in the first few months of life.

Here are some supporting studies. Bornstein (1984) presents evidence that children as young as two to four months can acquire identity concepts. Bornstein (1979) reports evidence of colour concepts in four-month-old infants. Strauss (1979) found evidence that ten-month-old infants can form prototype concepts of various schematic faces. Bomba and Siqueland (1983) found evidence of prototypes of dot pattern categories in even younger children – just three to four months old. Cohen and Strauss (1979) found that 30-week-old infants could learn the concept *female face in general* and could learn to respond to a particular female face. Golinkoff and Halperin (1983) found evidence that a child of eight months could form the concept of *animal*.

It is less clear when children first develop knowledge of partonomies and taxonomies. Partonomic structure is easier to learn and seems to develop earlier than taxonomic structure (Markman, 1984). Children often have trouble with the class-inclusion relation of taxonomies, because it requires knowing, for example, that a particular beast can be a dog, a mammal and an animal, but that not all animals and mammals are dogs. Estimates of when a child starts to acquire knowledge of class inclusion vary.

Markman (1984) argues that children have a fragmentary understanding of class inclusion at four or five years old; other estimates range to seven or eight years old (Mandler, 1983; Markman, 1984). The higher estimate may be due to procedures used in earlier studies, which relied heavily on language. Children often know much more than they can readily express, and studies using recognition and priming procedures show that they know more about class inclusion than they can say (Mandler, 1983).

## Language and concept development

The course of language development is quite well mapped. The first word generally appears at about the age of one year. The early words typically refer to objects with which the child frequently interacts (Anglin, 1977). These include proper names, such as 'Mama' and 'Dada', words that refer to interactions with adults, such as 'Hello', words related to basic needs, such as for food and clothing, names for interesting objects, such as animals and people, and simple verbs, such as 'give'. By the age of 18 months, the child knows an average of 50 words. Two-word utterances (e.g. 'no eat') typically appear at about the age of two, and the child's vocabulary grows immensely from there. By the age of four or five, the child is speaking in grammatical sentences and by the age of six knows an estimated 14 000 words (Clark, 1983). Many of these word meanings are learned from elaborate pointing and naming by the child's parents.

A major issue is the relation between language development and concept development. The issue can be framed as two opposing questions. Does the child learn concepts first and then later learn to attach words to them or, are concepts formed when a child tries to attach meanings to newly-encountered words (Kuczaj, 1982). Put another way, is the concept system built from words or is the word system built from concepts?

It seems likely that the answer lies somewhere in the middle. Concepts can be acquired from words and words may be attached to existing concepts (Kuczaj, 1982). Indeed, this possibility has been mentioned before. Chapter 2 described how repeatedly hearing the same word in several contexts may induce a child to try to see what the situations have in common and thus form a concept. Similarly, as we have just seen, children know some concepts before their first words are uttered, and development must partly involve mapping these concepts onto words. Such mapping may occur by hypothesis-testing. Indeed, Chapter 7 described how children may over-generalise the meanings of early words and then progressively refine them until they approximate the adult meaning. Thus, the word 'daddy' might initially refer to all men and gradually through discrimination training come to refer to the usual adult concept. One of Bowerman's children initially used the word 'moon' to refer to many objects. Children also may under-generalise word meanings and extend their range of applicability later (Anglin, 1977). Thus, a child may initially take 'car' to refer to only moving cars, or 'kitty' just to the family cat.

The onset of language introduces a major change in concept development (Ausubel, 1968; Sigel, 1983). The child has more ways of acquiring concepts. Markman (1984) suggests some further ways in which a child's knowledge of language can help it learn new concepts. She argues that children generally know that words refer to categories of stimuli and, so, when they hear a new word they look for a category. This phenomenon is readily demonstrated as follows. If we give young children a set of stimuli and ask them to put together those that 'seem the same', they tend to sort by *theme*. For example, if given a web, a spider and beetle, they will put together the web and the spider because the two interact (Tversky, 1985). If given two different dogs and some dog food, they will typically put together one dog and the food. However, if they are told that one dog is a 'dax' and they are then asked to find another dax, they are likely to select the other dog (Markman, 1984), which suggests that they know a word refers to a class. Markman further argues that knowledge of language also helps children acquire taxonomical relations as well. Understanding class inclusion is difficult, because it requires knowledge of transitivity and asymmetry of class relations, as mentioned earlier. Markman suggests that children eventually learn class inclusions through the simpler part/whole relation given by certain kinds of mass nouns (see Markman, 1984, for further details).

*Clark's semantic feature hypothesis*
Clark (1973) proposed that concepts can be learned from new words in a certain way. Her semantic feature hypothesis has provoked much research and criticism. While there is much evidence against it, it may apply to the learning of word meanings in some domains. She argued that word meanings (concepts) consist of features, each feature being one unit of meaning, as put forth by the classical view. When a child learns a word, it learns the set of features associated with it. Initially it may learn only one or two features (e.g. for 'dog' just 'alive' and 'barks') and others are added later. The first features acquired are perceptual ones, such as colour, shape, movement and size. Children also are supposed to learn the most abstract concept on a taxonomy first and then those concepts subsumed in it.

The hypothesis has problems when applied to the learning of all word meanings (Blewitt, 1982; Clark, 1983). A major problem is that it is based on the classical view, and the meanings of many words cannot be readily reduced to sets of defining features. In addition, children often learn basic-level concepts first, rather than more abstract ones as her theory holds. However, the hypothesis may apply to the learning of various relational words, such as kinship terms (Blewitt, 1982). Relational terms refer not to objects but to relations between them (e.g. 'up', 'down', 'uncle', 'author'). The simpler and more general kinship terms may be learned first, followed by the more complex ones.

## THEORIES OF COGNITIVE DEVELOPMENT

### Piaget's theory

'Cognitive development' refers to the changes in attention, memory, perception, etc that occur as a child ages. Jean Piaget in a long series of books and articles proposed a large-scale theory of cognitive development. It is a quite bold statement that has been very influential in developmental psychology and education, though parts of it have been much criticised of late (Scholnick, 1983). Much of developmental theorising and research has either examined some of Piaget's hypotheses or tested out others in reaction to them. Some of Piaget's ideas have been mentioned already, notably *accommodation* in this chapter's second section. The theory is complex and space permits just a brief survey of some relevant aspects. Then some more recent conceptualisations of cognitive development are mentioned.

Piaget was interested in cognitive growth, which is the course of a child's mental development from birth to adulthood. His general approach was biological. He stressed an organism's need to adapt to its environment, for which higher organisms need knowledge. We need to represent the external world and operate on our representations to adapt to the environment. Piaget also argued that we have an innate capacity to explore and try to make better sense of the world.

He proposed that a child's representation format and the operations available to work on the representations systematically change as the child gets older. The theory is thus *maturational*. A child is thought to go through an invariant sequence of four major stages. It is actually thinking differently at each stage, using different representation formats and operations. The analogy is often made to a developing embryo, which goes through a sequence of distinct stages rather than a steady progressive course of development. Each stage in Piaget's scheme builds on the accomplishments of previous ones and the child has certain cognitive capacities at given ages which were not present at earlier ones. Piaget also proposed that language development depends on cognitive development. Language becomes possible when certain cognitive capacities have developed.

Two important means by which a child's cognitive structures develop are *assimilation* and *accommodation*. Assimilation is taking in information about the outside world and incorporating it in existing schemata. Input is changed to fit existing cognitive structures. As we saw earlier, accommodation is the changing of existing schemata to fit the external world when such structures cannot handle various anomalies. These two processes operate throughout a person's lifetime.

Here is a description of the four stages. There are also a series of sub-stages within them, but these will not be considered here. The ages given below are only approximate. Some children may go through the stages at earlier or later ages.

### Sensory-motor (0–2 years)

Initially, the child has virtually nothing of the complex cognitive structure of the adult. It has no concepts, no representations, and therefore experiences only unconnected sensory impressions. Before the age of one, the child has no concepts of space, time, causality or object. The concept of *object* only develops slowly. When an object disappears from view, the child sees it as gone forever and cannot think about it. Only slowly does the child even realise that the self is separate from the external world.

The child can form mental representations only at the end of the stage. Earlier, objects can just be represented by the actions that can be performed on them – basic reflex actions like sucking, grasping and kicking. Thus, if an object such as a rattle is taken away, the child may continue to perform his shaking action. A child acquires knowledge about objects through his actions on them. With time, the action schemata become organised into larger units.

### Pre-operational stage (2–7 years)

At this stage a child can readily represent the world, but the child is still bound to perceptual features, taking appearance for reality. It cannot think in very abstract terms. Its thinking is greatly dependent on imagery. The child is also still *egocentric*. It has great trouble seeing things from other perspectives and great difficulty in relating ideas in meaningful ways. An example of limited mental capacity at this stage is the failure to *conserve* matter. Lack of conservation can be demonstrated with two beakers, one being much taller but thinner than the other. If the tall beaker is filled and then its water is poured into the second, the child will invariably say that the second beaker holds less water, thus failing to conserve quantity. Piaget argued that this finding shows that children cannot attend to all relevant dimensions (e.g. height and width here) at the same time.

*Concrete operations (7–11 years)*
By this stage, the child's cognitive capacities have improved a great deal. It can readily represent the world and operate on those representations. Objects are seen as concrete things that can be represented and the representations can be changed in logical ways. The child is no longer dominated by the way things look and can think more abstractly. It is no longer egocentric, and can readily shift from one viewpoint to another. While the pre-operational child thinks concepts such as *taller* refer to some absolute quantity, the child at the concrete operations stage knows that the concept is a relation that can change with context. Finally, the child can learn more abstract concepts at this stage and can do so without experiencing actual exemplars (Ausubel, 1968).

*Formal operations (11+)*
This stage is that of adults. A person can think and reason abstractly and can make inferences from hypothetical situations, being able to promptly set up and test hypotheses. Thinking is much more flexible than at earlier stages.

*Evaluation*
Though the theory has had enormous influence, parts of it have lately been challenged. Recent research has shown that Piaget greatly under-estimated the cognitive abilities of pre-school children (Mandler, 1983). For instance, the habituation studies have demonstrated that infants can form concepts and have some notion of object permanence at an earlier age than Piaget stated. The stages are also hard to demonstrate convincingly (Anderson, 1985), though there does seem to be a major shift in thinking at about the ages of five to seven years (Mandler, 1983). The idea that all adults get to the formal operations stage has also been questioned. Adults in some pre-literate cultures may not do so and the structures and thinking of that stage may be due to Western schooling rather than the unfolding of a genetic programme (Mandler, 1983).

Researchers in the information-processing tradition have argued that the amount of knowledge a child has could be responsible for age-related differences rather than children being at different stages (Anderson, 1985). Older children may perform certain tasks better because they know more, just as experts in a domain such as chess perform better than novices. Older children also have strategies such as rehearsal that improve their performance (Anderson, 1985).

**Bruner's theory**

Jerome Bruner has proposed a revision of Piaget's stage scheme (Bruner, 1966). Rather than there being invariant stages of development, he argued that the dominant format of representation changes with age. He proposed the existence of three types of format, which have been touched on earlier. The first type is *enactive*, which pertains to representation of procedural knowledge. An object is represented by the actions a person performs on it. The second type is *iconic*, in which knowledge is represented by imagery. Thus, a toy or a house can be represented by a mental image of each. Bruner argues that the ability to construct such images develops by the end of the first year, and thereafter a child represents most knowledge in this format. By the age of seven, the child relies much less on imagery and more on *symbolic* representation, which corresponds to the analytic mode (see Chapter 6). Here, a representation bears only an arbitrary relation to the object it represents. Thus, the leap from pre-operational to concrete operational thinking in Piaget's scheme can be seen as a shift from representing objects primarily in iconic format to predominantly using the symbolic format. Bruner also argues that language is very important in the five to seven-year-old shift, since the possession of language gives enormous power to symbolise.

## FURTHER READING

Concept development in general: Mandler (1983), Vygotsky (1962), Klausmeier *et al* (1974).
Theories of cognitive development: Bruner *et al* (1966), Mayer (1983a).

# Chapter 9

# How to Teach Concepts I: The Traditional Procedure

SUMMARY

1.  The concepts taught in school and the way they are learned tend to differ from the situation outside the classroom.
2.  The traditional procedure is a general method of teaching concepts of any discipline. It is based on the classical view.
3.  Instruction should have clear goals. With this procedure some goals when teaching concepts include knowing a concept's defining features, being able to categorise exemplars and non-exemplars, and using the concept to solve problems.
4.  The procedure involves analysis of a concept into defining features, presenting a set of exemplars and non-exemplars while pointing out the presence/absence of defining features in them, and giving practice at categorisation.
5.  The traditional procedure may be appropriate for teaching well-defined concepts to students who are old enough to readily learn and use a set of defining features and who can assimilate the concept easily into their existing conceptual structures.
6.  Concepts can also be taught by a discovery method, which involves teaching from instances rather than from an initial set of defining features.

## INTRODUCTION

This chapter summarises a general procedure for teaching concepts of any discipline. The method is based on many studies done over the years by educational psychologists, notably the following: Markle and Tiemann (1969), Clark (1971), Klausmeier et al (1974), Klausmeier and Sipple (1980), Eggen et al (1979), Merrill and Tennyson (1977), Tennyson and Park (1980) and Sowder (1980). The procedure is based on the classical view. It was described briefly in Chapter 6 and is analysed further as follows. The teacher first determines the defining features of the concept that is to be taught and teaches students this set of features and how to use it to categorise stimuli. The general method will be dubbed 'The traditional procedure' and this chapter presents a slightly updated version of it.

The view taken in this book is that the traditional procedure is one of several methods of teaching concepts and is only appropriate in certain circumstances. Only detailed research can reveal exactly when it is best to use it, but some likely cases are as follows. First of all, it is appropriate when the concept to be taught is well-defined and when the learners are old enough to acquire and use the defining features. Indeed, many school-taught concepts appear to be well-defined and to have reasonably clear-cut borders, often because they are so constructed. Such well-defined concepts predominate in the physical sciences and mathematics and are less common in the biological and social sciences, humanities and law. As a result, many concepts in these fields may need to be taught with a different procedure, as we see in Chapter 10. Secondly, the traditional procedure is appropriate when a new concept can be readily assimilated into a student's existing schemata. When a new concept is greatly discrepant to what a student already knows, instruction aimed at teaching it may simply be incomprehensible or just ignored (Anderson and Smith, 1984). In such a situation, both instructional aims and teaching methods need to be quite different. Chapter 11 describes a method of teaching concepts that can be used in such situations.

Despite some limitations, most aspects of the traditional procedure are useful in teaching all concepts. Such features as 'Decide if a concept lesson is needed' and 'Collect exemplars and non-exemplars' apply to just about any concept teaching situation. Only the method in its entirety may not always be appropriate.

Before describing the method, some preliminary issues need discussion. Then the procedure is covered, followed by a complete sample lesson.

## Some differences between school-taught and everyday life concepts

There appear to be several differences (Carroll, 1964; Skemp, 1971; Clark, 1971). Firstly, school-taught concepts tend to be more abstract and become more abstract as a student progresses in a discipline. Most everyday concepts are quite concrete. They are grounded in perceptual experience, while, as mentioned in Chapter 2, many abstract concepts are built up from complex component concepts. Many school-taught concepts are also based on relational rather than perceptual features (Carroll, 1964). Secondly, school-taught concepts tend to be part of a clear-cut conceptual structure and need to be related to other concepts in the system when being taught (Vygotsky, 1962). Thus, the physics student needs to relate concepts such as *quark, electron* and *electromagnetic radiation* to other important physics concepts. The biology student needs to learn that *species* fits into a taxonomy below *genera* and *family* and above *sub-species*. The psychology student needs to learn that *positive* and *negative reinforcement* relate to *punishment* in that each is a means of altering the rate of some response and also how they relate to other important concepts such as *stimulus control* and *operant* and *classical conditioning*. In contrast, many everyday concepts are not always clearly related to various taxonomies and theories in people's minds.

## Differences between school and everyday life learning situations

They differ in a number of ways (Vygotsky, 1962; Carroll, 1964). Some major ones are as follows.

### The conditions in which a concept is acquired
As mentioned earlier, in the real world we often have to abstract concepts just from exemplars. Sometimes we may just have a single instance to learn from, or a few

contexts in which a new word appears. There also may be long periods between exemplar presentations. Usually many other things are going on at the same time and we cannot devote our full attention to learning a given concept. We do, of course, often get some guidance from parents and peers. In contrast, the classroom situation is set up to make concept learning much easier. The teacher can alert the students to the fact that there is a concept to be learned, he can define it, relate it to other concepts, and slowly present exemplars and non-exemplars while pointing out defining and characteristic features. Learning purely from instances is not that common in the classroom, though it does occur in discovery learning as discussed later (see page 153).

In school, many concepts are also acquired from words. Indeed, as mentioned in Chapter 7, it is very hard to teach concepts such as *infinity, quark,* and *invisible export* (which has exemplars such as insurance, banking and tourism) in any other way (Skemp, 1979). As also mentioned in Chapter 7, purely verbal presentation may mean less depth of understanding (Serra, 1953). A person cannot fully understand *poverty* or *totalitarian society* simply by reading or hearing about them. Exemplars need to be actually experienced. Similarly, the words 'A tarn is a small mountain lake' are much less effective in learning the concept of *tarn* than actually seeing one (Carroll, 1964). Indeed, students often memorise a definition and some verbally presented instances without having any real understanding of the underlying concept. The practical implication is to try to arrange concrete exemplars when possible. They can be either real exemplars or pictures or diagrams. These may also induce students to pay more attention and to better recall the concept being taught.

*Differences in motivation*

In the world outside the classroom, we are often highly motivated to learn and use certain concepts; failure to do so can have quite dire consequences. A child is motivated to acquire such concepts as *fierce dog* and accurately categorise exemplars, a film producer of *this season's hit*, a salesman of his customers, and a department store buyer of customer's needs. An adequate concept of *suitable dating partner* or *marriage partner* is also extremely important for a person's wellbeing.

Conversely, there is often much less motivation in the classroom. While many students might be motivated by intrinsic interest or the chance of good grades, many clearly are not. No doubt much of the reason is that school-taught concepts and schemata are not seen as particularly relevant to their lives. They may be seen as too abstract to really apply to solving everyday problems (Schaefer, 1979). So, students may learn only as much as needed to pass exams. Such a lack of motivation can also lead to compartmentalisation, where school knowledge is separated from that learned and used in everyday life. This problem can be partially overcome by trying to emphasise the practical importance of some school-taught concepts. Practical components in vocational courses also help in inducing students to reorganise what they learn and to try to apply this knowledge.

The procedure itself is examined below.

## SOME PRELIMINARIES

### Introduction

The procedure to be described may seem quite complex and unwieldy, and indeed would not be practical to use in its entirety to teach all concepts. There simply would not be enough time. However, it is well worth using in complete form for important concepts in a discipline, those key ones that students really must understand to progress in the field. Examples are *mass* and *force* in physics, *gene* and *chromosome* in biology, *representation* in cognitive psychology and *significance test* and *correlation* in statistics. It also can be used for concepts that students find particularly difficult and that therefore need more instruction; for example *mole* in chemistry. In addition, teachers can use such parts of the procedure as they see fit, adapting the general method to time and resources available, the learners themselves and the importance of the concept.

The procedure has several distinct phases, with a choice between different methods in several phases. These can be divided into the preliminaries, which this section covers, the actual presentation and the evaluation of concept learning. The preliminary points that should be clarified are as follows.

### *Is a concept lesson needed?*

This is the first question to ask. Is there an important concept that the students must master? Is the textbook exposition of some concept inadequate or too difficult to understand, so that it needs more emphasis, explanation or some concrete exemplars? Table 4 gives some more examples of important concepts in several fields that might need a concept lesson.

**Table 4.** Some examples of important concepts in various disciplines which might when teaching need a concept lesson.

| Discipline | Concepts |
|---|---|
| Mathematics | Real number; limit; correlation; imaginary number. |
| Literature | Archetype; poetic metre; saga; satire. |
| Law | Tort; contract; habeas corpus; rule of law. |
| Physics | Energy; troposphere; electricity; force. |
| Chemistry | Ion; base; mole; solution. |
| Computer science | Algorithm; programming language; data structure. |
| Social science | Culture; political will; social structure. |
| Economics | Recession; supply and demand; command economy. |
| Music | Key; symphony; harmonic; sonata form. |

### *Decide your instructional objectives*

Instruction should have clear aims. An instructor needs a firm idea of just what knowledge or skills he aims to instil in students. As Mager (1962) puts it, 'When an instructor decides to teach something, he must determine his goals and then pick methods and content which can achieve them.'

Different instruction may have quite different aims. An art or literature course could aim mainly at a positive attitude towards art or literature, or at an interest in reading and going to art galleries. A politics course may aim at teaching some understanding of how governments work and a positive attitude towards democracy and regular voting. A physical education course could aim mainly at improving students' current fitness level. Thus, aims vary greatly according to subject matter and the time and resources available. Finally, any course's aims should be quite specific and at least potentially attainable (Gagné and Briggs, 1974). Vaguely stated objectives such as 'helping students develop their creative potential' and 'aiming to help students to moral and intellectual autonomy', are too hard to even understand, let alone actually meet.

What aims, then, should a concept lesson have? Again, the instructor's goals will vary according to the learners and the concept. With some concepts, the instructor may wish to instil an exemplar or prototype representation (see Chapter 10). Instruction according to the traditional procedure aims at instilling a classical-view representation and some other goals listed below. For advanced courses, when classical-view definitions do exist, these should be taught.

Some aims of concept teaching by the traditional procedure are as follows. Clark (1971) gives one set of aims, which is shown in Table 5.

**Table 5.** Examples of some instructional aims when teaching concepts by the traditional procedure, adapted from Clark (1971).

| Aims stated in simple terms<br><br>The student will have: | Aims stated in more technical terms | Evidence that a student has met the aims<br>The student can: |
|---|---|---|
| 1: Memorised a concept's definition. | 1. Memorised the defining features. | 1. State verbally the defining features. |
| 2. Applied the concept to a new situation. | 2. Used the defining features to accurately categorise exemplars and non-exemplars. | 2. Given any new stimulus, identify defining and irrelevant features in it. |
| 3. Discovered the concept without any instruction. | 3. Abstracted the defining features after a discovery-learning procedure. | 3. Correctly sort out exemplars and non-exemplars of the discovered concept. |

Markle and Tiemann (1969) give some aims as well. They argue that to really understand a concept, a learner must be able to do certain things. Instruction should aim at teaching these skills. The first two aims are also given by Clark and are shown in the table. Let us examine each in detail.

Firstly, the learner should be able to state the concept definition and its defining features. Thus, a student acquiring the concept of *square* should be able to define it as 'a plane, closed figure with four sides of equal length at right angles to each other'.

Secondly, the learner should be able to accurately categorise exemplars and non-exemplars, neither over- or under-generalising. Meeting this goal often requires experience with exemplars and non-exemplars. As mentioned, a definition alone is often not enough. Thus, most students when told that an analog representation is 'a relation between two things in which one in some way resembles the other' would probably be little wiser, and would be unlikely to be able to readily categorise exemplars. Experience with actual exemplars and non-exemplars is usually needed.

Thirdly, the learner should know how the concept relates to others in important taxonomies and theories. He should know the immediate superordinate concept and some important coordinates and subordinates, if these exist. Thus, a learner acquiring the concept of *mammal* should eventually be taught how it relates to *animal, reptile, bird* and perhaps *plant*. Such knowledge also allows inferences, as discussed in Chapter 1.

Fourthly, the learner should be able to actually *use* the concept, not just to categorise but also to solve problems that involve it and in applying principles and theories that it is part of. Too often students cannot readily apply concepts that they have acquired. Indeed, James (1958) discusses a teacher who asked a geography class the following question: 'If I dug a hole hundreds of feet deep would it be cooler or warmer at the bottom than on the top?' No one answered. Trying a different tack, she asked: 'In what condition is the interior of the globe?' More than half the class chimed: 'The interior of the globe is in a condition of igneous fusion.' Even if they understood what igneous fusion meant, they could not use the concept to solve a simple problem.

Finally, it is often useful before a concept lesson for the instructor to tell the students his or her aims. Thus, before teaching *mammal*, they could say, 'This lesson aims to teach you the defining features of mammal, give some idea of the diversity of its exemplars, teach how to categorise various animals as mammals and non-mammals, and teach you how the concept fits into the life form taxonomy.'

*Analyse the concept*
By working from textbooks, dictionaries, and other teaching materials the concept should be analysed to determine the following characteristics. Firstly, determine its name. Concepts that lack a single-word name can often be labelled with a short phrase. Secondly, determine an important taxonomy that it is part of, listing the immediate superordinate concept, some coordinates, and some subordinates if these exist. For example, say we are teaching the concept *triangle*. The immediate superordinate is *polygon*, a coordinate is *quadrilateral*, and a subordinate is *equilateral triangle*. For *alloy*, the superordinate is *metal*, a coordinate is *metal element*, and a subordinate is *bronze*. Thirdly, specify the concept's defining features and some characteristic ones if desired. Also determine some major irrelevant features that are likely to cause confusion and that could be mistaken for defining ones. Use the set of defining features to write a short definition, which states the name, some defining features and the immediate superordinate. Some examples of such definitions are as follows:

A square is a rectangle with four sides of equal length at right angles to each other.
A chord is a set of three or more notes sounded at the same time.
A positive reinforcer is a stimulus which increases the rate of a response it is contingent on.

The same concept can sometimes be defined in different ways, often by structure or function. Kagan and Lang (1978) give two definitions of chromosome:

A chromosome is composed of strings of genes.
Chromosomes are units which duplicate in our body cells and are responsible for what we inherit.

Kagan and Lang (1978)

Presenting a definition does indeed improve concept learning (Tennyson and Park, 1980). Table 6 gives three complete examples of concept analysis.

Once the analysis is complete, the instructor should ask several important questions if he has not already done so. First of all, have the students mastered the important component concepts that constitute the defining and irrelevant features? For example, to acquire the concept of *sonnet*, a student needs to know what *iambic pentameter*, *rhyme pattern* and even *poem* are. To acquire the concept of *melting*, a student must know what *solid* and *liquid* are. These component concepts also must be available to

**Table 6.** Three examples of concept analysis. The first is adapted from Markle and Tiemann (1969), the second from Klausmeier (1976b) and the third from Herron *et al* (1977).

---

*Sonnet*

Definition: a sonnet is a 14-line poem that expresses a single idea.
Defining features: definite rhyme pattern. Fourteen lines. Clear-cut formal divisions. Iambic pentameter.
Irrelevant features: subject matter. Development. Length. Author.
Immediate superordinate: poem.

*Observing scientifically*

Definition: observing scientifically is critically examining objects or events using one or more senses and recording those observations.
Defining features: using one or more senses. Critically examining data. Accurately recording data.
Irrelevant features: what particular objects or events are observed. The sense used. The method of recording data.
Immediate superordinate: observing.
Coordinate: non-scientific observing.

*Melting*

Definition: melting is the change of state from solid to liquid.
Defining features: solid form of the substance decreases and the liquid form increases. The overall composition of the substance is the same.
Irrelevant features: whether the substance is pure or impure. Whether the substance is an element or compound.
Immediate superordinate: physical change.
Coordinates: boiling; freezing; dissolving; condensing.
Subordinates: none.

---

students during instruction. The instructor may need to first review them before moving to the concept itself or be willing to backtrack during the lesson (Skemp, 1971). Secondly, is the students' cognitive developmental level sufficient for them to learn the concept? Sometimes a concept analysis reveals that a certain concept is much more complex than was thought and should be introduced later in the curriculum.

*Prepare instructional materials*

A set of exemplars and non-exemplars of the concept should be assembled. These are needed for several reasons. The first is to illustrate the concept. As mentioned earlier, presenting only a definition may mean that students just memorise words without understanding them. Secondly, the definition of some concepts is so vague or hard to understand that they can only really be taught with exemplars. Indeed, Skemp (1971) argues that many mathematical concepts can only be acquired in this way. Thirdly, exemplars and non-exemplars can help to highlight a concept's defining features, and help to establish a concept's boundaries. As Markle and Tiemann (1969) put it, 'Exemplars promote generalisation and non-exemplars promote discrimination'. An example should make this point clearer. If an instructor is teaching the concept of *square* and only presents instances that are oriented upright, students may under-generalise, excluding as instances squares that are tilted. Presenting exemplars at different angles while emphasising that they are instances should prevent this problem. Non-exemplars help in preventing over-generalisation. If in teaching the concept of *square* the instructor presented no non-square rectangles, a student might then conclude that a square was any rectangle. Again, experience with non-exemplars should help prevent such problems.

*The exemplars*

The instructor should pick more than he is likely to need. Some will be used to illustrate the concept and others in later categorisation practice. He should pick a *divergent* set whose stimuli range from clear, highly typical ones to less typical and atypical stimuli. Thus, for *mammal*, highly typical stimuli would be bear and sheep, and atypical stimuli would be whale, dolphin and kangaroo. The set of exemplars should be diverse, varying over such irrelevant dimensions as size, appearance, habitat, etc. (Tennyson and Park, 1980). A divergent set of exemplars for *dog* would include beagle, terrier, basset, poodle, boxer, Great Dane, and bloodhound. The set varies over such features as size, hair length and ferocity. A divergent range of exemplars for *set* would be as follows:

All known planets.
The living members of your family.
All cars with engine capacity over 1200 cc.
All female Colombians.
All train journeys of more than 60 kilometres.

They vary over such irrelevant factors as living/non-living, size and whether they are objects or events. To stress the point, a divergent set helps to ensure that learners do not conclude that an irrelevant feature is in fact a defining one (e.g. that 'living' is a defining feature of *set*, or 'lives on land' is a defining feature of *mammal*).

*The non-exemplars*

The instructor should pick a divergent set of these as well, which vary along many irrelevant dimensions. Each non-exemplar should not be too different from the exemplars, however. Using non-exemplars that are just too different is of little use. For instance, to teach the concept of *fish*, a poor set of non-exemplars would be planet, bicycle, year and socialist state. A good set would include whale, crab, barnacle and lobster, which are much more similar to exemplars of *fish*.

*Using matched pairs*

A good way to proceed is to arrange exemplars and non-exemplars in matched pairs (Markle and Tiemann, 1969). Here an exemplar and a non-exemplar are matched on as many irrelevant features as possible so that they are very similar. Thus, the presence of the defining feature in the exemplar is highlighted. Figure 29 presents some examples. The set of matched pairs used to teach *square* emphasises various defining features. Thus, stimuli are matched in orientation and size, such that the length of sides feature is highlighted. The same is true in teaching the concept of *mammal*. Whale and shark are quite similar in shape and habitat but differ in such defining features as 'delivers young alive' and 'breathes air'. Bat and hawk both have wings and fly, but again differ in some defining features. While most pairs should be so matched, include some pairs in which the exemplar is highly typical and obviously different from the non-exemplar.

How many pairs are needed? While Clark (1971) suggests that the optimum number for teaching many concepts is four, the total will vary greatly with the concept's complexity and the age and expertise of the learners. Abstract, complex, important concepts, such as *ecosystem*, may need many more pairs than simpler ones, such as *triangle* and *quadrilateral*. You need enough stimuli to cover a range of irrelevant features, prevent over and under-generalisation and to highlight defining features.

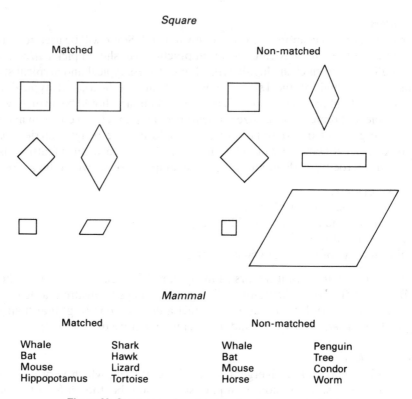

**Figure 29.** Some examples of matched and non-matched pairs.

*Arrangement of the matched pairs*

Tennyson and Park (1980) suggest arranging the pairs in an easy-to-hard sequence. Begin with one or two pairs that have a clear typical exemplar readily distinguishable from its matched non-exemplar. Thus, to teach *mammal*, a good pair to start with would be 'mouse–lizard'. Gradually work up to the more difficult peripheral exemplars (e.g. 'whale-shark'). Put another way, start with concrete familiar pairs and proceed progressively to the more abstract and unfamiliar.

*Format of stimuli*

Possible representation formats for exemplars and non-exemplars include the actual objects, schematic diagrams, photographs and words. The general rule is to use real instances if possible, especially for younger students. A trip to the zoo or an expedition to the forest are much more useful in illustrating various biological concepts than words or pictures, just as a cell seen through a microscope or a laboratory demonstration of operant conditioning is better than just words. Yet, we cannot always use real stimuli, of course. The instructor is often in practice restricted to words or diagrams. When restricted to words, he can often use 'mini-anecdotes' to illustrate concepts. These are like the verbal categorisation formats described in Chapter 7. Eggen *et al* (1979) give the following exemplar and non-exemplar for *apathy:*

1.  John and Mary were honeymooning and saw Niagara Falls at sunset. 'Oh, how beautiful', exclaimed Mary. But, John glanced briefly at the scene and resumed reading his newspaper.

2.   Jim and Sally at the same scene were overcome by its beauty. Shaking with emotion,
     they said, 'May all our times be as happy as this one.'

Eggen et al (1979)

Merrill and Tennyson (1977) suggest using a variety of different formats to teach a certain concept when possible. Thus, some stimuli can be represented by diagrams and others by photographs and words. To teach *mitosis* the instructor could present schematic diagrams of the process, film taken through a microscope as well as verbal descriptions. For the concept *liberal* the teacher could present a cartoon expressing a liberal idea (with one expressing a conservative idea as a non-exemplar), short political speeches with a liberal theme, and verbally-presented Acts passed by liberal governments. Again, some concepts lend themselves better to the use of a variety of formats.

*Attentional factors*

The stimuli should be as varied and interesting as possible. Such variation helps capture and hold the learners' attention. People like abrupt changes in stimuli, so the stimuli should be as surprising and unpredictable as possible. The teacher can also direct the students' attention to the more important aspects of the stimuli in several ways. The defining features can be made more salient by underlining them, colouring them differently, or even making them bigger than usual. Another method is to use schematic diagrams with all the extraneous information deleted. Thus, to teach the concept of *mitochondria*, a diagram of a cell with only this part shown could first of all be presented, and then later more detailed diagrams could be shown.

*Problems in generating exemplars and non-exemplars*

Finally, two possible problems in generating stimuli with certain concepts may be noted. Herron *et al* (1977) list several. The first case they cite is concepts that have no readily perceptible exemplars, such as *light year, universe* and *angstrom*. It is also hard to think of useful non-exemplars. As suggested above, models, diagrams, analogies and metaphors, and verbal descriptions must be used. The second case is concepts that have no clearly perceptible defining features. Examples they give are *element* and *compound* in chemistry. From such exemplars of *element* as iron, mercury and chlorine and non-exemplars as water and salt, students cannot see the defining features. The teacher cannot point to an iron bar and point out the defining features of *element* in it as he can so point to an exemplar of *square*. The defining features cannot be highlighted by colouring them or enlarging them. They must be explained with words.

THE ACTUAL PRESENTATION

The stimuli can be presented in one of two ways, which are called the expository and discovery methods (Ausubel, 1968; Woolfolk and McCune-Nicolich, 1984). In actual fact, these are two different ways of teaching almost any material. The *expository* method is highly directive. The teacher outlines the general principles and proceeds from them to specific cases, which illustrate the principles. It is often the method of choice, especially for older students, because it is quicker and easier to use. The *discovery* method involves working from the particular to the general. Cases are presented and students are induced to abstract general principles from them. When this method is applied to concept teaching, exemplars and non-exemplars are presented and students are encouraged to abstract a certain concept from them.

The traditional procedure usually involves straight expository presentation, as is demonstrated below. However, it can be adapted to discovery presentation by changing some details, as described later in this chapter.

### Establish a set to learn concepts

People have a set when they are primed to take in certain data. Thus, a radar operator may have a set to pick up blips from a certain direction, or a teacher may have a set to spot early signs of disciplinary trouble. Students should be directed towards learning a concept as follows (Klausmeier and Sipple, 1980). First of all, they should be told that there is a concept to be learned, and it should be pointed out that it fits into a previously learned taxonomy or that it is part of a certain theory. Secondly, the concept should be named to further focus the students' attention and set them towards picking out the defining and major irrelevant features.

### Present the exemplars and non-exemplars

The teacher should first of all say what the defining features of the concept are and then present the stimuli one pair at a time in either of the following two ways.

*Method A*
Clark (1971) suggests first showing two clear, typical exemplars (not matched pairs). Each is named as an instance ('these stimuli are both triangles') and then the defining features in each are identified and named. For example, if teaching the concept of *square*, two squares of different sizes could be shown and the teacher could state:

> These are squares. Each is a closed plane figure with four sides of equal length at right angles to each other. Such features as size and orientation are irrelevant. A square can be any size or at any tilt.

A second example is *mammal*. Two typical exemplars, such as bear and horse, are presented. The defining features are named, such as 'breathes air', 'delivers young live' and 'suckles young'. Size, habitat and overall shape are irrelevant features.

After showing the two typical exemplars, the teacher should start to present the matched pairs, one at a time, in an easy-to-hard sequence. He points out the defining feature/s in each exemplar and its/their absence in each non-exemplar. For instance, say an exemplar is a certain square and a non-exemplar is a rectangle with two sides longer than the other two. The teacher points out that the square has four sides of equal length while the non-exemplar does not. When all the matched pairs have been shown, some *practice* stimuli are presented. Some exemplars and non-exemplars are shown in a random sequence (not easy-to-hard), each stimulus being shown alone. The students are asked if each stimulus is an exemplar or not and for the reasons for their answers. After answering, the teacher should say if they are right or wrong, giving reasons, and then move to the next stimulus.

*Method B*

Merrill and Tennyson (1977) suggest a 'rule-examples-practice' procedure, which we can slightly adapt as follows. The teacher should not start with two typical exemplars. Instead, he should present the first matched pair as in the above method, and then follow the pair presentation with a practice stimulus. The students have to say whether the practice stimulus is or is not an exemplar and why it is or is not. The teacher gives the students feedback and presents the next matched pair, followed by another practice stimulus. This cycle is repeated until all the pairs have been shown. The pairs are arranged in an easy-to-hard sequence but the practice stimuli are arranged randomly. The defining features in each exemplar are identified as in Method A.

*Variants on matched-pair presentation*

The teacher does not have to use matched pairs, or necessarily present both members of a pair at the same time. He could just show one single exemplar or non-exemplar at a time. Whether matched pairs are used or not depends on time available and the concept itself.

*Some additional tips*

First of all, the students should have enough time to study each stimulus. A common error is to rush through them too quickly. Secondly, if possible, leave all the stimuli shown so far in full view during the lesson. Thus, students can refer back to them if they wish – their memories will be strained less, and the differences between exemplars and non-exemplars is made clearer. When stimuli cannot be left in full view be willing to review them or present some again if the students so wish. Thirdly, it is often useful to get students to label defining features in each exemplar during the lesson.

## EVALUATION OF CONCEPT LEARNING

The final step is to evaluate how well, or indeed whether, the students acquired the concept. Such evaluation has several uses. First of all, it can be useful feedback on the teaching method. If many or most students did not learn the concept, then the lesson needs to be examined to find out why. Had the students acquired the necessary component concepts? Was the teacher's analysis of the concept faulty or were the representation formats inadequate? Were students consistently over or under-generalising? If so, then more exemplars or non-exemplars are needed, or perhaps a more divergent set of each. Secondly, evaluation can grade students and thus meet institutional demands as well as help motivate students. Thirdly, a test or effort to apply what we have learned can help expose gaps in our understanding. Most of us have had the experience of believing that we have understood some material only to discover that this is not the case when confronted with problems to solve or an essay to write. Evaluation can, along with the practice stimuli, induce students to further think about the material and go over certain parts again if necessary.

There are a number of methods of evaluation. Which one is used largely depends on instructional objectives. If the instructor's aim is for students to just reasonably accurately categorise exemplars and non-exemplars, then a categorisation test with stimuli not shown in the learning phase is the best method to use. Stimuli are presented and the concept is judged as acquired if the student's accuracy meets some preset criterion.

Categorisation accuracy can be tested with questions using a variety of formats. A laboratory class could also have some actual exemplars of various concepts. Klausmeier *et al* (1974) and Klausmeier (1976b) give some examples which go along the following lines.

1.  Which of the life forms below is a reptile?
    a.  Whale
    b.  Horse
    c.  Turtle
    d.  Tarantula
    e.  Robin.

2.  Pick an instance and a non-instance of reptile from the following set.
    a.  Whale
    b.  Lizard
    c.  Condor
    d.  Ape.

3.  A dolphin is a:
    a.  Marsupial
    b.  Primate
    c.  Mammal
    d.  Reptile.

4.  What term applies to all these animals?
    a.  Tortoise
    b.  Lizard
    c.  Brontosaurus
    d.  Turtle
    e.  Frog.

Another useful device is to ask students to produce their own exemplars and non-exemplars:

1.  Give two examples of reptiles and two examples of animals that are not reptiles. Give two examples of reptiles likely to be found in your garden.

Ask questions which determine if students both know and can readily identify a concept's defining features. For example:

1.  What are the defining features of primate? Of immigrant? Of invisible export?
2.  Define invisible export in your own words.
3.  Which of the following animals lay eggs? Which deliver live young?
    a.  Lizard
    b.  Kangaroo
    c.  Robin
    d.  Whale.

More sophisticated evaluation methods are needed if the aim is to teach students to apply the concept to solve problems and use in various principles. Klausmeier (1976b) gives some examples of problems that can be set to assess whether students can use a given concept to solve them. These are shown in Table 7.

**Table 7.** Some examples of the kind of problems that can be set in order to test students' ability to use a newly-taught concept, adapted from Klausmeier (1976b).

---

*Triangle*

Principle 1 involving the concept: if the three sides are the same length then the three angles of the triangle are equal.
Problem involving principle 1: one angle in a triangle is 60° and the sides are all five centimetres long. What are the other two angles?
Principle 2: the perimeter of an equilateral triangle is three times the length of one side.
Problem involving principle 2: one side of an equilateral triangle is three kilometres. What is its perimeter?

*Observing scientifically*

Two drawings of a growing plant are shown. The growing plant was measured on Day 1 and Day 6. Which part grew the most in the first five days?
a. The leaf.
b. The stem.
c. The root.

---

## A SAMPLE CONCEPT LESSON

The concept is *rectangle*.
The aims of the lesson are to teach students the concept name, its defining features, some important irrelevant features, and to categorise any plane figure as a rectangle or non-rectangle.

### Concept Analysis

*Definition:*　A rectangle is a plane, closed figure with four sides of the same length, or of which parallel sides are equal, and which has four internal right angles.
*Defining features:*　Plane, closed figure.
　　　　　　　　　　Four sides of the same length or parallel sides equal.
*Irrelevant features:*　Size.
　　　　　　　　　　Tilt.
*Immediate superordinate:*　Quadrilateral.
*Subordinates:*　Square, oblong.

### Stimuli

These are arranged in an easy-to-hard sequence in matched pairs, roughly equated on size and tilt. They are shown in Figure 30.

### Presentation

Today we learn the concept of *rectangle*. A rectangle is a type of quadrilateral (which students have acquired already). It can be defined as a plane, closed figure with four

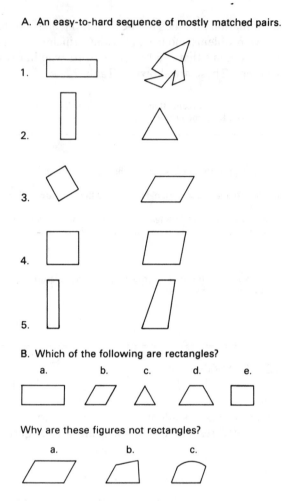

**Figure 30.** Stimuli presented in the sample concept lesson for both teaching and evaluation.

internal right angles. Here are two examples (shown in Figure 30). Each has four sides (pointing these out) with opposing ones of just the same length and four internal right angles (pointing these out). They can differ in size and orientation and still be rectangles. Here are some more examples (see Figure 30).

## Evaluation

1.  In your own words name the defining features of rectangle.
2.  What is the difference between a rectangle and a non-rectangular quadrilateral?

Figure 30 gives some more examples of questions for evaluation.

## TWO MODIFICATIONS OF THE BASIC PROCEDURE

This final section presents two variants of the traditional procedure. The first looks at teaching several coordinate concepts at the same time and the second at discovery learning.

### Teaching coordinate concepts

So far we have looked at the teaching of a single concept and mentioned the need to relate it to its fellows in a taxonomy or theory. Though it is often best to teach one concept at a time in order to reduce possible confusion, sometimes it is useful to teach several coordinate concepts at the same time. (Coordinates are concepts at the same abstraction level. Examples are *apple, pear* and *peach*, and *truck* and *bicycle*.) A common situation in which coordinate concepts are taught is when the concepts are very similar and thus easily confused. Examples are *mass* and *weight, tourist* and *immigrant, punishment* and *negative reinforcement* and *revolution* and *rebellion*.

Two important features of coordinate concepts are worth mentioning before proceeding further. Firstly, each coordinate concept that shares an immediate superordinate will have the superordinate's defining features (if the superordinate has them). Thus, *triangle* and *quadrilateral* both have all the defining features of *polygon*. They are both plane, closed figures with straight sides. *Reptile* and *bird* have the defining features of *animal*. They move about and are alive. Many coordinate concepts only differ from each other in the presence of one or a few defining features. For example, *triangle* and *quadrilateral* only differ in the number of sides and internal angles they have. Secondly, a non-exemplar of one coordinate concept may be an exemplar of another coordinate. Thus, penguin is a non-exemplar of *fish* but an exemplar of its coordinate, *bird*.

Tennyson and Park (1980) and Klausmeier (1976b) suggest some ways of teaching coordinate concepts which go as follows. The method is a simple extension of the expository procedure for teaching a single concept. Definitions are determined and presented, concepts are analysed, exemplars are generated and arranged in an easy-to-hard sequence. The major difference is in the presentation of stimuli. For each coordinate concept a divergent set of exemplars that vary over major irrelevant features and range from typical to atypical are chosen. They are then arranged as a series of exemplar *sets*, each set consisting of one exemplar of each coordinate. Exemplars within each set should be matched as closely as possible on irrelevant characteristics. Exemplars of one concept will serve as non-exemplars of the others and thus will highlight various defining features. Here is an example:

*Bird, Mammal and Reptile*

|        | Bird    | Mammal  | Reptile   |
|--------|---------|---------|-----------|
| Set A: | Robin   | Mouse   | Lizard    |
| Set B: | Hawk    | Wolf    | Crocodile |
| Set C: | Ostrich | Dolphin | Tortoise  |

Similarly, if teaching *triangle* and *quadrilateral* as coordinates, have a series of pairs of exemplars of each that are matched in size and orientation.

Then proceed as follows. First give the name of the immediate superordinate concept and then the names and defining features of each coordinate concept in turn. Then present the stimuli in each set according to the following plan:

Exemplar      1     2     3
Practice stimulus      1     2     3

In other words, first present an exemplar of coordinate concept 1, then of 2 and then of 3. Say that each stimulus in turn is an exemplar of each coordinate and why, pointing out the defining features. Then present a practice stimulus for each one. The practice stimuli can consist of both exemplars of the coordinates and exemplars of coordinates with a different immediate superordinate. An illustration is in Figure 2 in Chapter 1. If teaching the concepts of *element* and *alloy*, exemplars of their coordinate concepts *precious* and *common stone* could be used as practice stimuli. Present the exemplars in an easy-to-hard sequence and the practice stimuli in a randomised order.

**Two examples of the presentation of coordinate concepts**

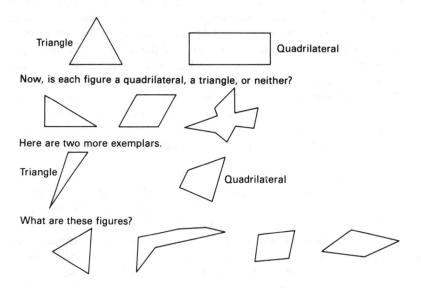

**Figure 31.** An example of the presentation of coordinate concepts.

*Triangle and quadrilateral*

Triangles and quadrilaterals are plane, closed figures and are instances of polygon. Triangles have three sides of any length, while quadrilaterals have four sides. They can be at any orientation or any size. An example of each is illustrated in Figure 31.

*Reinforcers and punishers*

Reinforcers and punishers are stimuli that affect the rate of the behaviour they follow. Reinforcers increase the rate of a behaviour and punishers decrease it.

Here is an example of a reinforcer – food. A rat was given food each time it pressed a bar. The rate of bar pressing went up. Here is an example of a punisher – electric shock. Every time a pigeon pecked a key for food, it was given an electric shock. Key peck rate went down.

Are the following cases examples of reinforcers or punishers?

a. Members of the sales force were given a free trip for every 100 cars they sold. Sales went up greatly.
b. Traffic fines for speeding were raised by 50%, but the rate of speeding violations remained the same.

## Discovery learning

In its pure form, the discovery method is quite a contrast to the expository one. As mentioned, material is not served up well-cooked but in a raw form, and the learner has to abstract general principles from it. The basic approach can be illustrated with a geography lesson, then we will look at how it applies to concept teaching.

If one wanted to teach students how human settlements are likely to develop in a certain region (Woolfolk and McCune-Nicolich, 1984), an expository approach would cite general principles of settlement, such as 'Settlements tend to develop around ports or rich farming areas'. Such tenets would then be illustrated with some concrete examples. A discovery approach might involve presenting a physical map of some territory (showing rivers, bays, etc) and asking where the students think the major settlements would be. With some prodding, they may go some way towards abstracting the principles.

One might use the procedure to teach a concept as follows. It is much like a typical laboratory experiment in which subjects are shown stimuli and have to abstract a concept from them. For example, if we are teaching the concept of *quadrilateral*, we could present a variety of four-sided plane figures, either at the same time or in a sequence, and ask what they have in common. After eliciting responses such as 'they have four straight sides', we can present some non-exemplars (a pentagon, circle, triangle) and can ask how these differ from the first set of figures. This question may induce the students to focus on the defining features in the exemplars and their absence in the non-exemplars. We can also ask how the figures in the first set differ from each other, eliciting such responses as 'size, length of sides', etc. We can sum up with the concept's name and its defining features.

Another example is from Gorman (1974) – teaching the concept of *island* to young children. The teacher can present maps or pictures of various islands and ask what they have in common. After eliciting features such as 'surrounded by water' and 'is a piece of land', the teacher presents some non-exemplars, such as a peninsula. He can ask how it differs from an island, again trying to focus the students' attention on the defining features. At the end, the concept's name and defining features are given. The teacher could then perhaps contrast the concept of *island* with that of *continent*.

Bruner has argued that the discovery method has distinct advantages over expository presentation. It actively involves students in learning. They are forced to think about the material and to try to understand it. As a result, their natural curiosity is harnessed, which helps them to learn, and their retention is supposed to be better. In contrast, expository presentation may be passively endured by students, who just rote-learn the material without thinking much about it.

The discovery method does have disadvantages, however. B. F. Skinner has pointed out, quite accurately, that original thoughts are quite rare. Progress in any field is often quite slow; a lot of hard work and thought by thousands of talented people is behind many advances. It is optimistic to believe that students in a short time can reproduce the products of years of hard work of experts. Also, discovery presentation can be cumbersome. It can take a long time to elicit responses from students or guide them in a given direction. The method also may favour the very bright pupils in a class, who learn more quickly than the less gifted students.

Despite such problems, the method can be used judiciously with certain material and certain younger students. For more difficult material and more advanced students, expository presentation may be better. As Mayer (1983b) has pointed out however, it should be determined which people would benefit most from discovery presentation and under what conditions.

A method of compromise is *guided discovery*. It uses some of the principles of the expository method and some of the discovery method. Students, therefore, do not need to do most of the abstracting themselves. For example, when teaching the concept of *island*, we could begin by giving the concept's name and perhaps a definition, then present instances and ask students what they have in common. Non-exemplars could be presented later, and students could be asked how these differ from the instances.

## FURTHER READING

The traditional procedure: Klausmeier (1976b); Merrill and Tennyson (1977).
Discovery learning: Gorman (1974); Mayer (1983b).

# Chapter 10

# How to Teach Concepts II: Some New Techniques and Implications of Recent Research

SUMMARY

1.  The traditional procedure seems inadequate for teaching some concepts in certain circumstances. New methods may thus be needed.
2.  Some aspects of concepts described in Chapters 4 and 6 have several educational implications. Basic-level concepts should usually be taught first. Advanced students sometimes need to be taught that a given concept's exemplars vary greatly in typicality in order that they have a better basis for dealing with a given domain. Students also need to know that concepts and schemata are constructions and never exactly fit the real world.
3.  Some concepts are better taught as prototypes rather than as sets of defining features. Students can be taught a best-example or a set of characteristic features and can practise categorisation with it.
4.  Metaphors can make instruction more interesting and help students to understand unfamiliar concepts. Complex concepts can be taught with a cluster of metaphors.
5.  Concept mapping involves use of the ELINOR and spreading activation theory notations in order to map out the students' existing conceptual structures or the conceptual structure of a domain one wishes to teach. Students also can learn to map domains in order to better understand them.
6.  Memory for concepts can be improved in several ways. Elaboration and organisation of material are two ways. The keyword technique can help students to more easily recall the name of a given concept.

## INTRODUCTION

The traditional procedure has several shortcomings. One major problem, dealt with in Chapter 11, is that it assumes students are empty vessels to be filled with knowledge. A second one, mentioned in Chapter 9, is that it can only be used with concepts that have clear defining features. While many school concepts are well-defined, many are not and so another teaching procedure is needed. A third problem is that it takes little account of phenomena such as typicality, fuzzy category boundaries, ill-defined category systems, and metaphorical definitions of complex concepts. Developmental factors, also, are often not emphasised. It is generally assumed that a concept is either learned or is not learned. Instead, the teacher needs to remember that conceptual development can be a long, slow process.

This chapter explores the implications of the phenomena listed above for concept teaching and also describes some new teaching techniques. These include teaching exemplar and prototype representations, concept mapping, and the use of analogies and metaphors to define complex concepts. Finally, the chapter examines some ways of ensuring that newly-acquired concepts are well retained by students.

## EDUCATIONAL IMPLICATIONS OF SOME CONCEPT CHARACTERISTICS

This section suggests some educational applications of material covered in Chapters 4 and 6. The following discussion is best regarded as somewhat speculative, because, with a few exceptions to be noted, there is little hard research to suggest how well this material applies in the classroom. The material can be seen as a set of useful ideas to test.

### Basic-level categories

The notion of a basic-level in some conceptual structures has several applications. As mentioned in Chapter 4, it seems best to teach basic-level concepts first and proceed upwards and downwards on a taxonomy from there. The example given in Chapter 4 was starting from familiar concepts, such as *dog* and *cat*, and from there moving to the concepts of *mammal* and *life form*. Such a procedure follows Ausubel's principle of beginning instruction with what students already know or can readily learn. It seems likely that experts have basic-levels in such fields as computer science, chemistry, and law, but research has not yet suggested what they might be.

A related point is to give extra instruction when teaching superordinate concepts. Basic-level concepts are easier to learn, because their instances are quite different from those of other basic-level categories and they look much alike. However, instances of superordinate concepts are often held together only by quite abstract functional features and they, therefore, tend to be more difficult to learn.

Mervis (1980) suggests some further implications. Firstly, she points out that younger children may not know superordinate or subordinate concepts on some taxonomies until the ages of eight or nine. A teacher should, therefore, try to use basic-level concepts in verbal and written instruction, unless sure that the students understand terms for other concepts or new terms are being introduced. Secondly, anaphoric references should be used sparingly. The latter is a reference to a previously cited stimulus, using a different name. For example,

> Bill ate a crab; seafood was his favourite dish.
> Sally tried to start her car, but her vehicle needed repairs.

Crab and seafood refer to the same object, but seafood is the name of the superordinate category. Similarly, car and vehicle refer to the same machine; vehicle is the name of the superordinate category. The anaphoric device is usually easy for adults to understand and it makes discourse more varied and interesting. However, a child who does not understand the more abstract term may not comprehend the sentences. Use the anaphoric device only when sure students will indeed understand it.

## Typicality and vague category boundaries

The traditional procedure has little to say about exemplar typicality, other than to suggest the use of typical and atypical instances when teaching a given concept. Here are some implications of typicality. One important point is to use highly typical exemplars so that students can readily generalise from them to less typical ones. The Mervis and Pani (1980) study found that subjects learn better from typical exemplars. It also is important to present peripheral exemplars and non-exemplars so that students can learn where the boundaries are with some concepts. A medical student learning to interpret X-ray patterns or ECGs needs to be acquainted with atypical exemplars of various disorders. Mervis (1980) also suggests using only typical exemplars for diagrams and other illustrations with young children (unless explicitly teaching that certain atypical exemplars are instances). Children may not know that the atypical ones are instances.

Concept teaching is sometimes not just a matter of teaching a given concept but of extending the boundaries of concepts that students already know to include atypical exemplars. Children may not include insects and one-celled animals as exemplars of *animal*, or whale and dolphin as exemplars of *mammal*, therefore they need to be taught that they are instances. A related point is to emphasise that concept boundaries in some cases can be extended or retracted according to one's purposes. For some purposes a teacher may see Yugoslavia as a member of the Eastern Bloc and for others as a non-member.

Another important implication is relevant for more advanced students. When teaching certain concepts, it is useful to point out that exemplars vary greatly in typicality. We tend to believe that a stimulus is either an instance or a non-instance in some cases, but students will form a more useful concept without making that assumption. This situation is most likely to occur in the social sciences.

An example is *democracy*. Teachers tend to suggest that a given state either is or is not a democracy, but it is not hard to think of good and poor exemplars of this concept. Holland and Denmark would be good exemplars. Every adult has an equal vote, parties get seats according to their share of the popular vote, parties regularly rotate in government, and citizens can readily eject an unwanted régime. Other states are not such good exemplars. Some régimes doctor the electoral boundaries for their own advantage. The government of one Australian state has so altered its electoral boundaries that it needs only about 36% of the vote to stay in office. Some nations fall near the periphery of the concept of *democracy*. For instance, Singapore has an elected Parliament, regular elections and each citizen's vote is of equal value. However, the same party has ruled for many years and it actively discourages any prominent opposition leaders from emerging. Also, any district that ventures to elect an opposition member is denied basic resources. While Singapore is arguably a democracy, it is a very poor exemplar of the concept. There are also good and poor exemplars of *non-democracy*. Many South and Central American nations have some trappings of democracy and regular elections, but the army and wealthy landowners exert great influence and the military at times takes direct control. Some nations such as Viet Nam and North Korea are good exemplars of *non-democracy*. The régime cannot be dislodged by elections, most citizens cannot even leave the country legally, and the people have few political rights. To sum up then, a student has a better understanding of the political world by recognising that concepts such as *democracy* have typical and atypical exemplars. In some cases, typicality seems to result from a family-resemblance structure, as we see a little later.

### Fuzzy category systems

A related point is to restate the importance of realising that concepts and concept systems may be fuzzy, with unclear boundaries and a lack of clear-cut defining features. We are generally taught that concepts should be well-defined with clear boundaries, so that a given stimulus is or is not an instance. Classical-view concepts may not be useful for dealing with some stimulus domains, at least not with current knowledge. Using prototype concepts may give a better basis for dealing with the domain. Here are some examples.

One example is the psychiatric taxonomy. For many years it was periodically criticised. Some researchers recommended that the whole system should be scrapped, because there were unclear cases and no clear-cut defining features shared by exemplars of some categories. However, as Cantor *et al* (1980) pointed out, the problem could lie with the assumption that such a complex domain can be usefully divided up into clear-cut classical-view concepts. Looking at the system as a set of prototype concepts gives a better basis for dealing with the diversity of mental disorders.

Another example is the concept of *totalitarian society* which has at times come under criticism (Lacquer, 1985). Critics pointed out that it was very hard to find any common features that supposed exemplars shared and there were no clear exemplars. States usually considered totalitarian differed in many ways, and so, they suggested scrapping the concept. As is shown later, totalitarian society might be better considered as a family-resemblance concept. A final example is from biology – the concept of *species*. I once did a university course on evolution, which included a number of lectures on the *species* concept, defining it and describing the various mechanisms of speciation. But, at the course's end, the lecturer pulled the notion itself apart, facetiously adding that he had left this topic until last; otherwise he would have had nothing to talk about. The criticism again went along the lines of its problems as a classical-view concept. Some different species can produce offspring, contrary to the definition (e.g. horses and donkeys to produce a mule), and the criteria for deciding if a given group of organisms constitutes an exemplar of *species* are somewhat vague. Therefore, some stimuli are hard to categorise as exemplars or non-exemplars.

### Concepts are constructions

One more related point needs to be made, which is also put quite strongly by Fensham (1983). Teachers need to emphasise that concepts and schemata are constructions. They are invented and generally over-simplify or idealise the real situation. Since they are constructions, they will never exactly fit the real world, and some fit better than others. People often overlook this point, expecting such constructions to fit perfectly. An example is from the social sciences. Some years ago, Elisabeth Kubler-Ross proposed a schema of the bereavement process. Persons dying of some incurable disease were supposed to go through a series of distinct stages in a fixed order. These ranged from initial 'denial', where a person simply denied any problem at all, to 'final acceptance', which was a calm, mature realisation and acceptance of his or her fate. While this schema gained widespread popularity among health and social workers, it only seems to apply to some people (Silver and Wortman, 1980). Many people do not deny anything, or go through any stage of the schema, or calmly accept their fate, often to the chagrin of the people looking after them. Indeed, nurses are reported to get greatly upset when their patients fail to 'die properly'. It must be emphasised that the model can only help people to understand the behaviour of some persons, as it is a construction.

## Teaching prototype and exemplar representations

The rest of this section describes some applications of the work on category representation, which was described in Chapter 6. As mentioned in that chapter, sometimes a teacher can aim for a prototype or exemplar representation of some categories rather than a set of defining features. A general procedure for teaching prototype or exemplar-based concepts is described as follows.

### A best-example procedure

Tennyson and his colleagues have modified the traditional procedure with the aim of instilling a prototype representation. Many steps in their 'best-example' procedure and in the traditional procedure are the same. A definition, a set of exemplars and non-exemplars are prepared; some are used in teaching and some in practice. The major difference is in the teaching itself. The teacher first presents one or two highly typical exemplars and instructs the students to remember them (e.g. by forming a visual image or memorising features). Then he presents a series of exemplars and non-exemplars and instructs students to categorise them by comparing them to the 'best-example'. Thus, they are explicitly trained to generalise and discriminate by reference to a prototype rather than to a set of defining features. The students, also, may be instructed to abstract the dimensions along which the exemplars vary from the best-example.

Here are some examples of this procedure. Tennyson *et al* (1983) taught third and fourth grade students (aged 8 or 9 years) the concept of *regular polygon*. First of all, the students were given the definition that regular polygons are 'plane, closed figures with all sides of equal length and equal internal angles'. Then they were shown two best-examples: an equilateral triangle and a hexagon. They were told, 'There are many examples of regular polygons. Here are two best examples.' Later, the set of exemplars and non-exemplars was shown and students were told to act as follows:

> The following figures will help you learn to tell whether a figure is a regular polygon. Read the definition and look at the two best examples shown on the sheet . . . Now look at the following figures. [A regular octagon was shown here.] Now look at this figure. It is a regular polygon . . . Even though it does not look exactly the same as example B [a best example] the figure matches the definition.
>
> Tennyson *et al* (1983)

Students who were given the best-example training performed better on a subsequent categorisation test than students who were taught with a set of defining features and a definition. Tennyson *et al* (1981) used a similar procedure to teach the concept of *equilateral triangle* and found it produced better classification than the traditional procedure. Dunn (1983) found a best-example procedure to be the best of six methods of teaching *nib* (a right triangle with a line perpendicular to the centre of the shortest line in the triangle).

Another detailed example is from Park (1984). He used the best-example procedure to teach older students (aged 17 or 18 years) some basic concepts in operant psychology. These concepts are more abstract than those used above. Each concept was defined and a best-example was then given. Thus, for the concept of *positive reinforcement*, students were given:

> *Definition*: when an organism's behaviour produces a desirable (or pleasant) outcome by obtaining an attractive stimulus, that behaviour is said to be positively reinforced.
> *Best example:* A mother asked her boy to clean his messy room, and he did. The mother gave him $1.00. The boy's behaviour was positively reinforced because he obtained $1.00.
> Park (1984)

Students were shown a set of verbal-format exemplars and non-exemplars and were instructed to categorise them by reference to the best-examples. Park found contrary results to those above, however. The performance of the best-examples group was inferior to that of a defining-features group when a categorisation test was given immediately after instruction. However, the best-examples group did relatively better when a test was given one week later, which suggests that best-example training might produce better retention of knowledge.

However, the Park study has some problems that may explain the discrepant results. Neither the examples nor the definitions are best, or even very good. Neither gets at the crucial feature of reinforcement, which is that the response rate must increase as a result of a contingent reinforcer. The example above might not be an example if the boy's rate of cleaning behaviour did not change. A better 'best-example' would be what seems to me the prototypical example – a rat pressing a bar for food with its response rate rising or falling depending on whether it receives food or not. That example can be more readily applied to categorisation than the exemplar above. This point suggests that great care needs to be taken in selecting very typical exemplars that students can readily apply.

### Teaching an idealisation

A modification of the best-example procedure is to use it to teach an idealisation, which is a set of characteristic features not present in any actual instance. An idealised case can be presented and illustrated with exemplars and non-exemplars, and students are taught to use this case to categorise stimuli. The procedure is otherwise the same as for teaching a highly typical exemplar.

For example, if teaching the concept of *lonely person*, the students are taught the 18 features of the prototype, and then exemplars and non-exemplars are presented so that they can categorise by reference to the idealisation. The teacher could point out that the concept is an abstraction and that various people will have differing numbers of these features. No one is likely to have them all. The student can conclude that a given person falls into the category if he has a certain number of such features.

This basic approach has been used to teach some concepts in certain disciplines for many years. Sociology teachers often present an 'ideal type', which is a kind of prototype that defines a category. Students learn the ideal type and then are shown some exemplars that have varying numbers of its features. A first example is *bureaucracy*. Many civil services, corporations, church organisations and charities fall into this category. Max Weber, who coined the term, originally listed five characteristic features. A lesson that teaches the concept as a prototype might go as follows, as adapted from an introductory sociology text (Rose *et al*, 1976):

> *Definition*: A bureaucracy is a formal organisation which has clearly defined tasks assigned to positions in an explicit hierarchy of authority.
> *The prototype has five characteristic features*
> 1.  Bureaucracies are organised into clearly defined offices, each of which has defined tasks. People perform their job according to its defined roles.
> 2.  Lines of authority are clearly defined from top to bottom. Ultimate authority rests at the top.
> 3.  Personnel are selected according to merit and training.
> 4.  Rules specify how the job is carried out. For example, a passport is issued according to such criteria as citizenship rather than looks or wealth.
> 5.  Promotion is made on merit, seniority or examination performance.

No organisation is likely to have all these features. For instance, informal leaders often develop who give guidance outside the formal hierarchy. Workers often use unofficial channels to get things done, and factors other than merit often enter into promotions. The teacher should stress these points and then present exemplars of bureaucratic and non-bureaucratic organisations. He can point out that a certain number of such features makes a given organisation an instance, and that typicality is likely to be correlated with the number of characteristic features an instance has.

Coordinate concepts can also be taught as idealisations. The teacher presents two prototypes and then asks students to practise categorising various stimuli as exemplars of one concept or the other. He might also point out that, if coordinates have family-resemblance structures, the border between them might be fuzzy and their exemplars might vary greatly in typicality. Placing a given stimulus in either category is a matter of matching it to the prototypes.

An example of teaching coordinate concepts from political science is *totalitarian/authoritarian society*. These concepts could be best considered as having family-resemblance structures, because it is very hard to find any defining features that all instances of either concept share (though it has been facetiously suggested that a given state is totalitarian if its régime consistently gets at least 99% of the vote). These examples of prototypes for the two concepts are adapted from an introductory political science text (Dickerson and Flanagan, 1982).

*Totalitarian state*
A state with several of the following features:
1.  A single mass political party which permeates all aspects of society.
2.  The régime has the utopian aim of remaking society on a grand scale.
3.  Domination by one all-powerful leader.
4.  Power is maintained by force.
5.  All ideas are controlled by total domination of the media.
6.  Power is maintained by secret police who act outside the legal system.
7.  Law is the tool of the state, and thus is subordinate to it.
8.  The economy is totally planned by a central authority.

No actual state has or has ever had all these features, though North Korea and the Soviet Union under Stalin's rule come close and are thus highly typical exemplars. Although the Soviet Union today probably would be considered a totalitarian state, it has only some of the above features. It lacks an all-powerful leader in the Stalinist mould. Ideas from outside do filter through via media broadcasts and underground publishing, and there is a sizeable black market. The old utopian aims of creating a 'new man' or 'classless society' also have been pretty much discredited among much of the elite. North Korea, however, has many of the features. It has an all-powerful leader, control over dissemination of ideas, etc. Hungary would be a peripheral instance, because it has few of the features of totalitarianism. Some free enterprise is allowed, there is no dominant leader, and many citizens can even leave the country.

The prototype for totalitarian society could be contrasted with that for authoritarian state, which would include the following characteristic features:

1.  No elaborate guiding ideology, or great drive to mobilise society for utopian ends.
2.  Has limited pluralism, and limited tolerance of opposition.
3.  Ill-defined but predictable limits to state power.
4.  Dominant role of the military.

Again, no state has all these features, though perhaps Chile comes close. Some of the states usually categorised as authoritarian have some of the above features and some of those of *totalitarian state* as well. For instance, Argentina from 1976–82 was ruled by the military and there were some limits to state power. However, the régime had the overriding goal of rooting out all leftist elements and it used the secret police, which operated outside the law, to do so. Similarly, Tanzania is usually considered authoritarian, but it has a powerful leader, little tolerance of dissent, and a state ideology (but one not pushed too hard).

To sum up then, each concept is better seen as an idealisation rather than a set of defining features. Concepts can be taught as coordinates, presenting the idealisations and stressing that no state will have all of them, and then students can be given practice in categorising various states by reference to the prototypes.

### When to use a best-example procedure

The obvious question is when this procedure should be used in preference to the traditional one. The question can only be answered by extensive research, but some possibilities can be suggested.

Firstly, the procedure may sometimes be useful for teaching concepts that have clear sets of defining features. An obvious case is with younger children. One might aim for an exemplar or prototype representation of concepts such as *square* and *triangle*. Children may have great trouble learning the component concepts, such as *angle, side,* and *perpendicular*, and have difficulty in using them to categorise, but they can more easily learn a prototype. Another case is when aiming for a multiple representation, which is a set of defining features and a prototype to be used for rough-and-ready categorisation. The concept of *positive reinforcement* mentioned above is one good example.

Secondly, the procedure can be used for ill-defined concepts such as those described above. Examples are various artistic and musical styles, many social science concepts, and even such medical concepts as X-ray and ECG patterns. Other examples are concepts that appear to be defined by a salient exemplar, such as *a Viet Nam, a Catch-22,* and *a thalidomide*. The exemplar could be explained in detail, and then practice in categorising stimuli could by reference to the exemplar be given. Another case is when a concept has a definition, but one so vague as to be nearly useless. Some legal concepts have this problem. In practice they are not well-defined – or the core is, but the boundaries are very unclear. They can often be defined by sets of court decisions, which can be viewed as categorisations of exemplars. Thus, a court decides if a given case is or is not an exemplar of, say, *cruel and unusual punishment, libel* or *defamation of character*. New cases are categorised by analogy to certain decisions that act as landmarks, just as a child may categorise an animal as a dog by reference to a few stored exemplars. Education, then, is in part a process of learning these important cases and how to categorise new ones by analogy to them, at least in part.

This point can be further illustrated by a legal concept called *fair use*. It pertains to how much of someone else's published work a person can copy verbatim without permission. Some uses are fair and fall into the category while others are unfair. How does one decide if a given use is fair? Some guidelines are given, which have partly been abstracted from various court cases. Some are as follows:

1.   Whether the use is for commercial or educational purposes.
2.   How much is used in relation to the whole copied work.
3.   The effect of your use on the market for the copyrighted work.
4.   An idea cannot be copyrighted, only a specific expression.
5.   The 'heart' of a work cannot be copied.

Some additional rules of thumb are also given. One is that a person can copy about 400 words without needing permission. The problem is that highly typical cases of *fair* or *unfair use* may be quite clear from the above, but many less typical cases are much harder to categorise. For instance, the distinction between educational and commercial purposes is quite hard to draw. Even a textbook publisher usually hopes to make a profit, and some advertising can be considered educational. It is also hard to decide what the 'heart' of a work actually is. An illustration of how hard the guidelines are to apply to some cases comes from a real lawsuit some years ago. A news-magazine reprinted six quotes from a book, and the book's author sued. He maintained that, though the quotes had all been made by other people and were not copyrighted by him, his selection of them was original work and should not be used without permission. (He lost.) Essentially, then, the law student is taught a series of exemplars of *fair use* and he reasons by analogy to them. Hypothetical exemplars and non-exemplars that could be used in a best-example procedure are as follows:

1.   A soap company used four bars of a popular song to advertise its new detergent. The court ruled that this use was commercial and thus was not fair.
2.   A philosophy professor made 30 copies of Chapter 10 of a well-known textbook for his course. The court ruled that the purpose was educational and was thus fair.

Here is a case that needs to be categorised by reference to exemplars:

An article in a popular educational journal used much material from a book without permission to liven up its writing.

## TEACHING CONCEPTS WITH METAPHORS AND ANALOGIES

Metaphors and analogies are important tools for all teachers. As mentioned in Chapter 4, they provide interesting ways to communicate. Just as the poet or novelist embellishes text with metaphors, so a teacher can use them to brighten written and oral instruction. In addition, they can bridge the familiar and unfamiliar, thus providing learners with a springboard to better understanding difficult concepts and schemata. They can be used along with the traditional procedure or the best-example method. One can use a metaphor to either initially define a concept or some way into a lesson to clarify difficult points. Though there is little hard evidence on the effectiveness of metaphors, some is described below.

## Using one metaphor or analogy to teach a concept

Chapter 4 gave several examples of the use of familiar concepts to help learners to understand complex, unfamiliar ones. For instance, the immune system was likened to an army defending territory and an atom was likened to a miniature solar system. Petrie (1979) has argued that a person can only learn very unfamiliar concepts by analogy to old, known ones. Indeed, the concept of a fourth spatial dimension is very hard to grasp and is usually explained by analogy to a two-dimensional flat-lander. Objects going up or down from his two-dimensional world would seem to just disappear, as objects going into a fourth spatial dimension would to us. Similarly, the current cosmological concept of a finite but unbounded four-dimensional universe is very hard to grasp. It is usually explained by analogy to a sphere, with the galaxies all on the outside surface and rushing away from each other because the 'sphere' is expanding like a balloon.

Gordon (1973) gives more examples of the use of metaphors to bridge the known and unknown and to make instruction more vivid and memorable. Sound waves can be likened to ripples in a pond. An amoeba's behaviour can be likened to the advance of an army. The nucleus corresponds to the general, the false foot to the advance guard, and the creature's method of 'eating' (surrounding its food) is like an army surrounding its enemy. He uses an exploding volcano as a vivid metaphor to help students to understand the concept of *revolution*. Pressure building up inside the volcano is likened to increasing social dissatisfaction, which grows until the pressure is so great that violence explodes and the existing order is overthrown. The volcano metaphor also helps a person to understand and better appreciate pieces of music; for example, part of Wagner's 'Tannhäuser' overture. It begins with low bass rumbles, which gradually get more intense, representing Tannhäuser's increasing dissatisfaction. The rumbles grow and grow until the music comes to a typical Wagnerian climax, analogous to the volcano exploding. Similarly, the opening strains of Wagner's opera *Das Rheingold* can be better understood and appreciated from the metaphor of the flow of a mighty river, with the appearance of the villain, Alberich, introducing discordant eddies.

Gordon suggests the use of three types of metaphor in instruction. The first type he calls 'direct analogy', which is a simple comparison of two concepts. Examples are 'A crab walks like a sneaky burglar' and 'The telephone works like the tiny bones in the inner ear'. The teacher simply takes a concept from one well-understood domain and uses it to teach another, as in all the examples given so far in this section. The second type is 'personal analogy'. Here the teacher encourages students to identify with an exemplar of a concept, to put himself into its position and try to discern what it would be like. An example he gives is, 'Be a crab and describe what it would be like'. This identification might increase the student's understanding of the crab and its life.

Gordon describes a scientist who uses this method in his field, trying to think like an electron or a light beam. Indeed, Einstein worked out much of his theory of relativity by imagining himself voyaging through the universe at the head of a beam of light. The third type is 'compressed conflict', in which two contradictory concepts are combined. An example is, 'Sellotape is imprisoned freedom'. How can something be both free and imprisoned? Well, the freedom part refers to the capacity of tape to 'heal' broken things (making them free), and the imprisoned part refers to the tape being coiled up. Gordon suggests that compressed conflict metaphors induce students to learn when they try to work out how the metaphor applies to the referent. He also suggests asking students to develop their own compressed conflict metaphors for certain objects, so that they are better motivated to learn and remember material (see Petrie, 1979).

*Effectiveness of metaphors and analogies*

How well do they actually work? Some recent studies suggest that they do indeed aid understanding and recall. Reynolds and Schwartz (1983) found that analogies improved recall of text. Shustack and Anderson (1979) asked subjects to learn brief biographies of fictional people. Some subjects learned them by analogy to famous people they already knew. Thus, a fictional Japanese politician's history might be compared to that of former US President Lyndon Johnson. The analogy improved recall of details in the biographies. The experimenters suggested that the analogies encouraged subjects to elaborate on the data in the texts, and they therefore saw more connections between details.

Mayer (1975) taught students a new programming language with a concrete 'model' of a computer, which is a set of analogies used to understand parts of it. The input window was likened to a ticket window, executive control to a shopping list, and output to a message pad. Students who were given such analogies learned the language better than those students who were not given the analogies.

Finally, Beeson (1981) used an analogy to teach the concept of *electrical circuit*. He likened a circuit to a water-pump arrangement, with various parts of the circuit corresponding to various parts of the pump set-up (see Figure 32). The battery is likened to the pump itself, the flow of water to the flow of electricity, and an on/off switch to a tap. Again, students given this analogy learned the concept better. The analogy is from Beeson and the figure is from Gagné (1985).

**Figure 32. An analogy used to teach the concept of an electrical circuit***

*Electric Circuits*

In an *electric circuit* electric charges move around the circuit. The battery supplies the energy to keep the charges moving. This movement of electric charges is called an electric current.

Here is a diagram of an electric circuit and the corresponding water circuit. We use simple symbols to stand for the parts of the electric circuit.

* This analogy is reproduced from Short, Edmund C., Knowledge Production and Utilization in Curriculum: A Special Case of the General Phenomenon. *Review of Educational Research*, Summer 1979, pp. 237–301. © 1979, American Educational Research Association, Washington DC.

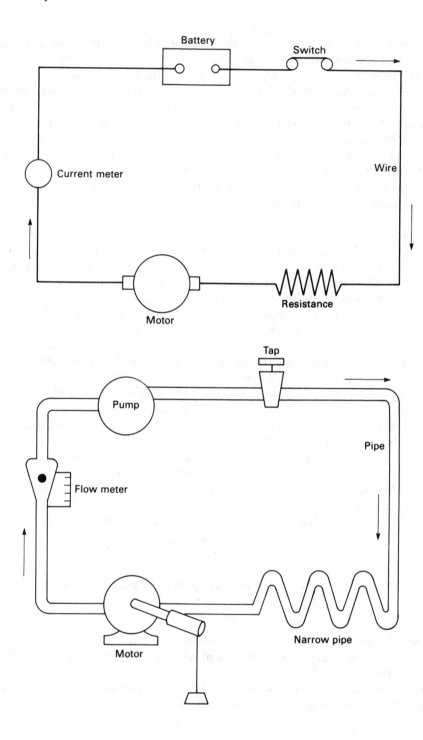

An electric circuit and the corresponding water circuit.

We can see that certain parts of the electric circuit correspond to parts of the water circuit, as follows:

| Electric circuit | | Water circuit |
|---|---|---|
| battery | corresponds to | pump |
| connecting wires | ,, | pipes |
| switch | ,, | tap |
| motor | ,, | motor |
| resistance | ,, | narrow pipe |
| electric current | ,, | flow of water |
| current meter | ,, | flow meter |

In the electric circuit we can measure the *current* in the circuit. We could also measure the *potential difference* across parts of the circuit (compare with pressure differences in a water circuit).

In both electric circuits and water circuits we could also work out the *resistance to flow* that a particular appliance caused.


**Using a cluster of metaphors**

As two of the above examples suggest, one can use a cluster of metaphors to define some complex concepts. Chapter 4 described at length Lakoff and Johnson's thesis that many complex concepts are comprehended with a series of metaphors. Thus, the concept of *mind* is understood as a container, a brittle object, a machine, etc. Otherwise, how could we teach such concepts as *infinity* and *mind*? Certainly it would be hard to draw up a set of defining features and exemplars and teach students to categorise by reference to the set. We can also use this technique along with the traditional procedure or best-example method when using the technique is indicated.

A good illustration of this technique is given by Rumelhart and Norman (1981) – teaching how to use a computer text editor. They taught students to understand the unfamiliar editor by using a series of analogies. None by itself was perfect, but each covered some aspect of the editor. Consider the following:

1. *The text editor is like a secretary.*
   This analogy covers some aspects of the mixing of commands and text material. But, unlike a secretary, the editor is not intelligent and understanding. It does not allow certain errors that a real secretary would remedy.
2. *The text editor is like a tape recorder.*
   Once it is in 'record' mode, it takes in every input verbatim, unlike a secretary who could distinguish between the actual text and extraneous material.
3. *The text editor is like a filing-card system.*
   Information can be removed or added, just as a card can be taken from or added to a card file.

With practice, the learner gets more adept at selecting the right analogy for a certain action.

**Requirements for effective use of metaphors and analogies**

Rumelhart and Norman (1981) suggest several. Firstly, make sure that students are indeed quite familiar with one domain. Thus, if using the metaphor 'an atom is like a solar system', make sure the students have a sound knowledge of the solar system and can readily apply that knowledge. Secondly, use a domain as similar to the unfamiliar one as possible, so most relations between the parts of one are likely to be applicable to the other as well. Thirdly, make sure that students actually understand the metaphor or analogy itself. The teacher often needs to carefully show students how an analogy applies and what parts of one domain can be carried over.

**Problems with metaphors**

Several described in Chapter 4 can arise in teaching situations.

*Reification*
An over-zealously applied metaphor may be *reified*, or treated as the thing itself rather than just an aid to understanding it. Examples given were 'the mind is a computer' and 'behavioural disorders are mental illnesses'. *Intelligence* is sometimes treated as a personal trait like height or weight, rather than as an abstraction from behaviour, which is understood by using a metaphor based on physical traits. To avoid such problems, carefully explain to students that a metaphor is being used and warn them against reification.

*Transferring incorrect features*
No metaphor fits exactly, and some fit better than others. However, students may take inappropriate parts or relations from one domain to another. For example, in the Shustack and Anderson study, subjects sometimes falsely recalled facts that were true in one biography but not present in the one they learned. Similarly, the metaphor 'an atom is a solar system' has flaws. Electrons do not rotate around the nucleus in fixed orbits, as planets revolve around the sun. An electron moves in unpredictable paths, and the physics of such movements is complex enough to give anyone a headache.

*Existing metaphors can interfere with instruction*
Rumelhart and Norman (1981) and Skemp (1971 and 1979) give examples of early metaphors or analogies interfering with later instruction. For example, many people learn fractions from an analogy to a pie. The analogy works well for adding and subtracting but not for multiplying and dividing. How does one divide one piece of pie into another? Students who stick to the pie analogy then encounter difficulties. Another example came from the text-editor study above. Some students used faulty metaphors to understand it and their error patterns were largely predictable from their metaphor. Gagné (1985) suggests that people may use an inappropriate typewriter analogy to understand a text editor, thereby overlooking the text editor's memory system, which a typewriter, of course, lacks. Students, therefore, often need to be convinced that they must abandon inappropriate metaphors for better ones.

## CONCEPT MAPPING

As we saw in Chapter 5, concepts are usually linked together within various structures, such as taxonomies and partonomies. Chapter 5 also described two ways of representing the maze of relations between concepts. A technique called 'concept mapping' uses notation systems to represent the structure of some domain to be taught or learned. Concept mapping has been widely applied in education (e.g. Novak and Gowin, 1984; Stuart, 1985).

The basic method is as follows. Firstly, take the major concepts in a domain and simply draw a map, linking the concept nodes with labelled pointers, such as 'is a', 'has a' and whatever other relations exist between them. Indeed, the taxonomies in Chapter 1 are essentially concept maps with the concepts connected by an unlabelled 'is a' relation. Some more examples are as follows. Figure 33 illustrates a concept map for *food chain*. Component concepts include *producer, consumer* and *omnivore*. Note the wide variety of relations, such as 'are eaten by', 'used by', 'broken down by', etc. Figure 34 illustrates a concept map of knowledge about the oceans, which was constructed by some students from pages of a science textbook. Any domain can be represented as such; it is thus made more comprehensible. It is simply a matter of labelling the important concepts and their relations. The amount of detail in the map depends on the intended use.

Here are some possible uses of the technique, mostly derived from Novak and Gowin (1984), Sutton (1980), Preece (1978) and Gagné (1985). They can be divided into uses for the teacher and uses for the student.

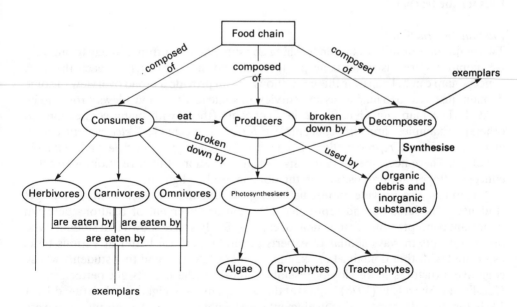

**Figure 33.** A sample concept map. The component concepts are represented by nodes and are linked in a variety of ways to form a conceptual structure for food chain. From Novak, J. D. and Gowin, D. B. *Learning how to learn*. New York: Cambridge University Press, 1984. Reproduced with permission.

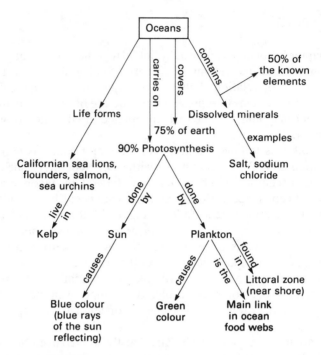

**Figure 34.** A concept map. From Novak, J. D. and Gowin, D. B. *Learning how to learn*. New York: Cambridge University Press, 1984. Reproduced with permission.

### Uses for the teacher

*Planning instruction*

Two major questions to ask when teaching any subject matter from ecology to auditory psychophysics are just what concepts to teach and in what order to teach them. A concept map can help answer these questions. It can provide a broad overview of some domain, just as a road map gives an overview of some territory and allows a route to be plotted. The map can identify the key concepts (those with many connections to others). Examples are the concepts of *force* in mechanics, *electric current* in electromagnetism, *representation* in cognitive psychology, and *role* and *status* in sociology. These need special emphasis and an exposition of their relations with other concepts. Important propositions in the domain are highlighted.

A map can also provide an instructional goal. One aim of teachers may be to get students to understand and reproduce a certain arrangement of relations between important concepts – the arrangement of experts. Studies have shown that students who order concepts in ways similar to experts generally perform better at various tasks associated with that domain. For example, Fenker (1975) found that students whose cognitive structures more closely resembled those of the experts got better grades. Geeslin and Shavelson (1975) looked at the concept maps of eighth graders (aged 12 or 13) before and after instruction in elementary probability. The concepts involved were *probability, event, independent, trial* and a few others that were related in certain ways. Overall, the organisation of their knowledge after instruction was closer to that of the experts and those students whose knowledge most closely resembled that of the experts achieved better test results.

### To diagnose what students already know

Ausubel's principle of determining what a student already knows and teaching from that point was mentioned earlier. Asking students to draw a concept map can help to determine just what they do know about some domain and what therefore needs to be taught. If a student draws a map with key concepts or relations missing, then these need to be dealt with. If students do not connect two sets of related concepts (say *plant* and *animal* taxonomies), then the teacher can focus on their relationship. Indeed, students often do report that concept maps help them to link concepts, because they make clear the need to relate new and old knowledge. The method also makes teachers aware of the vast differences in the maps of each student and that they, therefore, have to adapt instruction to an individual's cognitive structure.

### To evaluate instruction

As mentioned in the last chapter, evaluation provides feedback on a teacher's method of instruction as well as providing a means of assessing and grading students. One way of evaluating instruction is to ask students to draw maps at various points of the lesson. Examine these maps and see if the students' concept organisations grow closer to those of the experts. Are important links that were previously missing now present? Are various misconceptions still there? If the structure hardly changes, then the methods of instruction need to be examined to see why this is so. Instruction can be evaluated in two major ways. The first way is to give students a set of unlinked concepts in some domain to relate, and the second way is to give them one important concept (e.g. *force*, *life*, *ecosystem*) and ask them to draw a map from it, adding concepts and links that they themselves know.

## Uses for the students

Novak and Gowin (1984) suggest several. The first is similar to that for the teacher. A map helps to represent some complex domain and thus helps a student to make better sense of it. Such a map can thus help a student to write a paper, study for an exam, or provide a schema to relate course material to. A map also can force students to think through their ideas and make gaps in their knowledge and their understanding clear.

How should concept mapping be introduced to students? Novak and Gowin suggest several methods. The first, and perhaps the best, is to teach them the concept of concept. Discuss why concepts are important and illustrate the notion with 10–12 familiar nouns and verbs, pointing out that they represent categories. Then ask students to connect these concepts in a map, adding any other concepts that they think of themselves, appropriately labelling relations between them. Then ask them to draw a concept map of a domain of special interest, such as music or football. Secondly, ask the students to read a few pages from a standard textbook and then draw a map of the important concepts discussed in it, as in Figure 34. Students should draw at least two maps of each domain, because the first is usually flawed. However, they are usually loath to draw three. Novak *et al* (1983) suggest that students as young as seventh graders (aged 11 or 12 years) can be profitably taught concept mapping.

**Dangers in using concept maps**

Avoid two possible pitfalls. First of all, make sure that the students actually connect the concept map to the real world (Driver and Erickson, 1983). A student may be able to draw an internally-consistent expert-like map but not really understand how to use it. Thus a student may acquire models of the atom or the food chain but not know what to do with them. Secondly, make sure that students understand the concepts and the relations between them. Students may simply rote-learn all the material and produce a list-like map (Stuart, 1985).

## ENSURING THAT CONCEPTS ARE WELL-RETAINED

This final section looks at the question of how to ensure that concepts are well-retained. How can a teacher improve the likelihood that students will retain what they have acquired? There are two general approaches to meeting this goal. The first involves the teacher presenting material so that it is memorable. Some suggestions made so far include presenting material so that it can be readily assimilated into students' existing schemata (also see Chapter 11), to use metaphors and analogies to make material more vivid and comprehensible, and to use highly typical exemplars. It is also useful to use a lot of examples from many realms to illustrate various points.

The second approach is to teach students some general learning strategies, which are methods of acquiring any meaningful material (e.g. Pressley *et al*, 1982). Some standard mnemonic devices have been known for centuries (see Howe, 1984), and are taught in countless articles, books and memory-improvement courses. Three general strategies are elaboration, organisation and imagery, which are described below.

**Elaboration**

To elaborate is to add to. A person elaborates a plan by putting in more details and contingencies and elaborates a pattern by making it more complex. As a memory strategy, elaboration can be defined as adding facts to material at the time of learning (Reder, 1982). Many studies have suggested that getting students to so elaborate can aid both learning and retention (Howe, 1984; Gagné, 1985). Encourage students to think about the material, rework it, and connect it to other areas of their knowledge. Ask them to draw pictures of aspects of the material they are learning, summarise part of a text in their own words, or give their own definitions and exemplars of particular concepts. If, for instance, we were teaching the concept of *a skewed distribution* in statistics (where most instances occur at one end of the scale), the students should be asked to produce their own exemplars of such distributions. Metaphors may improve memory, partly because they induce students to think more about the material in order to understand the metaphor, as does producing their own metaphors. We can also ask students to make inferences from the material. For example, if teaching the concept of *revolution*, ask them which nations are likely candidates for future revolutions and why, or if their own nation has ever had one. Ask about revolutions in social and technological spheres and ask how a new concept relates to other concepts.

## Organisation

Organised material is generally much easier to learn and recall. Indeed, schemata promote learning and retention, partly because they enable people to impose an organisation on the material. It is often useful to encourage students to impose organisations on material they are learning. Indeed, many do so spontaneously, and the use of such strategies increases as people get older (Gagné, 1985). The simplest kind of study that demonstrates the effects of organisation on recall usually provides subjects with a set of words to learn. A sample list is: horse, apple, car, paper, truck, wolf, Beethoven, peach, pair. When asked to recall the list, people usually do so not in the order in which the words were presented but according to category membership. Thus, a person might recall the fruits first, then the animals and then the vehicles. A category organisation is therefore imposed on the list. Analogies and concept maps also might promote retention, partly because they organise material.

There are a variety of organisational devices students can use. Here are two simple ones.

### Using narratives
A simple device is to put information into an easily-recalled story. If we had to learn the words in the list above, we could proceed by making up a story that included all the words. We would therefore be imposing an organisation on them. We could then remember the story rather than a random list of words.

### Using chunking
Chunking is the organisation of material into larger units. A simple example is as follows. If a person had to remember the following digits: 3—6—5—5—2—1—9, rather than remembering seven separate pieces of information, he could combine them into three units. The numbers 3—6—5 could be combined to 365, the number of days in the year, 5—2 as 52, the number of weeks, and 1—9 as 19, perhaps his current age. In Chapter 3, we saw how a chessmaster has much better recall of piece formations, because he can chunk piece placements into larger units of information.

## Imagery

Imagery can greatly improve memory, and children as young as five and six can be profitably taught imagery strategies (Pressley *et al*, 1982). Indeed, most training programmes that promise a 'photographic' or 'super-power' memory generally teach imagery strategies. A simple demonstration of the power of imagery is a study by Bower (1972). Subjects learned sets of paired associates (e.g. horse–kettle; car–house). One group was instructed to create a mental image that linked the two words in each pair. Thus, when given horse–kettle, a person might visualise a kettle riding a horse. Subjects who were instructed to use imagery recalled many more pairs than those who were not instructed. Luria (1968) reports a case of a man whose imagery was so vivid that he found it hard to forget anything. The teacher can use this device to encourage students to visualise exemplars or prototypes of important concepts.

*The keyword technique*

This method is a specific imagery strategy that can help students to associate a concept and its name. It is derived from foreign-language instruction, but it can be applied to teaching English vocabulary (e.g. Levin *et al*, 1982). They report that schoolteachers like the method. Sweeny and Bellezza (1982) suggest that it is used to teach scientific terminology. Here is an example of the procedure from Levin *et al*.

The use of the keyword technique is quite simple, though it means a little more work in preparing vocabulary items. Start with a new word and its definition. Then take a familiar word that sounds like the first one, and that has one or two of the first syllables of the word to be taught. For example:

| | |
|---|---|
| carline | car |
| poteen | pot |
| persuade | purse |

The students are then instructed to form an image that involves the referent of the keyword (the second word) and the meaning of the first. For example, 'carline' above means 'old woman' and we could visualise an old woman driving a car. 'Poteen' is an Irish whiskey, which we could imagine in a pot. For 'persuade', we could imagine two women looking at a purse, one trying to induce the other to buy it. The new word is thus connected to its definition by two links. One is *imaginal* and the other is *phonetic*. The keyword technique greatly improves retention.


FURTHER READING

Basic level categories and typicality: Mervis (1980).
The best-example procedure: Tennyson *et al* (1981).
Metaphors and teaching: Gordon (1973), Petrie (1979).
Concept mapping: Novak and Gowin (1984).
Mnemonic devices: Howe (1984).

# Chapter 11

# Schemata and Teaching

SUMMARY

1. The notion of schema when applied to teaching suggests a number of ways to improve instruction.
2. New material taught needs to be consistent with students' existing schemata to be understood and retained. One way to make material consistent is to use an advance-organiser, which either elicits an existing schema or provides a new one. Instruction should also be sequenced so that students have the schemata needed to understand material at progressively more advanced levels.
3. Students can be directly taught certain abstract schemata to improve comprehension and memory for many kinds of material. Some examples are schemata for scientific theories, change and various types of text.
4. Students cannot readily acquire some concepts through the traditional or best-example procedures, because they are too discrepant from existing schemata. These 'misconceptions' also greatly interfere with later instruction, making much of it incomprehensible. Such schemata must be directly confronted using a procedure that induces cognitive conflict and accommodation.

## INTRODUCTION

Learning a new concept may allow us to look at the world in a different way and perhaps behave more adaptively. This chapter suggests some ways in which holding the concept of *schema* may alter the way we look at both learning and classroom interactions, and perhaps allow us to improve instruction as a result. Research on schemata has been recently applied to many areas of education, but space permits just a sampling and a discussion of some important aspects. The application is also quite new and not yet rigorously tested.

This chapter is organised as follows. Firstly, some main characteristics of schemata are reviewed. Then follows a discussion of some general applications to teaching. These include planning and organising instruction and classroom interactions. The rest of the chapter examines the direct teaching of certain schemata in two situations. The first is the value of teaching students a certain schema that they can use to better comprehend and recall certain classes of information. The schema taught in such situations is unlikely to greatly conflict with any existing schemata that students hold and so can be readily learned. The second situation is when a new schema does greatly conflict with a student's existing one, which indeed occurs with much instruction. A special teaching procedure is needed to deal with this problem, and one is described in detail.

**Some main points about schemata**

Here is a summary of some important characteristics of schemata as discussed in Chapter 3. A schema is a mental representation of some aspect of the world. It has slots that are related to each other in prescribed ways and that are filled by stimuli to create an instantiation of the schema. Schemata are used in perception, comprehension, learning, remembering and problem-solving. They can be acquired from instances, words, or through metaphors, and may evolve. Finally, people may greatly resist efforts to change their existing schemata. Discrepant data may be ignored, compartmentalised, or only partially absorbed, which means that the schema is changed in idiosyncratic ways.

## SOME GENERAL APPLICATIONS TO TEACHING

**Planning and organising a course**

The most general point to keep in mind is to relate information taught to students' existing schemata, or to teach them schemata that they can use to assimilate new material. Material that cannot be readily assimilated will be poorly understood and poorly retained (Skemp, 1979). Students who cannot apply a given schema may just learn by rote or opt out of the learning situation in some way. Therefore, structure material as closely as possible to students' existing frameworks, or teach them a broad framework that they can hang new material on.

Too often this basic principle is not followed. Everyone has experienced a poorly organised course or textbook that seems to start in mid-air. The learner discovers little on how the topics or chapters relate, which parts are important and which are mere detail, and how the whole course or book relates to anything else he knows. I took various undergraduate courses, which were taught in such a fragmented way, and have tried to read many difficult textbooks. In some courses, a series of topics was presented with no indication of how they fitted together, what researchers in the field concerned were trying to find out, and why the area was worth studying. Some textbooks in the behavioural sciences are particularly guilty of this sin, and the average reader gets little notion of what the field is all about. Glass *et al* (1979) in their foreword mention this problem when describing the stock organisational devices of many experimental psychology textbooks,

> Lengthy descriptions of the procedures and results of specific experiments are grouped so that one type of paradigm follows another. Our experience has been that students find such texts exceedingly dull, for the good reason that the point of all the experiments is seldom clear.
>
> Glass *et al* (1979)

Presentation may be fragmented for several reasons. Firstly, teachers and textbook writers may erroneously assume that students have the appropriate schemata or can readily link the topics themselves. Secondly, teachers and textbook writers may not think through to the foundations of their field fully, or are not very interested in starting at the very beginning and moving from there. The moral is to structure a course so that topics cohere, students can see how they cohere and how the material relates to other areas, and why the field exists at all. In a science course, the fundamental questions that researchers in the field are trying to answer form one basis of organisation. Efforts to answer these questions provide a framework from which most of the material taught can be understood. When using such a device, present the basic questions in some detail and explain why they are worth answering. Other frameworks are possible, of course. Basic principles can be taught by organising them around their applications, for instance.

A closely related point was made in Chapter 1. The goal of much instruction is not to impart a set of poorly organised facts about some domain, but to teach concepts and schemata. These allow students to look at the world in a different way, to make better sense of it, to readily understand and retain new material, and to solve problems. A course should therefore emphasise basic concepts and schemata and how to use them. A basic goal of education is to teach a wide variety of schemata, some means of relating them to the world, and how and when to use particular ones (Calfee, 1981).

## Advance-organisers

An advance-organiser provides a framework that students can relate new material to (Ausubel, 1968). An organiser can bridge the known and unknown, which means that certain information is easier to understand and recall. Advance-organisers can be verbal or visual. Two major types are as follows.

### An organiser which activates an existing framework
The simplest kind is one that activates a known framework that a learner can then use to assimilate new material. A prototypical example is the 'washing clothes' passage on page 39. Without a title, the material was incomprehensible. The title activated a person's schema of *washing clothes* and that framework allowed the material to be assimilated. Also, the headings in textbooks can be regarded as organisers, because they give clues to the information to follow. The metaphors and analogies discussed in Chapter 10 can also serve as this type of organiser. Thus, the metaphor 'A revolution is an exploding volcano' gives a framework on which to hang data about political revolutions. The water-pump analogy provides a framework on which material about the electrical circuit can be organised. In Chapter 4, an analogy to the boundaries between nations was made as an organiser for material on boundaries between concepts.

Keep the following points in mind when using this method. Pick an organising framework that learners know well, that maps onto the target body of knowledge in as many respects as possible, that is actually elicited, and that the learners are induced to actually use.

### An organiser which provides a new framework
Often, the learners have no schema to organise new material and so one must be provided. A prototypical example is the balloon passage in Chapter 3 on page 40. The

passage again makes little sense, because we cannot readily relate it to a schema. However, the illustration of the amplifier suspended by balloons in Figure 9 gives such a schema. The illustration can thus be seen as providing an organisational framework. Another such organiser is a concept map showing the pattern of relationships between concepts that are to be taught.

Ausubel proposed giving abstract verbal information as an organisational framework, which relates the main concepts taught in a body of material. It summarises the main propositions in the material to follow. The summaries at the start of each chapter in this book are examples.

### *When to use advance-organisers*

They take a lot of time to write or construct and may not always be useful. They are most likely to be useful when very new or difficult material is introduced. Mayer (1979) gives a checklist of points to note when using an advance-organiser. Firstly, ensure that the organiser allows the learner to see the important logical relations between concepts in the new material. Secondly, ensure that it does actually bridge the gap between the familiar and unfamiliar. Can the learner readily connect the new material and the organiser? Thirdly, make sure the organiser is easy to learn and use. Fourthly, use one only when sure that the learners would not normally use their own frameworks. Mayer further suggests that they are likely to be most useful in science and mathematics instruction.

## Classroom interaction between teacher and students

A little-developed but promising application of the schema notion is in understanding what goes on in a classroom from the teacher's and the students' viewpoints. Teachers and curriculum developers often have one set of schemata that relate various lessons and the material within a given lesson and therefore provide a rationale for the teacher's classroom behaviour. But students may hold a quite different set of schemata and interpret many events quite differently. They may not see links between lessons, or the reasons for particular laboratory exercises, and may come to quite unintended conclusions. One aspect of this problem is covered in the final section.

An interesting study that underlines the importance of understanding both the teacher's and the student's existing schemata was carried out by Tasker (1981). Though he does not use the term 'schema', the notion provides a good account of his observations. He observed many science classes, which involved nine teachers and many students aged between 11 and 14 years. He also interviewed both students and teachers during lessons. He examined how teachers and students perceived the tasks set, how the tasks were actually carried out, and how each saw the significance of results of laboratory experiments performed in the classroom.

They seemed to assimilate classroom experiences quite differently. Also, the teachers were often quite unaware of the students' existing schemata and their differing interpretations. Firstly, students often saw lessons as isolated events, not linking them to previous work. For example, one lesson was the third of a series on the particle model of matter. The teacher saw it as a direct follow-on, concerning the contraction and expansion of substances, but the students lacked an appropriate schema and saw it differently:

Observer: 'What was today's one all about?'
Student: 'What crystals can do . . . we get a card every so often . . . and we copy from the card. Do an experiment maybe, with crystals . . .'
Observer: 'Does today's lesson have anything to do with the other work?'
Student: 'No, not really . . . no.'

Tasker (1981)

The practical implication reiterates a point made earlier. The teacher needed here to use advance-organisers or more instruction to get students to link up the topics. Students' schemata need to be activated to increase the chances that new material is assimilated to them.

Secondly, the students often saw a lesson's purpose as quite different from the teacher's purpose. The students' main purposes were 'getting the right answer' or 'following instructions' rather than observing a certain phenomenon or learning a new concept. Again, more explicit instruction in the reasons for classroom actions was needed here, which requires relating activities to schemata.

Thirdly, students doing an experiment were often unclear as to what results to expect, as they again lacked the appropriate schema. In many cases, the teachers did not recognise this problem. They rarely fully explained the nature of the experiment done and what students should look for. Fourthly, the students often did not relate classroom experiences to the outside world, a point mentioned in earlier chapters. They saw the classroom and what happened in it as quite isolated from the real world. They had one schema for classroom events and another for real world events. Data that did not readily fit their real world schema were ignored or simply consigned to a general schema for formal science learned in classrooms. Students operated on this secondary framework in class and it had little impact on their other schemata.

Osborne and Schollum (1983) discuss in detail a science lesson observed by Tasker. They highlight some very common problems it reveals, which can be summarised as a set of mismatches that greatly hinder instruction. The first is a mismatch between the students' existing schemata and those the teacher assumed they had, which meant lessons were not connected and were not related to the outside world. The second was a mismatch between a laboratory problem that the teacher wanted the students to investigate and the one they actually did investigate. When unable to understand what the teacher wanted them to do, they made up their own study from their existing schemata. The third was a mismatch between the conclusions that the teacher wanted them to draw and those they actually did draw. Despite all these mismatches, the pupils did 'cope':

> In general what we find is that pupils cope . . . if necessary they make up their own investigation, they make up their own activity, they draw their own conclusions and . . . they often further develop their own ideas.

Osborne and Schollum (1982)

The practical implication is to try to be aware of students' schemata, tailor instruction to them or provide a new schema that they can use, and ensure that tasks are understood and carried out in terms of the appropriate schemata.

## TEACHING ABSTRACT SCHEMATA

It is sometimes useful to teach students a quite abstract schema that they can use to comprehend and recall certain types of material. These schemata are usually more general than those typically taught, since they can be applied to a wide range of material types. The slots are taught, the relations between them, and examples and practice in instantiating the schema are given. Abstract schema of this type were described in Chapter 3 – text structures, such as the story schema. Often students are left to abstract the schema from instances or they get only cursory instruction. One schema that can be taught is *nation*. It has slots for type of government, population, exports, etc. Students learning about any particular nation could relate its details to their *nation* schema. Another example is *science*, with slots for subject matter, methodology, applications, etc. There are many other examples. These schemata can be distinguished from advance-organisers, though the two are clearly closely related. An advance-organiser is usually content-specific, i.e. it is used to teach a certain piece of material. These schemata are more general and more widely applicable. The story schema, for example, can be applied to a very wide range of materials. Students are also not likely to resist learning schemata in this category. They may have no existing schema for the domain, so the new schema may readily fit into what they already know. These schemata can be taught by using the best-example or traditional procedures; a definition, exemplars and non-exemplars, and practice in using them are given. Here are some examples. The first is a prototypical one.

**A schema for medical information**

Patients often have great trouble understanding and remembering medical data, and therefore may not follow their doctor's orders. One reason is that their doctor may give disorganised or incomplete data that cannot be readily assimilated. Ley (1978) suggests teaching both doctor and patient a simple schema that has slots for certain information, which are placed in a fixed order. Studies show that using this schema can improve recall. It goes as follows. The doctor says:

> 'First I am going to tell you:
> What is wrong with you.
> What tests we are going to carry out.
> What I think will happen to you.
> What treatment you will need.
> What you must do to help yourself.

Ley (1978)

After presenting this framework, the doctor fills in each slot in turn. 'First what is wrong with you . . .'

**A schema for definitions**

This can be seen as a schema for concepts. Schwartz and Raphael (1985) suggest teaching students a given schema that they can use to think about and assimilate the meanings of new words. Figure 35 presents a somewhat adapted version. It has slots for the name, a superordinate, coordinates and three exemplars. An illustration of its use they give is with the word 'sandwich'. The superordinate slot can be filled with 'food', the 'what is it like' slots with 'soup', 'steak', and 'corn chips', and the exemplar slots with 'ham sandwich', etc. They taught it to fourth-grade (aged 9 years) students in a series of lessons. The children were first told what a concept is and why concepts are important, and the idea of using strategies to learn concepts was expounded. Then the schema was shown, the slots were explained, practice in using it was given and the students were later taught to fill in the slots without actually using paper and a pencil. The experimenters are enthusiastic about the schema, but present no hard evidence for its efficacy.

A. What is it?

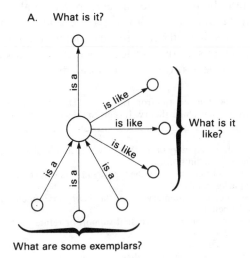

A. What is it?

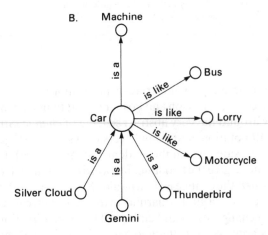

B. Machine

**Figure 35.** A schema for word definitions (A), adapted from Schwartz and Raphael (1985), and an instantiation (B) of it. Students are taught to assimilate details of new words to this schema.

## A schema for scientific theories

Scientific theories come in many sizes, fields, degrees of plausibility and degrees of complexity. Although students in every science learn a variety of different theories, they often get little explicit training in understanding scientific theories in general. Thus, they may or may not abstract their useful characteristics from the exemplars encountered. A promising counter to this problem is to teach a *scientific theory* schema that students can use to take in information about any particular theory. Brooks and Dansereau (1983) taught students a structure with six major slots, which is shown in Table 8. Students also practised using it. Thus, when reading about the big bang theory and the steady-state theories of the universe, psychoanalysis, evolution, and Marxism, material can be re-organised to fit the slots in the schema. Students who used it to read a text on plate tectonics showed better recall of details than those who did not. However, the schema took some six hours to learn, which is a possible practical drawback. It probably would only be appropriate for more advanced students.

**Table 8.** A schema for scientific theories from Brooks and Dansereau (1983). It has six slots, each of which is instantiated by details of a particular theory. It is given the acronym DICEOX to promote easy retention.

1. *Description*. A short summary of the theory, which should include (a) phenomena (b) predictions (c) observations (d) definitions.
2. *Inventor/history*. A brief account of the theory's history, which should include (a) name(s) (b) date (c) historical background.
3. *Consequences*. A concise summary of how the theory has influenced man. This should include (a) applications (b) beliefs.
4. *Evidence*. A short summary of facts that support or refute the theory. This should include (a) experiments (b) observations.
5. *Other theories*. A concise summary of theories dealing with the same phenomena. These are usually of two types: (a) competing theories (b) similar theories.
6. *X-tra information*. An open category that should include any important information not in one of the other five DICEOX categories.

### A schema for change

This example is quite complex, but it illustrates a more ambitious use of a specific schema – to organise an entire course. Hewson and Posner (1984) taught an introductory physics course at a university around the very abstract schema of *change*. Students were taught the schema in ELINOR notation, and a simple version is shown in Figure 36. The concept node is linked to various slots, which the student instantiates with various stimuli. For instance, the slots $X_i$ and $X_f$ give the two states involved in a change. If one instantiates the schema with *boiling water*, the change is from liquid ($X_i$) to gas ($X_f$). The 'is caused by' slot is filled with 'heat'. The schema guides learning in that a student can ask what is changing and what is not, when change starts and ends, and in which direction change goes. For instance, consider its application to *fading jeans*. The colour is changing rather than 'jeanness'. The beginning is dark blue and the end is white.

Students used the change schema to develop a coherent view of the topics covered. Some of their comments after the course are worth noting. Hewson and Posner describe two undoubtedly extreme cases. One student found the schema helpful, because it enabled him to organise the course material and relate it to the world. It also gave him a framework for understanding various laboratory classes, 'When you don't know what is happening, you know where to begin. You ask what is changing, what is causing the change.' But a second student found the schema unhelpful. She seemed little interested in organising the course material and may not have used the schema to

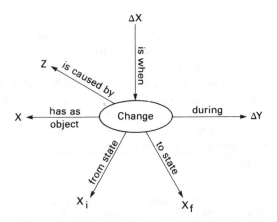

**Figure 36.** A schema for *change* used by Hewson, P. W. and Posner, G. J. The use of schema theory in the design of instructional materials: a physics example. *Instructional Science* **13**, 1984. Reproduced with permission.

do so. These reports seem to be tapping different *learning styles* (Entwhistle, 1981), which are related to the cognitive styles described in Chapter 7. Students differ in the extent to which they organise material. Those with a *holist* learning style look at an entire area, using analogies and other means to try to connect the material with what else they know. Those with a *serialist* style do not, and they are more likely to learn by rote. It seems likely that an abstract schema would be more useful for holists, because they aim for knowledge of a broad framework.

## Schemata for text

Much of what a student acquires is from textbooks and they become more important as the educational ladder is ascended. Text is usually organised in certain ways. A prototypical example is the written story, which is usually structured so that it has a setting, a development, episodes, etc. Other text structures, which were mentioned in Chapter 3, are for letters and newspaper and scientific reports.

There is a burgeoning literature on text structures and ways of training students to identify and use them (e.g. Mandl *et al*, 1984). The basic idea is to teach a student various text structures as sets of slots and to train him to identify and use a given text's structure or to assimilate poorly written material to one of his own schemata. Such training often improves both comprehension and recall. Here are some examples.

### Teaching a story schema
Fitzgerald and Spiegel (1983) studied some fourth-grade students (aged 9 or 10 years) who lacked a strong story schema. They were taught one as follows. The slots for setting, development, etc. were explained and illustrated with numerous examples. The students were then shown how each slot related to the others (e.g. how resolution related to development in a certain way). Then they practised using the schema, reading parts of stories and trying to predict what would happen next. They also read whole stories and identified the parts, and re-ordered scrambled stories. This training did indeed improve their subsequent understanding of stories.

*Teaching schemata for reports*

Barnett (1984) taught university students schemata for scientific and news reports. As mentioned in Chapter 3, a scientific report consists of four main slots, each of which contains certain data about the reported study. Table 9 presents an example. The news report is typically structured as an inverted pyramid. The first sentence summarises the event reported, and more and more detail is added in subsequent paragraphs. All too often such structures are not directly taught and students have to abstract them from exemplars. Barnett taught these schemata as sets of interrelated slots and trained students to assimilate material in specific reports to them. Such training did indeed improve recall and comprehension.

**Table 9.** A schema for scientific reports. Adapted from Barnett J. E., Facilitating retention through instruction about text structure. *Journal of Reading Behaviour* **16**: 1–13, 1984. Reproduced with permission.

---

*Outline for a Research Report*

Introduction
    Rationale for the study
    Review of related literature
    Hypothesis
Methods section
    Participants
    Materials
    Procedures
Results
Discussion
    Summary
    Interpretation and integration
    Implications

Communication of research findings to other members of the scientific community is an important task for researchers. To aid such communication, a set of rules that govern the organisation of research reports has evolved. Any reader familiar with this structure can use it to read any report.

Research reports are organised into four major sections: an introduction, a method section, the results and a discussion. Each is explained in detail below.

The introduction gives the background needed to understand the experiment. It is divided into three unlabelled sections. The first defines key concepts and explains why the experiment was actually done. The rationale often is posed as a question or explains the problem the research hopes to solve. The second section of the introduction reviews the findings of past research on related topics. Since research is often designed to test a theory, the section may explain what theory is being tested. The final section states the author's hypotheses, which are statements of the outcome he hopes to observe.

The method section gives precise details about how the experiment was carried out. Another researcher should be able to replicate the experiment from the information given. The section has three parts. The first explains who took part in the experiment. The number of subjects should be listed. The second part describes the materials, such as the room, equipment and any tests used. Finally, the procedure part gives a step-by-step account of exactly what happened during the course of the experiment.

The third section summarises the results of the experiment. The results are described in words, and usually statistics, diagrams and tables are included to help the reader understand the outcome of the experiment.

The final section is a discussion of the experiment. This part often begins with a summary of the purpose and outcome of the experiment, or an evaluation of hypotheses given at the end of the introduction. The discussion then focuses on interpretation of the results – explaining what they mean. The results need to be integrated with those of other experiments, explaining why they contradict other studies, how the research helps to evaluate a given theory or change a theory. Finally, a last segment may explain the implications of the findings for therapy, education, or business and industry.

---

An additional important use of such schemata is that one need not read all of a report in order to find certain information. I rarely read every word of a scientific report unless dubious about the study. I generally just read the abstract and, if interested, part of the introduction (if necessary) and glance at the tables and figures and read the discussion.

*Teaching schemata for instructional text*

The above are relatively simple text structures. Textbooks usually rely on a number of complex structures to present information. Some textbooks are also quite poorly organised, making it difficult to extract their message. An approach to dealing with instructional text is to teach students the various structures used, how to identify the ones a specific book is using, how to find the important information, and how to use structures they know to re-organise poorly written text. Below are a few examples of this approach (see Mandl *et al*, 1984; Burnes, 1985 for further details).

Students are first taught that they need to look for 'macropropositions'. These are the main points of a text – the superordinate ideas. Below these come supporting details and then specific details. Students often focus on the wrong parts, the details, rather than the macropropositions. They miss the important points and may just read what is familiar. Good texts often explicitly state the main propositions, or they can be readily inferred from headings or summaries. Students also need to monitor their comprehension. They often do not know when they are not understanding a text.

Meyer (1975 and 1984) points out that authors use stock devices that give clues to the macropropositions. One common one is problem/solution. A problem is stated and then the solution to it given (as in the start of the first chapter of this book). Another is comparison/relationship, which elaborates on the similarities and differences between two topics. Thus, a text might say 'Theory 1 proposes a, b, and c, while Theory 2 proposes a, disputes b, and is not applicable to c.' An antecedent/consequent relationship organisation shows a causal relationship between topics (e.g. 'If you fail to fill your car with oil, then the engine will seize up.'). Students are taught to identify such devices, hunt for key words that signal which one is being used, and use the structure to identify main ideas.

*How to teach text schemata*

They can be taught as any concept. Teach the parts as features, show how the slots relate, give exemplars and non-exemplars to illustrate the schema and for practice, and give practice in re-organising poorly written material in terms of schemata.

## CHANGING STUDENTS' EXISTING SCHEMATA

Much instruction aims at teaching a new schema to students who have a competing schema that they are loath to give up. Many recent studies have shown that students have their own schemata to understand particular domains that are often quite different from those of experts and their teachers. These schemata greatly resist change and make much instruction incomprehensible, because the existing schemata cannot assimilate it. Special procedures are needed to alter them. This growing area in education uses terms such as 'alternative frameworks', 'misconceptions' and 'preconceptions'. The word 'schema' is not often used, but the work can be readily translated into schematic terms. These alternative conceptions will be referred to here as 'misconceptions', as well as concepts and schemata.

## The concept of misconception

There is an apocryphal story about a government that planned to introduce daylight-saving time. It asked citizens for their views and someone strongly protested on the grounds that an extra hour of sunlight every day would fade her curtains more rapidly! She had odd notions about daylight-saving time and indeed, the power of government legislation. Her personal concept, so different from that of experts (and in fact most people), is a *misconception*. Others have been mentioned in previous chapters. Chapter 3 described the Nussbaum (1979) study, which showed that children held various misconceptions of the Earth as a cosmic body. Indeed, a standard device in a lecture is to present some early and once widely held schemata in that subject. With present-day knowledge, such misconceptions seem quaint and, when the audience stops chuckling, it wonders how anyone ever could have held them. Thus, chemists talk about the early concept of *combustion* as involving 'phlogiston'. Very combustible materials, such as wood, had a lot of phlogiston, while non-combustible ones had little. Burning was the loss of phlogiston to the air. Astronomers discuss the *ether* – a mysterious substance once thought to permeate the cosmos. It provided a medium in which light could travel, just as a wave such as sound needs a medium like air. Neuropsychologists discuss phrenology, the 'science' of judging character from bumps on the head (which Bierce (1906) defined as 'the science of picking the pocket through the scalp').

However, such misconceptions are still very common among students and they actively resist any effort to alter them. Studies show that many believe matter to be completely solid, that gravity depends on air, and that worms are not animals. Such misconceptions have been demonstrated mainly in the sciences (Freyberg, 1985). As mentioned earlier, scientists' schemata of their field are more likely to greatly differ from the schemata of the layperson than will the schemata of the expert in a non-scientific area. It may be, however, that later research shows serious misconceptions in areas such as the humanities, law and music.

## Characteristics of misconceptions

Driver and Erickson (1983) and Fisher (1985) summarise some major characteristics. Firstly, the schemata are quite different from those held by experts in the field (the difference is the defining feature). The schema is thus less adequate, and teachers are very often unaware of them. Secondly, certain misconceptions are not completely idiosyncratic. Many children at a certain age may hold them. For instance, Nussbaum (1979) showed that many children of a certain age held a reasonably similar schema of the Earth; as a flat disc, for example. The likely reason for this commonality is that the concept arises directly from the evidence of our senses. The world is conceptualised as flat because it looks flat. Thirdly, misconceptions are very hard to change. Teaching either does not affect them or alters them in unintended ways. Again, we saw how some children integrated the idea of the Earth being round in odd ways – by making it a flat disc, for example. As also mentioned in Chapter 3, much later instruction may simply be incomprehensible, because it assumes that students hold certain schemata which they do not (Osborne and Wittrock, 1985).

A final characteristic is that the misconception may once have been held by the general population (and may still be) or by early-day experts in a given field. Again, the likely reason is that the schema derives directly from the evidence of our senses. Although some scholars had known from the time of the Ancient Greeks that the Earth was round and even how big it was, most people around AD 500 probably thought it was flat. Another example is *natural selection*. As proposed by Darwin, selection operates by differential survival. A species has a wide range of variation in inherited characters (size, speed, colour) and a particular character comes to predominate because species members with it tended to survive and reproduce while those without it did not. Yet, Brumby (1984) found that many medical students appear to hold a Lamarckian view, which predates Darwin's and is now generally discredited. Lamarck held that species change because individuals alter within their lifetimes and pass that changed trait onto offspring. When the students were asked why doctors should use antibiotics only sparingly (the reason is that continual use selects for drug-resistant bacteria and the drug will eventually become ineffective), some implied that the human body adapted to drugs rather than the bacteria. Many thought that the body was therefore the target of antibiotics. One even said that he avoided using them in case he was sick later and really needed them.

### Some examples of common misconceptions

A wide variety of studies has shown misconceptions among students in many fields (see Driver and Erickson, 1983; Gilbert and Watts, 1983). Here are some examples.

*Price*
Economists generally consider an item's price to derive from its supply and demand. Price goes up as demand increases and goes down as supply increases. Yet some first-year economics students at a university, examined by Dahlgren and Marton (1978), held a different concept. They did not generally refer to *price* as a result of supply and demand, but conceptualised it as an intrinsic property of items, like size or colour. For example, when asked what determined the price of a bun, two commented as follows:

1.  'Yes, there is a lot of stuff in it, it's the material that costs money, the wheat, flour and then to have it baked and wages . . . and . . . the costs of selling it.'
2.  'Because the producers have set a price. They have included all costs.'

Dahlgren and Marton (1978)

The authors point out that the same concept of *price* was held by early economists, is assumed in Marx's theory of labour value, and is probably that held by most people.

*Light*
A common misconception about light and vision is that one sees an object itself rather than the light reflected off it. Also, an object is typically thought to appear red because it *is* red, rather than because the red wavelengths are reflected off it. Anderson and Smith (1984) studied a fifth-grade class (aged 10 or 11 years) and the science textbook they read. They found that both expository and discovery teaching by several teachers and

even a clear exposition in the textbook had little effect on the students' misconceptions. Also, the students could not comprehend most of their textbook's discussion of light and vision, because the details could not be assimilated with their schemata.

## Matter

Nussbaum and Novick (1981) suggest that 13 and 14-year-old students cannot readily conceive of empty spaces between molecules and so find the particle model of matter very difficult to comprehend. Many conceive of matter as completely solid and assimilate the idea of it being composed of particles in odd ways. They conceive of the spaces between molecules and atoms as filled with air, dust or water. Driver (1983) describes a student who believed that these particles were embedded in an unspecified substance and that heat induced the particles themselves to expand rather than the spaces between them.

## Mass, volume and density

Hewson and Hewson (1983) looked at various schemata held by students ranging in age from 13 to 20 years. Table 10 presents the scientific definitions of these concepts and some reported misconceptions.

**Table 10.** Scientific concepts and some misconceptions of *mass, volume* and *density*, from Hewson, P. W. and Hewson, M. G. Effect of instruction using students' prior knowledge and conceptual change strategies on science learning. *Journal of Research in Science Teaching* **20,** © 1983 John Wiley & Sons Inc. Reproduced with permission.

| Scientific concept | Misconceptions |
|---|---|
| Mass is a measure of the amount of matter in an object. All matter has mass. Units of measurement are grammes and kilogrammes. | Mass/weight = heaviness. Some objects have mass/weight (brick) while others do not (pin, hair). Change shape = change mass. Mass/weight = density. |
| Volume is the amount of space occupied by matter. All matter has volume. Units of measurement are millilitres or cubic centimetres. | Volume = size or quantity. Volume = capacity. Some objects have volume (water in cup) while others do not (cup, pin). Change shape = change volume. |
| Density is the ratio of the mass per unit volume of a substance. Unit of measurement is grammes per cubic centimetre. | Density = mass/weight. Density = denseness + crowdedness. Density = packing of particles i.e. closely packed = dense loosely packed = not dense |

## Gravity

Several studies have shown misconceptions of *gravity*. A very common one is that gravity results from the Earth's atmosphere rather than its mass. In other words, gravity only occurs where there is air. For example, Kreyenberg (1974) found that many 13-year-olds believe that air causes gravitational attraction and that astronauts are therefore weightless on the Moon (sic) because it has no air. Gravity thus does not exist in space or even underwater. Some believe that gravity acts differently on objects according to their weight. They do not relate differential air resistance to the rates at which objects fall.

Some students conceive of gravity as only relevant to falling objects. Watts and Zylbersztajn (1981) found that some students regarded gravity as only operating at the maximum height of a projectile's flight, and Gunstone and White (1981) note some misconceptions held by university students when solving problems involving the gravity concept.

## Natural selection

This example was mentioned before but is worth expanding on. As well as the antibiotics problems, Brumby (1984) set students these ones:

1. Why are insecticides much less effective nowadays than when first introduced?
2. If a white couple moved to Africa, what would happen to the skin colour of a child born to them there?

As mentioned, some responses revealed a Lamarckian view. Some students said the above child would be slightly darker at birth, and that insects become more immune to insecticides rather than those insects with an inborn resistance becoming more numerous.

## Life

Studies suggest that children have many misconceptions about life but, in many cases, the problem seems to be boundaries that are too narrow (see Chapter 4). Piaget (1929) asked children of varying ages if certain objects were alive. The children had various notions. Very young ones saw movement as a defining feature. Anything that moved was alive, which included fire. Older ones saw only things that moved by themselves as alive, such as the sun and rivers. From about the age of 11, only plants and animals were categorised as alive.

Tamir *et al* (1981) looked also at criteria children have for life. The subjects were aged in grades 5 to 7 (aged 10–14 years). Many believed that plants and animals were different kinds of life, and some thought seeds were not alive but later grew into something living. Movement and growth were the most common criteria for life.

Brumby (1982) looked at the concepts of life held by an older group – first year biology students at a university. They were given various problems involving the concept to be solved, and their schemata were inferred from their answers. Some questions were:

1. To a small child, fire seems alive. Why? Why do you feel fire is not alive?
2. How would you determine if there were life on Mars if you arrived in a spaceship?

Students tended to answer by referring to seven textbook criteria for life, such as growth, respiration, and locomotion. Few mentioned the DNA molecule or the importance of energy transformation. Brumby suggests that most of the students did not have a well-developed concept and had just rote-learned the textbook characteristics.

However, this study has some difficulties and it is not clear just what it reveals. *Life* is a very tricky concept. Biologists do not agree on its definition. The 'life on Mars' question is also tricky. Scientists much debated what life-seeking experiments to put on the Viking landers that arrived on Mars in 1976, and those that were sent yielded results that were very hard to interpret. Brumby also does not allow for extraterrestrial life forms based on quite different chemicals (such as silicon) and processes, which some students may have. The study suggests another point that will be taken up later.

*Other misconceptions*
Pervasive misconceptions have been found with many other concepts. Examples are *electricity, heat, energy,* and *force* (Gilbert and Watts, 1983; Osborne and Freyberg, 1985), *amino acid translation* in molecular biology (Fisher, 1985), and *food web* (Griffiths and Grant, 1985).

## Some reasons why misconceptions occur

Why do these misconceptions occur and why do students resist instruction to change them? Here are some possible reasons.

*The schemata are still evolving*
As noted in Chapter 8, acquiring an adequate concept may take much time, acquisition of a great deal of background knowledge, and reorganisation of people's existing schemata. A concept may thus take a long time to evolve. Conceptual change is often quite difficult as well. Indeed, that appears to be the case with the complex concept of *life*, which evolves over a long period. Bell and Freyberg (1985) also suggest that the concept takes much time to evolve. Children aged between 9 and 15 years had a somewhat different concept of life than many adults. Early bases of categorisation were the presence of fur, size, and whether the creature lived on land.

*Existing schemata are seen as sufficient*
A student may see his existing schemata as adequate for his everyday purposes and consign all school-taught schemata to a separate mental compartment. For almost all everyday purposes it is more useful to see matter as completely solid or an object as having a colour. Many school-taught concepts have little intrinsic interest to many students and they may see little reason to go to the great trouble of trying to understand them. McClelland (1984) even argues that students are often not convinced that teachers have much worthwhile to offer. (Misconceptions prevail even in domains of great intrinsic interest and practical importance. Consider *sex*. Surveys consistently reveal numerous misconceptions of this topic. Teenagers and some adults commonly believe that girls cannot get pregnant the first time they have intercourse and are uncertain about fertile days in the oestral cycle and about means of contraception, even after formal instruction in the area.)

Another major reason why existing schemata are seen as sufficient is that students' experience in some domains is much more limited than that of scientists (Osborne and Wittrock, 1983 and 1985). They cannot see the full range of phenomena that need to be accounted for by a given schema and so do not need to change those they have. For example, an everyday schema of *gravity* does not have to account for frictionless situations or have to be used to plot spacecraft orbits. A child does not normally have to explain various pressure phenomena and may thus account for objects such as boards floating in water by just saying that no gravity exists in water.

*Pressure of time and work*

Some courses cover many concepts in a short time, and students may just be unable to think deeply and understand them all (Fisher, 1985). They may, therefore, resort to rote-learning simply to survive the course. Also, examinations often reward rote-learning rather than understanding and students may study simply to pass examinations. Teachers also may devote too little time to teaching understanding of material; instead they stress the memorisation of formulas, algorithms and facts.

*Them and us*

This problem is a variant of compartmentalisation. A 'them and us' attitude is quite common in social studies (Freyberg, 1985). Students may learn such concepts as *customs, traditions, rituals,* etc. but simply refuse to apply them to their own or other advanced industrial cultures. As a result, the concept is inadequate.

*Some new schemata are hard to accept*

New schemata may be hard to accept because they are just too discrepant from existing schemata and accepting them requires a major reorganisation of one's cognitive structure. For example, many people refused to accept Darwin's theory of evolution in the nineteenth century, because they saw humanity as entirely distinct from animals and the idea of species remaining the same throughout time was axiomatic. Even today, many students refuse to accept the theory because of perceived conflict with religious schemata. Anthropology students often find the concept of *cultural relativism* hard to accept. The notion that right and wrong are largely culturally dependent and that standards of behaviour are also is discrepant from the usual societal view of absolute standards of right and wrong. The notion that all scientific knowledge is provisional and should never be believed is also hard to accept. Many students prefer just to be taught 'the facts'.

Posner *et al* (1982) found that students had great trouble learning the theory of relativity, because some tenets were just too contrary to existing schemata. The ideas of space being curved and time running at different rates are just too discrepant from the fundamental assumptions we make. The philosopher Bertrand Russell (1925) summarised this problem well some sixty years ago when explaining why the theory of relativity can be so hard to understand:

> What is demanded is a change in our imaginative picture of the world – a picture which has been handed down from remote, perhaps pre-human ancestors . . . A change in our imagination is always difficult . . . The same sort of change was demanded by Copernicus, who taught that the earth is not stationary . . . Our whole conception of what exists outside us is based upon the sense of touch . . . much of what has been learned from the sense of touch was unscientific prejudice, which must be rejected if we are to have a true picture of the world . . . The theory of relativity depends, to a considerable extent, upon getting rid of notions which are useful in ordinary life . . . Circumstances on the surface of the earth, for various more or less accidental reasons, suggest conceptions which turn out to be inaccurate, although they have come to seem like necessities of thought . . . the whole notion that one is always in some definite 'place' is due to the fortunate immobility of most of the large objects on the earth's surface . . . If we were not much larger than an electron, we should not have this impression of stability, which is only due to the grossness of our senses. King's Cross, which to us looks solid, would be too vast to be conceived except by a few eccentric mathematicians . . . The world of our experience would be quite as mad as the one in which the different parts of Edinburgh go for walks in different directions.
>
> Russell (1925, Chapter 1)

Current theorising in subatomic physics is very far removed from everyday notions. Indeed, the physicist Niels Bohr once said of early quantum theory that 'Anyone who is not profoundly disturbed by it has not understood it'.

**Ways to determine students' misconceptions**

Teachers need to know what existing schemata students hold and then tailor instruction accordingly. The textbooks and curriculum materials of the future may list the common misconceptions of important concepts at various ages and what to do about them, but now some methods of determining what they are are needed. This is very important. Many teachers assume that students are empty vessels to be filled with knowledge. Practice in diagnosing misconceptions is not usually part of teacher training. But it should be. A study by Nussbaum (1981) suggests that student teachers are not very adept at such diagnosis. They could not readily detect misconceptions such as matter being completely solid, or of laws in science determining phenomena rather than merely summarising observations. Some reasons for this lack of perception mentioned by Nussbaum are worthy of note. Firstly, the misconceptions were often masked by the students' use of technical terms and their rote recitation of material. Secondly, some teachers were just too distant from the basics of their field. The idea of matter being composed of particles seemed so fundamental that the teacher trainees just did not consider that students could believe otherwise. Thirdly, a few student teachers lacked the necessary knowledge to detect them, sometimes sharing the misconception themselves.

There are a number of methods to diagnose misconceptions (e.g. Sutton, 1980). One is the clinical interview. See students individually and probe for their ideas on various topics. Another is concept mapping. Give students a set of concepts to link up. An odd pattern of relations or the lack of important connections may indicate misconceptions. A third method is to give students a series of problems as in the Brumby studies mentioned above. Carefully scrutinise their answers and the reasoning behind them for misconceptions.

A more complex method uses word association (Preece, 1978; Sutton, 1980). A particular word usually triggers off a string of associations. Thus, 'cat' may elicit such associates as 'dog', 'kitten', etc. The teacher can thus give a student a concept name and ask him to write down associates and thus tap the underlying conceptual structure. For example, Schaefer (1979) asked students to write down words that came into their minds in response to certain words. Thus, when given 'growth', a student might write down 'energy' and 'disturbance', and when given 'learning' he might write down 'memory' and 'training'. The researcher then applies statistical techniques to the data, which assess how often two particular terms are linked directly or through an intermediate word. This method is probably too cumbersome for extensive classroom use, however.

One more point may be made here, which has been mentioned earlier. Children often know a lot more than they can clearly express, and a person should not rely too much on purely verbal diagnostic techniques. Indeed, Mandler (1983) has argued that many of Piaget's studies underestimated children's abilities, because the interviews relied too much on words. Children were asked anomalous questions that they may never have thought about before (e.g. Are clouds alive?).

**Instruction to change misconceptions**

How should such misconceptions be attacked? This section describes a basic procedure that can be used when students have a schema that seems impervious to instruction with the traditional or best-example procedures. The main principle behind it derives from Piaget's notion of accommodation and Kuhn's (1962 and 1970) philosophy of science. The teacher presents *anomalies* to induce *cognitive conflict*. The students are confronted with data that their existing schemata cannot handle so that they see the need for a new schema. The specific procedure described here derives from several sources, notably Posner *et al* (1982), Hewson and Hewson (1983 and 1984) and Nussbaum and Novick (1981). Two sample lessons based on it are presented at the end of this chapter.

It should be noted that the method has not yet been widely applied and there is as yet little hard evidence for its effectiveness. Only two recent studies give evidence that a procedure based on cognitive conflict is better than other methods (Anderson and Smith, 1984; Rowell and Dawson, 1985). However, the procedure seems eminently plausible. It is closely related to attitude-change methods used by missionaries, salesmen, revolutionaries and politicians. It consists of three main phases. (A useful preliminary to Phase 1 is an open discussion with students on conceptual change in general and how difficult it can be.)

*Elicit students' existing schemata and have them examine them.* The first step is to get students to verbalise or map their existing schemata and then study them. Their views will be the starting point of instruction. They can be elicited in a number of ways in a classroom situation. Have a general class discussion and write down various students' schemata on the blackboard. Conduct a Socratic dialogue, posing various problems and asking a variety of questions. Try to distil their answers to one or two schemata if possible and then ask students if these are indeed what they hold. If students do insist on different views, put them all on the board. It is important to be non-judgmental at this point. Encourage a free expression of opinions in an atmosphere in which students are not afraid to be wrong. Be non-committal about each view shown, just giving the usual responses, such as 'That's interesting', etc.

After the views are listed, if desired, ask the students to discuss them in detail. Get them to support their own schema or point out problems with other ones. This part may help capture their attention and increase their commitment to a given schema.

*Confront students' schemata with anomalies.* Revolutionaries and union organisers often work by stirring up dissatisfaction with things as they are. They confront people with anomalies in their life situation, with contradictions that they may never even have thought about before. Thus, a Communist revolutionary may point out the great poverty of the people contrasting to the immense wealth of a few, their lack of power and few rights. The revolutionary may further say that such discrepancies are not necessarily the natural order of things, since they do not exist elsewhere. The union organiser might call attention to certain workers' lower pay, poorer working conditions and fewer fringe benefits compared to unionised colleagues. Once dissatisfaction is elicited, the targets are told that the anomalies can be resolved by a new order of things that eliminates all such contradictions – a Communist society or unionised factory.

The teacher also needs to be a revolutionary, or a troublemaker, making students dissatisfied with their current schemata by showing them anomalies the misconceptions cannot handle. The dissatisfaction may then motivate students to acquire a new schema that can resolve the contradictions. Learning some new schemata can only be considered as a revolution in everyday thinking. The notions of matter consisting of particles or the continents on floating, moving plates are indeed revolutionary. The teacher also must *persuade* and *convince*, not simply present facts.

Let us elaborate on the notion of anomaly. An anomaly is a datum that an existing schema cannot account for. Thus, the schema of the Earth as the centre of the universe met with various anomalies – with astronomical observations that did not fit it. The after-effects of natural disasters are anomalous with people's *just world* schemata (see Chapter 3). A common feature of murder mysteries is where the detective constructs a plausible schema of the crime but is dissatisfied because it cannot explain just one fact.

Anomalies fall into two basic categories (Stavy and Berkovitz, 1980). The first type is a discrepancy between a schema and an observation. Thus, a person who believes in a flat Earth when taken into space would encounter an observation inconsistent with his schema of the Earth. The second type is one between two schemata a person holds, which may be so compartmentalised that they are rarely put together. We saw earlier that students may have one mental compartment for the real world and another for the classroom. An Amazonian Indian whose schema for the world populated it with numerous spirits and demons might also hold a quite different but compartmentalised schema based on Western science. It seems certain that most of us hold various contradictory schemata for certain domains. Often, however, no problem is posed, as long as we select an appropriate schema for a given purpose. Thus, a doctor may use the Western system of medicine to treat some patients but may use other systems for other patients. Similarly, the relativity model of gravity is generally recognised as more adequate than the Newtonian model. But, Newton's one is simpler to use and is employed to calculate spacecraft orbits. Relativity only becomes more useful in certain circumstances, such as at speeds approaching that of light.

Let us now return to the teaching procedure. After the students' schemata have been elicited and discussed, confront each one with anomalies. Thus, if teaching the particle model of matter, confront students' schema of matter as one full of anomalies. Ask how matter can be compressed. If teaching the theory of plate tectonics, determine if students believe that the continents are stable. Confront this view with anomalies such as the distribution of species and the discovery of fossils in such lifeless places as the interior of Antarctica. Try to provoke their curiosity.

Here are some examples of the use of anomalies. They are sometimes used to explain the concept of *frame-of-reference* (Petrie, 1979). A teacher might put a chair on the floor and ask if it is moving. The students will typically say 'No' and an anomaly can then be introduced. Is the Earth not moving through space? Is the solar system not rotating around the centre of the galaxy? Is the galaxy not moving through space? Minstrell (1982) describes the use of anomalies to explain the concept of the *at rest* state of an object. He first elicited various views on why a book stays at rest on a table rather than falling through it. These views ranged from air pressure to there being no gravity exerted on an object located off the ground. These were then challenged by various demonstrations. The idea of there being no gravity off the ground was countered by placing the book on a bendable table, for instance. Eventually the students became convinced that some upward force was exerted on the book. Rowell and Dawson (1981) used various anomalies to teach eighth-grade children (aged 13 years) the concept of *volume of non-compressible substances*.

Such anomalies may not induce schema change unless presented under certain conditions. These are as follows.

(a)   The students must see that the datum is an anomaly. They must see that their existing schema cannot handle it. Careful explanation is often needed and the anomaly must be directly related to the schema. Often much background knowledge is needed to see that an anomaly is indeed an anomaly. For instance, Posner *et al* (1982) found that students often had trouble seeing that certain phenomena were inconsistent with Newtonian mechanics. Provide such knowledge if necessary.

(b)   The anomalies must be strongly presented. People who dearly hold a certain schema may not be encouraged to alter it unless the anomalies are so strongly presented that they cannot be ignored or dodged. An example is the survivors of the Nazi concentration camps. As mentioned in Chapter 3, many people hold a *just world* schema, built up from years of experience, which is not easily changed. The schema also provides a rationale and a 'meaning' for life. The experiences of many survivors were so strongly anomalous to their *just world* schema that they lost it. It could not account for what had happened to them, and disappeared along with their religious schema. Some could not believe that their god would allow such a thing to happen and so rejected their religion. Life thus lost its 'meaning' (Dimsdale, 1974).

(c)   Avoid possible dodges by students. Ensure that students do not escape conceptual change by one of several routes. Firstly, do not allow them to compartmentalise the anomalies. Use many examples to get them to apply what they have learned to the real world. A common dodge is: 'Science does not have anything to do with the real world'. Secondly, do not allow them to simply accept the anomalies as mysteries that do not need to be explained. Thirdly, guard against a partial accommodation, as in Nussbaum's (1979) study.

*Present a new schema that accounts for the anomalies*. The first two phases are mainly concerned with convincing students of the *need* for a new schema. Once they see that need, present a new schema, just as the revolutionary presents a revolution and a new order of society as means of resolving the contradictions in society. Present the new schema and carefully explain why it is better than the old ones, demonstrating how it can account for the anomalies.

Posner *et al* (1982) suggest that three conditions promote its acceptance. Firstly, and not too surprisingly, the new schema should be readily understandable. It needs to be intelligible and clearly explained. Use analogies and metaphors as needed. Secondly, the new schema must appear plausible. It must seem to make sense and thus not be too discrepant from what students already know. If it is, then the schema may be summarily rejected. They give two examples. Before 1900, physicists were loath to accept geologists' estimate of the Earth's age, because their model of the Sun could not explain how it could produce energy for so long. Similarly, students are reluctant to accept aspects of relativity, because they are so discrepant from everyday experience. Again, use analogies and images and other special efforts to make the new schema seem plausible. Thirdly, students should see the new schema as potentially fruitful, as having some useful applications. Thus, the teacher can explain applications of the theory of relativity in designing nuclear accelerators and calculating life expectancies of stars.

After the schema is presented, give the students a chance to consolidate the new ideas. Elaborate on them and show how the schema applies to a wide range of situations. If possible, get students to use it to solve practical problems, to apply the new schema to parts of the world and see it work.

Here are two sample lessons based on the above procedure. The first is adapted from Nussbaum and Novick (1981) and teaches the particle model of matter to seventh-grade students (aged 13 years). The second teaches the concept of *significance test* to first and second-year university students. Both have been slightly adapted to fit the above model (and so are not accurate in all details), since they are intended to illustrate it.

**Sample lesson 1** (adapted from Nussbaum and Novick, 1981 with permission)

The basic schema of *matter* held by physicists is that it is composed of tiny particles with empty spaces between them. As mentioned earlier, students often have great trouble acquiring this model. Many conceive of matter as completely solid. Therefore, their existing schemata need to be elicited, confronted with anomalies, and then the particle schema needs to be presented.

*Elicit students' existing conceptions.* The students are shown a flask containing air which is attached to a pump. Some air is pumped out of the flask and a basic problem is then set: 'Which part of the flask is left without air?' The teacher then asks the students to draw their conception of what the air would look like (by colouring it in) on the blackboard. Their responses are shown in Figure 37. The figure reveals a variety of different conceptions. Some students thought the air would sink to the bottom of the flask, leaving a vacuum at the top. Others thought the air would rise, leaving a vacuum at the bottom. The teacher gives no quality judgments at this stage. The students are then asked to give reasons for their conceptions. Why do they think the flask would look as they have drawn it when half the air has been pumped out? Some reasons given by students are shown in Figure 37.

The teacher then emphasises the diversity of views and poses the question: 'Which view is correct?' A poll reveals that drawings 1, 3, and 4 are most favoured. The common factor between these views is that the air stays in one large chunk and leaves a vacuum elsewhere. The students are separated into small groups to debate the issue. They also discuss whether the various conceptions would be consistent with various other experiments that could be done with air.

*Produce dissatisfaction by citing anomalies.* The teacher asks: 'What makes air compressible?', demonstrating that air can be compressed in a cylinder but that a liquid or solid cannot be. How can one compress part of the air in the cylinder into a space which already contains air? The teacher points out that two people cannot occupy the same space at the same time so how can some air occupy the same space as other air?

The students hunt for an explanation among the drawings.

*Present a new schema to account for the anomalies.* Only drawing 6 can readily explain the compressibility of air and the teacher shows how. The idea of air being made of small particles with spaces between them can account for compressibility by supposing

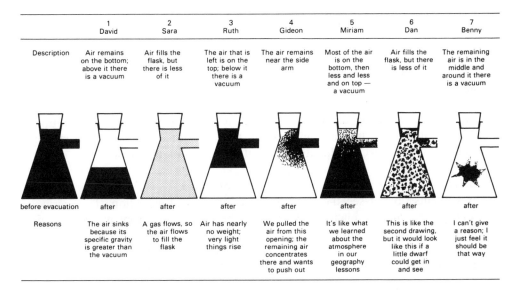

| | 1<br>David | 2<br>Sara | 3<br>Ruth | 4<br>Gideon | 5<br>Miriam | 6<br>Dan | 7<br>Benny |
|---|---|---|---|---|---|---|---|
| Description | Air remains on the bottom; above it there is a vacuum | Air fills the flask, but there is less of it | The air that is left is on the top; below it there is a vacuum | The air remains near the side arm | Most of the air is on the bottom, then less and less and on top — a vacuum | Air fills the flask, but there is less of it | The remaining air is in the middle and around it there is a vacuum |
| | before evacuation    after | after | after | after | after | after | after |
| Reasons | The air sinks because its specific gravity is greater than the vacuum | A gas flows, so the air flows to fill the flask | Air has nearly no weight; very light things rise | We pulled the air from this opening; the remaining air concentrates there and wants to push out | It's like what we learned about the atmosphere in our geography lessons | This is like the second drawing, but it would look like this if a little dwarf could get in and see | I can't give a reason; I just feel it should be that way |

**Figure 37.** The various conceptions and explanations for them given by students in the Nussbaum and Novick (1981) study. From Nussbaum and Novick (1981). Reproduced with permission.

that the particles are pushed closer together. An analogy is made to a sponge consisting of much empty space – space that can be filled with water. The teacher presses further, pointing out that the other conceptions on the board cannot readily account for compressibility or air evacuation.

The teacher can then explain the schema in detail and extend the students' understanding of it. He compresses 100 cm³ of air into a 20 cm³ (5:1) space and asks what this compressibility suggests about the amount of space taken by the particles compared to the empty spaces between them. The students suggest that the particles occupy much less space. The teacher talks about compressing the air even further and asks why the air could not be compressed to zero volume. The pupils suggest that the limit is reached when no empty space is left between the particles. The teacher could then show how the particle model accounts for a wide range of phenomena. Future lessons using the same teaching method could cover other aspects of the particle model, such as the particles being in constant motion.

## Sample lesson 2

*Significance test* is a fundamental concept in statistics and it is widely used in disciplines from psychology and education to agriculture. It has instances such as the chi-square and t-tests and the analysis of variance. Students often have great trouble acquiring the concept. They find it hard to understand what a test does and how it does it. Usually the concept is extensively taught by straight textbook and lecture exposition, but such teaching is often not very comprehensible to students. Many become quite adept at rote-learning various tests and when to use them, while having little understanding of what they are doing and why they need to do it.

My several years of teaching introductory statistics to first and second-year university students has suggested a major reason why many students have trouble. They do not see the *need* for a significance test because of two basic misconceptions. These misconceptions need to be elicited and then confronted with anomalies for the concept to make sense. The following lesson also shows the importance of teaching a basic schema of *significance test*. Specific exemplars can be acquired and better understood once this basic concept has been acquired. The following lesson is somewhat simplified and leaves out some aspects of the statistical test schema (such as a description of confidence intervals). The main aim is to illustrate the procedure of eliciting students' existing misconceptions and directly confronting them with anomalies.

*Misconception 1: you do not need a sound control group*
Many students do not see the need for a sound control condition. This pervasive misconception can be elicited by posing the following problem. Say a drug manufacturer wants to know if a new drug affects reaction-time and he does the following experiment. He tests a group of rats in a reaction-time task first without the drug and then one week later with the drug. His results are these:

| Without drug | With drug |
| --- | --- |
| Mean time = 1.92 seconds | Mean time = 1.24 seconds |

What can he conclude about the drug? Someone will say that the drug speeds up reaction-time. I ask how many agree and usually most of the class do.

This misconception is then confronted with anomalies. I point out that many factors differed between the two test conditions aside from the presence/absence of the drug. One or more of these factors may have produced the apparent difference. The rats might have become more practised at the task and therefore faster at doing it. Perhaps they were less anxious because the test situation was more familiar and they were therefore more active. Perhaps the room temperature was a lot higher on the first day and slowed them down. We cannot be certain that the drug and not something else was responsible for the apparent difference. I say that conclusions from such a paradigm are therefore quite hazardous, yet making them is a common error. A good source of examples of this mistake is the letters to the editor page in a newspaper. I then explain how this problem is often solved by having a control group and randomly assigning subjects to either it or the experimental group. That way the groups will only differ in the presence/absence of the drug. A difference in their reaction-times must then be due to the drug rather than any extraneous variable. When the students are convinced, we move to the next misconception.

*Misconception 2: any difference between means that seems sizeable shows the effect of the variable*
Students commonly believe that almost any obtained difference between the two group means shows the effect of the independent variable. This view can be elicited as follows. Say that we did the drug experiment with a control group and got these results:

| Without drug | With drug |
| --- | --- |
| Mean = 3.98 seconds | Mean = 1.68 seconds |

What can we conclude? Someone will say that the drug speeds up reaction-time and most of a now slightly suspicious class agree. Then some anomalies are introduced. The students are asked what we could conclude if we got these results instead:

| Without drug | With drug |
| --- | --- |
| Mean = 1.0000000002 seconds | Mean = 1.0000000001 seconds |

It may also help to review notions of measurement error here. Students will usually agree eventually that the tiny difference obtained cannot show the effect of the drug. The results suggest that the drug had no effect at all. Then they are induced to think about how large a gap between the obtained group mean times there needs to be before they will consider the difference to show that the drug had an effect. How about 1.0000002 and 1.0000001? How about 1.003 and 1.002? How about 1.1 and 1.0? How about 2.1 and 1.3? How big does the obtained difference have to be? Where is the cut-off point between deciding whether the drug had an effect or not? Why put the cut-off at that point? Would my cut-off point be the same as yours?

This anomaly to their conception usually induces students to see the need for some way of deciding if a given obtained difference is in fact large enough to show that the drug had an effect. I then ask what basic approach we can use. What principle can be applied? The usual response is blank faces, but the students are then ripe for acquiring the schema. I say, let us assume that the drug has no effect at all. Given that assumption, what is the likelihood that we obtained the difference in mean times that we did? If that likelihood is below a certain cut-off point (say one chance in 20) then we can accept that the drug probably had an effect. The concept of a statistical test can then be explained in detail, because the class is ready to take it in. We can also later explain that there are various types of test, the use of which depends on the nature of a person's data, and we can also describe the theoretical basis of each test. Students can use the schema to assimilate all this new information.

## FURTHER READING

Schemata and teaching in general: Skemp (1979), Anderson (1977).
Advance-organisers: Ausubel (1968), Mayer (1979).
Schemata for text: Mandl *et al* (1984).
Misconceptions: Driver (1983), Osborne and Freyberg (1985).

# References

Anderson, C. W. and Smith, E. L. (1984) Children's preconceptions and content-area textbooks. In G. G. Duffy, C. R. Roehler and J. Mason (Eds) *Comprehension instruction: perspectives and suggestions*. New York: Longman.

Anderson, J. R. (1976) *Language, memory and thought*. Hillsdale, N. J.: Erlbaum.

————— (1978) Arguments concerning representations for mental imagery. *Psychological Review* **85**: 249–277.

————— (1980) *Cognitive psychology and its implications*. San Francisco: Freeman. First edition.

————— (1985) *Cognitive psychology and its implications*. San Francisco: Freeman. Second edition.

Anderson, R. C. (1977) The notion of schemata and the educational enterprise. In R. C. Anderson, R. T. Spiro and W. E. Montague (Eds) *Schooling and the acquisition of knowledge*. Hillsdale, N. J.: Erlbaum.

Anderson, R. C. and Kulhavy, R. W. (1972) Learning concepts from definitions. *American Educational Research Journal* **9**: 385–90.

Anglin, J. M. (1977) *Word, object and conceptual development*. New York: Norton.

Armstrong, S. E., Gleitman, L. R. and Gleitman, H. (1983) What some concepts might not be. *Cognition* **13**: 263–308.

Attneave, F. (1957) Transfer of experience with a class schema to identification of patterns and shapes. *Journal of Experimental Psychology* **54**: 81–88.

Ausubel, D. P. (1968) *Educational psychology: a cognitive view*. New York: Holt, Rinehart and Winston.

Barnett, J. E. (1984) Facilitating retention through instruction about text structure. *Journal of Reading Behaviour* **16**: 1–13.

Barsalou, L. W. (1983) Ad hoc categories. *Memory and Cognition* **11**: 211–27.

————— (1985) Ideals, central tendency and frequency of instantiation as determinants of graded structure in categories. *Journal of Experimental Psychology: Learning, Memory and Cognition* **11**: 629–49.

Bartlett, F. C. (1932) *Remembering: a study in experimental and social psychology*. Cambridge: Cambridge University Press.

Beck, A. T. (1976) *Cognitive therapy and the emotional disorders*. New York: International Universities Press.

Beeson, G. W. (1981) Influence of knowledge context on the learning of intellectual skills. *American Educational Research Journal* **18**: 363–79.

Bell, B. and Freyberg, P. (1985) Language in the science classroom. In R. Osborne and P. Freyberg (Eds) *Learning in Science*. Auckland: Heinemann.

Berlin, B. (1978) Ethnobiological classification. In E. Rosch and B. B. Lloyd (Eds) *Cognition and categorisation*. Hillsdale, N. J.: Erlbaum.

Berlin, B and Kay, P. (1969) *Basic colour terms: their universality and evolution*. Berkeley: University of California Press.

Bierce, A. (1906) *The devil's dictionary*. New York: Doubleday.

Blewitt, P. (1982) Word meaning acquisition in young children: a review of theory and research. In H. W. Reese (Ed.) *Advances in child development and behaviour*. New York: Academic Press, vol. 17.

Bolton, N. (1977) *Concept formation*. Oxford: Pergamon.

Bomba, P. C. and Siqueland, E. R. (1983) The nature and structure of infant form categories. *Journal of Experimental Child Psychology* **35**: 294–328.

Borges, J. L. (1966) *Other inquisitions 1937–1952*. New York: Washington Square Press.

Bornstein, M. H. (1979) Effects of habituation experience on post-habituation behaviour in young infants-discrimination and generalisation among colours and notes. *Developmental Psychology* **15**: 348–9.

———— (1984) A descriptive taxonomy of psychological categories used by infants. In C. Sophian (Ed.) *Origins of cognitive skills*. Hillsdale, N. J.: Erlbaum.

Bower, G. H. (1972) Mental imagery and associative learning. In L. W. Gregg (Ed.) *Cognition in learning and memory*. New York: Wiley.

Bowerman, M. (1980) The structure and origin of semantic categories in the language learning child. In M. L. Foster and S. H. Brandes (Eds) *Symbol as sense*. New York: Academic Press.

Bransford, J. D. and Johnson, M. K. (1972) Contextual prerequisites for understanding: some investigations of comprehension and recall. *Journal of Verbal Learning and Verbal Behaviour* **61**: 717–26.

———— (1973) Consideration of some problems in comprehension. In W. G. Chase (Ed.) *Visual information processing*. New York: Academic Press.

Brooks, L. (1978) Non-analytic concept formation and memory for instances. In E. Rosch and B. B. Lloyd (Eds) *Cognition and Categorisation*. Hillsdale, N. J.: Erlbaum.

Brooks, L. W. and Dansereau, D. F. (1983) Effects of structural schema training and text organisation on expository prose processing. *Journal of Educational Psychology* **75**: 811–20.

Brown, R. (1958) How shall a thing be called? *Psychological Review* **65**: 12–21.

Brown, R. and McNeill, D. T. (1966) The 'tip-of-the-tongue' phenomenon. *Journal of Verbal Learning and Verbal Behaviour* **5**: 325–37.

Brumby, M. N. (1982) Students' perceptions of the concept of life. *Science Education* **66**: 613–22.

———— (1984) Misconceptions about the concept of natural selection by medical biology students. *Science Education* **68**: 493–503.

Bruner, J. S. (1966) On cognitive growth. In J. S. Bruner, R. R. Olver and P. M. Greenfield (Eds) *Studies in cognitive growth*. New York: Wiley.

Bruner, J. S. and Potter, M. C. (1964) Inference in visual recognition. *Science* **144**: 424–25.

Bruner, J. S., Goodnow, J. J. and Austin, G. A. (1956) *A study of thinking*. New York: Wiley.

Bruner, J. S., Olver, R. R. and Greenfield, P. M. (1966) *Studies in cognitive growth*. New York: Wiley.

Burnes, D. (1985) Comprehending text. In D. Burnes and G. Page (Eds) *Insights and strategies for teaching reading*. Sydney: Harcourt Brace Jovanovich.

Calfee, R. (1981) Cognitive psychology and educational practice. *Review of Research in Education* **9**: 3–73.

Cantor, N., Mischel, W. and Schwartz, J. C. (1982) A prototype analysis of psychological situations. *Cognitive Psychology* **14**: 45–77.

Cantor, N., Smith, E. E., French, R. and Mezzich, J. (1980) Psychiatric diagnosis as prototype categorisation. *Journal of Abnormal Psychology* **89**: 181–93.

Carey, S. (1982) Semantic development: the state of the art. In E. Wanner and L. R. Gleitman (Eds) *Language acquisition: the state of the art*. New York: Cambridge University Press.

———— (1983) Constraints on word meaning – natural kinds. In Th.B. Seiler and W. Wannenmacher (Eds) *Concept development and the development of word meaning*. Berlin: Springer-Verlag.

Carmichael, L. L., Hogan, H. P. and Walter, A. A. (1932) An experimental study of the effect of language on the reproduction of visually presented form. *Journal of Experimental Psychology* **15**: 73–86.

Carraher, R. G. and Thurston, J. B. (1966) *Optical illusions and the visual arts*. New York: Reinhold.

Carroll, J. B. (1964) Words, meanings and concepts. *Harvard Educational Review* **34**: 178–202.

Cearella, J. (1979) Visual classes and natural categories in the pigeon. *Journal of Experimental Psychology: Human Perception and Performance* **5**: 68–77.

Chaffin, R. and Herrmann, D. J. (1984) The similarity and diversity of semantic relations. *Memory and Cognition* **12**: 134–41.

Champagne, A. B., Klopfer, L. E., Desena, A. T. and Squires, D. A. (1981) Structural representations of students' knowledge before and after science instruction. *Journal of Research in Science Teaching* **18**: 97–111.

Chi, M. T. H., Feltovich, P. J., and Glaser, R. (1981) Categorisation and representation of physics problems by experts and novices. *Cognitive Science* **5**: 121–152.

Chiesi, H. L., Spilich, G. J. and Voss, J. F. (1979) Acquisition of domain-related information in relation to high and low domain knowledge. *Journal of Verbal Learning and Verbal Behaviour* **18**: 257–74.

Clark, D. C. (1971) Teaching concepts in the classroom: a set of prescriptions derived from experimental research. *Journal of Educational Psychology* **62**: 253–78.

Clark, E. V. (1983) Meanings and concepts. In P. H. Mussen (Ed.) *Handbook of child psychology*, vol. 3. New York: Wiley.

Clark, H. H. and Clark, E. V. (1977) *Psychology and language*. New York: Harcourt Brace Jovanovich.

Cohen, B. and Murphy, G. L. (1984) Models of concepts. *Cognitive Science* **8**: 27–58.

Cohen, G. (1983) *The psychology of cognition*. London: Academic Press. Second edition.

Cohen, L. B. and Strauss, M. S. (1979). Concept acquisition in the human infant. *Child Development* **50**: 419–24.

Collins, A. M. and Loftus, E. F. (1975) A spreading activation theory of semantic processing. *Psychological Review* **82**: 407–28.

Collins, A. M. and Quillian, M. R. (1969) Retrieval time from semantic memory. *Journal of Verbal Learning and Verbal Behaviour* **8**: 240–47.

Conrad, C. (1972) Cognitive economy in semantic memory. *Journal of Experimental Psychology* **92**: 149–54.

Dahlgren. L. O. and Marton, F. (1978) Students' conceptions of subject matter: an aspect of learning and teaching in higher education. *Studies in Higher Education* **3**: 25–35.

Deno, S. L., Jenkins, J. R. and Marsey, J. (1971) Transfer variables and sequence effects in subject-matter learning. *Journal of Educational Psychology* **62**: 365–70.

De Groot, A. D. (1965) *Thought and choice in chess*. The Hague: Mouton.

de Silva, W. A. (1979) The formation of historical concepts through contextual cues. In A. Floyd (Ed.) *Cognitive development in the school years*. London: Croom-Helm.

Dickerson, M. O. and Flanagan, T. F. (1982) *An introduction to government and politics*. Toronto: Methuen.

Dimsdale, J. E. (1974) The coping behaviour of Nazi concentration camp survivors. *American Journal of Psychiatry* **131**: 792–97.

Dougherty, J. W. D. (1978) Salience and relativity in classification. *American Ethnologist* **5**: 66–80.

Driver, R. (1983) *The pupil as scientist*. Milton Keynes: The Open University.

Driver, R. and Erickson, G. (1983) Theories-in-action: some theoretical and empirical issues in the study of students' conceptual frameworks in science. *Studies in Science Education* **10**: 37–60.

Duffelmeyer, F. A. (1985) Teaching word meaning from an experience base. *The Reading Teacher* **39**: 6–8.

Dunn, C. S. (1983) The influence of instructional methods on concept learning. *Science Education* **67**: 647–56.

Eggen, P. D., Kauchak, D. P. and Harder, R. J. (1979) *Strategies for teachers: information processing models in the classroom*. Englewood Cliffs, N. J.: Prentice-Hall.

Elio, R. and Anderson, J. R. (1981) The effects of category generalisations and instance similarity on schema abstraction. *Journal of Experimental Psychology: Human Learning and Memory* **7**: 397–417.

Ellis, H. C., Bennett, T. L., Daniel, T. C. and Rickert, E. J. (1979) *Psychology of learning and memory*. Monterey: Brooks/Cole.

Engelkamp, J. (1983) Word meaning and recognition. In Th.B. Seiler and W. Wannenmacher (Eds) *Concept development and the development of word meaning*. Berlin: Springer-Verlag.

Entwhistle, N. J. (1981) *Styles of learning and teaching*. Chichester: Wiley.

Farah, M. J. and Kosslyn, S. M. (1982) Concept development. *Child Development and Behaviour* **16**: 125–67.

Fehr, B., Russell, J. A. and Ward, L. M. (1982) Prototypicality of emotions: a reaction time study. *Bulletin of the Psychonomic Society* **20**: 253–54.

Fenker, R. M. (1975) The organisation of conceptual materials: a methodology for measuring ideal and actual cognitive structures. *Instructional Science* **4**: 33–57.

Fensham, P. J. (1983) A research base for new objectives of science teaching. *Science Education* **67**: 3–12.

Fisher, K. M. (1985) A misconception in biology: amino acids and translation. *Journal of Research in Science Teaching* **22**: 53–62.

Fitzgerald, J. and Spiegel, D. L. (1983) Enhancing children's reading comprehension through instruction in narrative structure. *Journal of Reading Behaviour* **15**: 1–17.

Flavell, J. H. (1963) *The developmental psychology of Jean Piaget*. New York: Van Nostrand Reinhold.

———— (1970) Concept development. In P. H. Mussen (Ed.) *Carmichael's manual of child psychology*, vol 1. New York: Wiley. Third Edition.

Freyberg, P. (1985) Implications across the curriculum. In R. Osborne and P. Freyberg (Eds) *Learning in Science*. Auckland: Heinemann.

Gagné, E. D. (1985) *The cognitive psychology of school learning*. Boston: Little, Brown.

Gagné, R. M. and Briggs, L. J. (1974) *Principles of instructional design*. New York: Holt, Rinehart and Winston.

Gardner, R. W. (1953) Cognitive styles in categorising behaviour. *Journal of Personality* **22**: 214–33.

Garis, L. (1975) The Margaret Mead of Madison Avenue. *Ms*, 47–48.

Geeslin, W. E. and Shavelson, R. J. (1975) Comparison of content structure and cognitive structure in high school students' learning of probability. *Journal for Research in Mathematics Education* **6**: 109–20.

Gibbons, H. (1940) The ability of college freshmen to construct the meaning of a strange word from the context in which it appears. *Journal of Experimental Education* **9**: 29–33.

Gilbert, J. K. and Watts, D. M. (1983) Concepts, misconceptions and alternative conceptions: changing perspectives in science education. *Studies in Science Education* **10**: 61–98.

Glass, A. L., Holyoak, K. J. and Santa, J. L. (1979) *Cognition*. Reading, Mass.: Addison-Wesley.

Goldman, D. and Homa, D. (1977) Integrative and metric properties of abstracted information as a function of category discriminability, instance variability and experience. *Journal of Experimental Psychology: Human Learning and Memory* **3**: 375–85.

Golinkoff, R. M. and Halperin, M. S. (1983) The concept of animal: one infant's view. *Infant Behaviour and Development* **6**: 229–33.

Gordon, W. J. J. (1973) *The metaphorical way of learning and knowing*. Cambridge, Mass.: Porpoise Books.

Gorman, R. M. (1974) *Psychology of classroom learning*. Columbus, Ohio: Merrill.

Greenberg, J. and Kuczaj, S. (1982) Toward a theory of substantive word-meaning acquisition. In S. Kuczaj (Ed.) *Language Development Volume 1: Syntax and semantics*. Hillsdale, N. J.: Erlbaum.

Griffiths, A. K. and Grant, B. A. C. (1985) High school students' understanding of food webs: identification of a learning hierarchy and related misconceptions. *Journal of Research in Science teaching* **22**: 421–36.

Gunstone, R. F. and White, R. T. (1981) Understanding of gravity. *Science Education* **65**: 291–99.

Halford, G. H. (1982) *The development of thought*. Hillsdale, N. J.: Erlbaum.

Hampton, J. A. (1979) Polymorphous concepts in semantic memory. *Journal of Verbal Learning and Verbal Behaviour* **18**: 441–61.

————— (1981) An investigation of the nature of abstract concepts. *Memory and Cognition* **9**: 149–56.

Hartley, J. and Homa, D. (1981) Abstraction of stylistic concepts. *Journal of Experimental Psychology: Human Learning and Memory* **7**: 33–46.

Hastie, R. (1981) Schematic principles in human memory. In E. T. Higgins, C. D. Herman and M. P. Zanna (Eds) *Social Cognition: the Ontario Symposium*. Hillsdale, N. J.: Erlbaum.

Herrnstein, R. J. and de Villiers, P. A. (1980) Fish as a natural category for people and pigeons. In G. H. Bower (Ed.) *Psychology of Learning and Motivation*, vol. 14. New York: Academic Press.

Herrnstein, R. J. and Loveland, D. H. (1964) Complex visual concept in the pigeon. *Science* **146**: 549–51.

Herron, J. D., Cantu, L. L., Ward, R. and Srinivasan, V. (1977) Problems associated with concept analysis. *Science Education* **61**: 185–99.

Hewson, M. G. and Hewson, P. W. (1983) Effect of instruction using students' prior knowledge and conceptual change strategies on science learning. *Journal of Research in Science Teaching* **20**: 731–43.

Hewson, P. W. and Hewson, M. G. (1984) The role of conceptual conflict in conceptual change and the design of science instruction. *Instructional Science* **13**: 1–13.

Hewson, P. W. and Posner, G. J. (1984) The use of schema theory in the design of instructional materials: a physics example. *Instructional Science* **13**: 119–39.

Homa, D. (1984) On the nature of categories. In G. H. Bower (Ed.) *The Psychology of Learning and Motivation*, vol. 18. New York: Academic Press.

Homa, D., Rhoads, D. and Chambliss, D. (1979) The evolution of conceptual structure. *Journal of Experimental Psychology: Human Learning and Memory* **5**: 11–23.

Homa, D., Sterling, S. and Trepel, L. (1981) Limitations of exemplar-based generalisation and the abstraction of categorical information. *Journal of Experimental Psychology: Human Learning and Memory* **7**: 418–39.

Honeck, R. P., Kibler, C. T. and Sugar, J. (1985) The conceptual base view of categorisation. *Journal of Psycholinguistic Research* **14**: 155–74.

Horowitz, L. M., French, R. de S., and Anderson, C. A. (1982) The prototype of a lonely person. In L. A. Peplau and D. Perlman (Eds) *Loneliness*. New York: Wiley.

Howe, M. J. A. (1984) *A teacher's guide to the psychology of learning*. Oxford: Basil Blackwell.

Hull, C. L. (1920) Quantitative aspects of the evolution of concepts. *Psychological Monographs* **28**: number 123.

James, W. (1958) *Talks to teachers*. New York: Norton.

Janis, I. L. (1965) Psychodynamic aspects of stress tolerance. In S. A. Klausner (Ed.) *The quest for self-control*. New York: The Free Press.

Johnson, D. D. and Pearson, P. D. (1978) *Teaching reading vocabulary*. New York: Holt, Rinehart and Winston.

Johnson, D. M. and Stratton, R. P. (1966) Evaluation of five methods of teaching concepts. *Journal of Educational Psychology* **57**: 48–53.

Johnson, P. E., Duran, A. S., Hassebrock, F., Moller, J., Prietula, M., Feltovich, P. J. and Swanson, D. B. (1981) Expertise and error in diagnostic reasoning. *Cognitive Science* **5**: 235–83.

Kagan, J. and Lang, C. (1978) *Psychology and education: an introduction*. New York: Harcourt Brace Jovanovich.

Keil, F. C. and Batterman, N. (1984) A characteristic-to-defining shift in the development of word meaning. *Journal of Verbal Learning and Verbal Behaviour* **23**: 221–36.

Kemler-Nelson, D. G. (1984) The effect of intention on what concepts are acquired. *Journal of Verbal Learning and Verbal Behaviour* **23**: 734–59.

Kempa, R. F. and Hodgson, G. H. (1976) Levels of concept acquisition and concept maturation in students of chemistry. *British Journal of Educational Psychology* **46**: 253–60.

Klausmeier, H. J. (1976a) Conceptual development during the school years. In J. R. Levin and V. L. Allen (Eds) *Cognitive learning in children*. New York: Academic Press.

————— (1976b) Instructional design and the teaching of concepts. In J. R. Levin and V. L. Allen (Eds) *Cognitive learning in children*. New York: Academic Press.

Klausmeier, H. J. and Sipple, T. S. (1980) *Learning and teaching concepts*. New York: Academic Press.

Klausmeier, H. J., Ghatala, E. S. and Frayer, D. A. (1974) *Conceptual learning and development: a cognitive view*. New York: Academic Press.

Kossan, N. (1981) Developmental differences in concept acquisition strategies. *Child Development* **52**: 290–98.

Kreyenberg, L. (1974) Bedingungsanalyse zum Themenbereich Raumfahrt in 8. Schuljahr der Hauptschule unter besonderer Berucksichtigung der damit verbundenen methodologischen und methodischen Probleme als Voraussetzung für eine adequate planung ven Unterricht. Ph.D. thesis, Universität der Osnabruck. (Cited by Gilbert and Watts, 1983).

Kuczaj, S. A. (1982) Acquisition of word meaning in the context of the development of the semantic system. In C. J. Brainerd and M. Pressley (Eds) *Verbal processes in children*. New York: Springer-Verlag.

Kuhn, T. S. (1962) *The structure of scientific revolutions*. Chicago: University of Chicago Press. First edition.

——— (1970) *The structure of scientific revolutions*. Chicago: University of Chicago Press. Second edition.

Labov, W. (1973) The boundaries of words and their meanings. In C.–J. N. Bailey and R. W. Shuy (Eds) *New ways of analysing variations in English*. Washington: Georgetown University Press.

Lachman, J. L. and Lachman, R. (1979) Theories of memory organisation and human evolution. In C. R. Puff (Ed.) *Memory organisation and structure*. New York: Academic Press.

Lachman, R., Lachman, J. L. and Butterfield, E. C. (1979) *Cognitive psychology and information processing: an introduction*. Hillsdale, N. J.: Erlbaum.

Lacquer, W. (1985) Is there now, or has there ever been, such a thing as totalitarianism? *Commentary* **80**: 29–35.

Lakoff, G. (1973) Hedges: a study in meaning criteria and the logic of fuzzy concepts. *Journal of Philosophical Logic* **3**: 458–508.

Lakoff, G. and Johnson, M. (1980) *Metaphors we live by*. Chicago: University of Chicago Press.

——— (1981). The metaphorical structure of the human conceptual system. In D. A. Norman (Ed.) *Perspectives in cognitive science*. Norwood, N. J.: Ablex.

Landau, B. (1982) Will the real grandmother please stand up. *Journal of Psycholinguistic Research* **11**: 47–62.

Langer, E. J. and Abelson, R. P. (1974) A patient by any other name . . . Clinician group differences in labelling bias. *Journal of Consulting and Clinical Psychology* **42**: 4–9.

Leinhardt, G. and Smith, D. A. (1985) Expertise in mathematics instruction: subject matter knowledge. *Journal of Educational Psychology* **77**: 247–71.

Levin, J. R., McCormick, C. B., Miller, G. E. and Berry, J. K. (1982) Mnemonic vs. non-mnemonic vocabulary-learning strategies for children. *American Educational Research Journal* **19**: 121–36.

Levine, M. (1975) *A cognitive theory of learning: research on hypothesis-testing*. Hillsdale, N. J.: Erlbaum.

Levine, M., Miller, P. and Steinmeyer, C. H. (1967) The none-to-all theorem of human discrimination learning. *Journal of Experimental Psychology* **73**: 568–73.

Ley, P. (1978) Memory for medical information. In M. M. Gruneberg, P. E. Morris and R. N. S. Sykes (Eds) *Practical aspects of memory*. London: Academic Press.

Loftus, E. F. (1979) *Eyewitness testimony*. Cambridge, Mass.: Harvard University Press.

Loftus, E. F. and Palmer, J. C. (1974) Reconstruction of automobile destruction: an example of the interaction between language and memory. *Journal of Verbal Learning and Verbal Behaviour* **13**: 585–89.

Lubow, R. E. (1974) Higher-order concept formation in the pigeon. *Journal of the Experimental Analysis of Behaviour* **21**: 475–83.

Luria, A. R. (1968) *The mind of a mnemonist*. New York: Basic Books.

McClelland, J. A. G. (1984) Alternative frameworks: interpretation of evidence. *European Journal of Science Education* **6**: 1–6.

McCloskey, M. E. and Glucksberg, S. (1978) Natural categories: well-defined or fuzzy sets? *Memory and Cognition* **6**, 642–72.

Macnamara, J. (1982) *Names for things*. Cambridge, Mass.: MIT Press.

Mager, R. (1962) *Preparing instructional objectives*. San Francisco: Fearon.

Malott, R. W. and Malott, R. K. (1970) Perception and stimulus generalisation. In W. C. Stebbins (Ed.) *Animal psychophysics*. New York: Appleton-Century-Crofts.

Mandl, H., Stein, N. L. and Trabasso, T. (1984) *Learning and comprehension of text*. Hillsdale, N. J.: Erlbaum.

Mandler, J. M. (1979) Categorical and schematic organisation in memory. In C. R. Puff (Ed.) *Memory organisation and structure*. New York: Academic Press.

———— (1983) Representation. In P. H. Mussen (Ed.) *Handbook of Child psychology*, vol. 3. New York: Wiley.

———— (1984) *Stories, scripts and scenes: aspects of schema theory*. Hillsdale, N. J.: Erlbaum.

Markle, S. M. and Tiemann, P. W. (1969) *Really understanding concepts*. Champaign, Ill.: Stipes.

Markman, E. M. (1983) Two different kinds of hierarchical organisation. In E. F. Scholnick (Ed.) *New trends in conceptual representation: challenges to Piaget's theory?* Hillsdale, N. J.: Erlbaum.

———— (1984). The acquisition and hierarchical organisation of categories by children. In C. Sophian (Ed.) *Origins of cognitive skills*. Hillsdale, N. J.: Erlbaum.

Martin, R. C. and Caramazza, A. (1980) Classification in well-defined and ill-defined categories: evidence for common processing strategies. *Journal of Experimental Psychology: General* **109**: 320–53.

Mayer, R. E. (1975) Different problem-solving competencies established in learning computer programming with and without meaningful models. *Journal of Educational Psychology* **67**: 725–34.

———— (1979) Can advance-organisers influence meaningful learning? *Review of Educational Research* **49**: 371–83.

———— (1981) Frequency norms and structural analysis of algebra story problems into families, categories and templates. *Instructional Science* **10**: 135–75.

———— (1983a) *Thinking, problem-solving, cognition*. San Francisco: Freeman.

———— (1983b) What have we learned about increasing the meaningfulness of science prose? *Science Education* **67**: 223–37.

Medin, D. L. (1983) Structural principles of categorisation. In T. J. Tighe and B. E. Shepp (Eds) *Perception, cognition and development: an interactional analysis*. Hillsdale, N. J.: Erlbaum.

Medin, D. L. and Schaffer, M. M. (1978) Context theory of classification learning. *Psychological Review* **85**: 207–38.

Medin, D. L. and Smith, E. E. (1984) Concepts and concept formation. *Annual Review of Psychology* **35**: 113–38.

Medin, D. L., Altom, M. W. and Murphy, T. D. (1984) Given versus induced category representations: use of prototype and exemplar information in classification. *Journal of Experimental Psychology: Learning, Memory and Cognition* **10**: 333–52.

Merrill, M. D. and Tennyson, R. D. (1977) *Concept teaching: an instructional design guide*. Englewood Cliffs, N. J.: Educational Technology.

Mervis, C. B. (1980) Category structure and the development of categorisation. In R. Spiro, B. C. Bruce and W. F. Brewer (Eds) *Theoretical issues in reading comprehension*. Hillsdale, N. J.: Erlbaum.

Mervis, C. B. and Pani, J. R. (1980) Acquisition of basic object categories. *Cognitive Psychology* **12**: 496–522.

Mervis, C. B. and Rosch, E. (1981) Categorisation of natural objects. *Annual Review of Psychology* **32**: 89–115.

Messick, S. (1976) Personality consistencies in cognition and creativity. In S. Messick (Ed.) *Individuality in learning*. San Francisco: Jossey-Bass.

Meyer, B. J. F. (1975) *The organisation of prose and its effects on memory*. New York: American Elsevier.

———— (1984) Organisational aspects of text: effects on reading comprehension and applications for the classroom. In J. Flood (Ed.) *Promoting reading comprehension*. Newark, Del.: International Reading Association.

Meyer, D. E. and Schaneveldt, R. W. (1971) Facilitation in recognising pairs of words: evidence of a dependence between retrieval operations. *Journal of Experimental Psychology* **90**: 227–34.

Millward, R. B. (1980) Models of concept formation. In R. E. Snow, P. Federico and W. E. Montague (Eds) *Aptitude, learning and instruction: cognitive process analyses of learning and problem solving*. Hillsdale, N. J.: Erlbaum.

Minstrell, J. (1982) Explaining the 'at rest' condition of an object. *The Physics Teacher* **20**: 10–14.

Muensterburg, H. (1908) *On the witness stand*. New York: McClure.

Murphy, G. L. and Smith, E. E. (1982) Basic-level superiority in picture categorisation. *Journal of Verbal Learning and Verbal Behaviour* **21**: 1–20.

Murphy, G. L. and Wright, J. C. (1984) Changes in conceptual structure with expertise: differences between real-world experts and novices. *Journal of Experimental Psychology: Learning, Memory, and Cognition* **10**: 144–55.

Nebelkopf, E. B. and Dreyer, A. S. (1973) Continuous– non-continuous concept attainment as a function of individual differences in cognitive style. *Perceptual and Motor Skills* **36**: 655–62.

Neisser, U. (1967) *Cognitive psychology*. New York: Appleton-Century-Crofts.

Norman, D. A. (1982) *Learning and memory*. San Francisco: Freeman.

Norman, D. A. and Rumelhart, D. E. (1975) *Explorations in cognition*. San Francisco: Freeman.

Novak, J. D. and Gowin, D. B. (1984) *Learning how to learn*. New York: Cambridge University Press.

Novak, J. D., Gowin, D. B. and Johansen, G. T. (1983) The use of concept mapping and knowledge vee mapping with junior high school teachers. *Science Education* **67**: 625–45.

Nussbaum, J. (1979) Childrens' conceptions of the Earth as a cosmic body: a cross age study. *Science Education* **63**: 83–93.

——— (1981) Towards the diagnosis by science teachers of pupils' misconceptions: an exercise with student teachers. *European Journal of Science Education* **3**: 159–69.

Nussbaum, J. and Novick, S. (1981) Brainstorming in the classroom to invent a model: a case study. *School Science Review* **62**: 771–78.

Olson, D. (1970) Language and thought: aspects of a cognitive theory of semantics. *Psychological Review* **77**: 257–73.

Ortony, A. (1980) Metaphor. In R. J. Spiro, B. C. Bruce and W. F. Brewer (Eds) *Theoretical issues in reading comprehension*. Hillsdale, N. J.: Erlbaum.

Ortony, A., Reynolds, R. E. and Arter, J. A. (1978) Metaphor: theoretical and empirical research. *Psychological Bulletin* **85**: 919–43.

Orwell, G. (1933). *Down and out in Paris and London*. London: Gollancz.

Osborne, R. and Freyberg, P. (1985) *Learning in science*. Auckland: Heinemann.

Osborne, R. and Schollum, B. (1983) Coping in chemistry. *Australian Science Teachers Journal* **29**: 13–24.

Osborne, R. and Wittrock, M. C. (1983) Learning science: a generative process. *Science Education* **67**: 489–508.

——— (1985) The generative learning model and its implications. *Studies in Science Education* **12**: 59–87.

Osherson, D. N. and Smith, E. E. (1982) Gradedness and conceptual combination. *Cognition* **12**: 299–318.

Palermo, D. S. (1982) Theoretical issues in semantic development. In S. Kuczaj (Ed.) *Language development vol. 1: syntax and semantics*. Hillsdale, N. J.: Erlbaum.

Palmer, S. E. (1978) Fundamental aspects of cognitive representation. In E. Rosch and B. B. Lloyd, (Eds) *Cognition and categorisation*. Hillsdale, N. J.: Erlbaum.

Park, O. (1984) Example comparison strategy versus attribute identification strategy in concept learning. *American Educational Research Journal* **21**: 145–62.

Petrie, H. G. (1979) Metaphor and learning. In A. Ortony (Ed.) *Metaphor and thought*. New York: Cambridge University Press.

Piaget, J. (1929) *The child's conception of the world*. London: Paladin.

Pichert, J. W. and Anderson, R. C. (1977) Taking different perspectives on a story. *American Educational Research Journal* **69**: 309–15.

Pines, A. L. and Leith, S. (1981) What is concept learning in science? *Australian Science Teachers Journal* **27**: 15–20.

Posner, G. J., Strike, K. A., Hewson, P. W. and Gertzog, W. A. (1982) Accommodation of a scientific conception: toward a theory of conceptual change. *Science Education* **66**: 211–27.

Posner, M. I. (1973) *Cognition: an introduction*. Glenview, Ill.: Scott, Foresman.

Posner, M. I. and Keele, S. W. (1968). On the genesis of abstract ideas. *Journal of Experimental Psychology* **77**: 353–63.

———— (1970) Retention of abstract ideas. *Journal of Experimental Psychology* **83**: 304–8.

Preece, P. F. W. (1978) Exploration of semantic space: review of research on the organisation of scientific concepts in semantic memory. *Science Education* **62**: 547–62.

———— (1984) Intuitive science – learned or triggered? *European Journal of Science Education* **6**: 7–10.

Pressley, M., Heisel, B. E., McCormick, C. B. and Nakamura, G. V. (1982) Memory strategy instruction with children. In C. J. Brainerd and M. Pressley (Eds) *Verbal processes in children*. New York: Springer-Verlag.

Pulman, S. G. (1983) *Word meaning and belief*. Norwood, N. J.: Ablex.

Quine, W. V. O. (1960) *Word and object*. Cambridge, Mass.: MIT Press.

———— (1977) Natural kinds. In S. P. Schwartz (Ed.) *Naming, necessity and natural kinds*. Ithaca, N. Y.: Cornell University Press.

Reder, L. M. (1982) Elaborations: when do they help and when do they hurt? *Text* **2**: 211–24.

Reed, S. K. (1972) Pattern recognition and categorisation. *Cognitive Psychology* **3**: 382–407.

Rey, G. (1983) Concepts and stereotypes. *Cognition* **15**: 237–62.

Reynolds, R. E. and Schwartz, R. M. (1983) Relation of metaphoric processing to comprehension and memory. *Journal of Educational Psychology* **75**: 450–59.

Riley, D. A. (1968) *Discrimination learning*. Boston: Allyn and Bacon.

Riley, D. A. and Lamb, M. R. (1979) Stimulus generalisation. In D. Pick (Ed.) *Perception and its development*. Hillsdale, N. J.: Erlbaum.

Rips, L. J., Shoben, E. J. and Smith, E. E. (1973) Semantic distance and the verification of semantic relations. *Journal of Verbal Learning and Verbal Behaviour* **12**: 1–20.

Rosch, E. (1973) On the internal structure of perceptual and semantic categories. In T. E. Moore (Ed.) *Cognitive development and the acquisition of language*. New York: Academic Press.

———— (1975) Cognitive representations of semantic categories. *Journal of Experimental Psychology: General* **104**: 192–233.

———— (1978) Principles of categorisation. In E. Rosch and B. B. Lloyd (Eds) *Cognition and categorisation* Hillsdale, N. J.: Erlbaum.

Rosch, E. and Mervis, C. B. (1975) Family resemblance: studies in the internal structure of categories. *Cognitive Psychology* **7**: 573–605.

Rosch, E., Mervis, C. B., Gray, W. D., Johnson, D. M. and Boyes-Braem, P. (1976) Basic objects in natural categories. *Cognitive Psychology* **8**: 382–439.

Rose, P. L., Glazer, M. and Glazer, P. M. (1976) *Sociology: inquiring into society*. San Francisco: Canfield Press.

Rowell, J. A. and Dawson, C. J. (1981) Volume, conservation and instruction: a classroom based Solomon four group study of conflict. *Journal of Research in Science Teaching* **18**: 533–46.

———— (1985) Equilibration, conflict and instruction: a new class-oriented perspective. *European Journal of Science Education* **7**: 331–44.

Rumelhart, D. E. (1980) Schemata: the building blocks of cognition. In R. J. Spiro, B. C. Bruce and W. F. Brewer (Eds) *Theoretical issues in reading comprehension*. Hillsdale, N. J.: Erlbaum.

———— (1984) Understanding understanding. In J. Flood (Ed.) *Comprehension*. Newark, Del.: International Reading Association.

Rumelhart, D. E. and Norman, D. A. (1981) Analogical processes in learning. In J. R. Anderson (Ed.) *Cognitive skills and their acquisition*. Hillsdale, N. J.: Erlbaum.

Rumelhart, D. E. and Ortony, A. (1977) The representation of knowledge in memory. In R. C. Anderson, R. J. Spiro and W. E. Montague (Eds) *Schooling and the acquisition of knowledge*. Hillsdale, N. J.: Erlbaum.

Russell, B. (1925) *ABC of relativity*. London: Allen and Unwin. (Fourth edition published 1985).

Schaefer, G. (1979) Concept formation in biology: the concept 'growth'. *European Journal of Science Education* **1**: 87–101.

Schank, R. C. and Abelson, R. P. (1977) *Scripts, plans, goals and understanding*. Hillsdale, N. J.: Erlbaum.

Scholnick, E. F. (1983) *New trends in conceptual representation: challenges to Piaget's theory?* Hillsdale, N. J.: Erlbaum.

Schwartz, B. (1984) *Psychology of learning and behaviour*. New York: Norton. Second edition.

Schwartz, R. M. and Raphael, T. E. (1985) Concept of definition: a key to improving students' vocabulary. *The Reading Teacher*: 198–205.

Seligman, M. E. P. (1970) On the generality of laws of learning. *Psychological Review* **77**: 406–18.

Serra, M. C. (1953) How to develop concepts and their verbal representations. *The Elementary School Journal* **53**: 275–85.

Shavelson, R. J. (1972) Some aspects of the correspondence between content structure and cognitive structure in physics instruction. *Journal of Educational Psychology* **63**: 225–34.

Shoben, E. J. (1980) Theories of semantic memory. In R. J. Spiro, B. C. Bruce and W. F. Brewer (Eds) *Theoretical issues in reading comprehension*. Hillsdale, N. J.: Erlbaum.

Shustack, M. W. and Anderson, J. R. (1979) Effects of analogy to prior knowledge on memory for new information. *Journal of Verbal Learning and Verbal Behaviour* **18**: 565–83.

Skemp, R. R. (1971) *The psychology of learning mathematics*. Harmondsworth: Penguin.

———— (1979) *Intelligence, learning and action*. Chichester: Wiley.

Sigel, I. E. (1983) Is the concept of concept still elusive or what do we know about conceptual development? In E. K. Scholnick (Ed.) *New trends in conceptual representation: challenges to Piaget's Theory?* Hillsdale, N. J.: Erlbaum.

Silver, R. L. and Wortman, C. B. (1980) Coping with undesirable life events. In J. Garber and M. E. P. Seligman (Eds) *Human helplessness*. New York: Academic Press.

Smith, E. E. (1978) Theories of semantic memory. In W. K. Estes (Ed.) *Handbook of learning and cognitive processes*, vol. 6. Hillsdale, N. J.: Erlbaum.

Smith, E. E. and Medin, D. L. (1981) *Categories and concepts*. Cambridge, Mass.: Harvard University Press.

Sokal, R. R. (1974) Classification: purposes, principles, progress, prospects. *Science* **185**: 1115–23.

Sowder, L. (1980) Concept and principle learning. In R. J. Shumway (Ed.) *Research in mathematics education*. Reston, Virg.: National Council of Teachers of Mathematics.

Spiker, C. C. and Kantor, J. H. (1979) Factors affecting hypothesis testing in kindergarten children. *Journal of Experimental Child Psychology* **28**: 230–48.

Spiro, R. J. (1977) Remembering information from text: the 'state of schema' approach. In R. C. Anderson, R. J. Spiro and W. E. Montague (Eds) *Schooling and the acquisition of knowledge*. Hillsdale, N. J.: Erlbaum.

Stasz, C. (1974) Field independence and the structuring of knowledge in a social studies minicourse. Masters thesis, Rutgers University.

Stasz, C., Shavelson, R. J., Cox, D. L. and Moore, C. A. (1976) Field independence and the structuring of knowledge in a social studies minicourse. *Journal of Educational Psychology* **68**: 550–58.

Stavy, R. and Berkovitz, B. (1980) Cognitive conflict as a basis for teaching quantitative aspects of the concept of temperature. *Science Education* **64**: 679–92.

Stokes, T. F. and Baer, D. M. (1977) An implicit technology of generalisation. *Journal of Applied Behaviour Analysis* **10**: 349–67.

Stones, E. (1984) *Psychology of Education*. London: Methuen.

Strauss, M. S. (1979) Abstraction of prototypical information by adults and 10-month-old infants. *Journal of Experimental Psychology: Human Learning and Memory* **5**: 618–32.

Stuart, H. A. (1985) Should concept maps be scored numerically? *European Journal of Science Education* **7**: 73–81.

Sutton, C. R. (1980) The learner's prior knowledge: a critical review of techniques for probing its organisation. *European Journal of Science Education* **2**: 107–20.

Sweeny, C. A. and Bellezza, F. S. (1982) Use of the keyword mnemonic in learning English vocabulary. *Human Learning* **1**: 155–63.

Szasz, T. S. (1974) *The myth of mental illness*. New York: Harper and Row. Second edition.

Tamir, P., Gal-Choppin, R. and Nussinovitz, R. (1981) How do intermediate and junior high school students conceptualise living and non-living? *Journal of Research in Science Teaching* **18**: 241–8.

Tasker, R. (1981) Children's views and classroom experiences. *Australian Science Teachers Journal* **27**: 33–37.

Taylor, S. E. and Crocker, J. (1981) Schematic bases of social information processing. In E. T. Higgins, C. D. Herman and M. P. Zanna (Eds) *Social cognition: the Ontario symposium.* Hillsdale, N. J.: Erlbaum.

Tennyson, R. D. and Park, O. (1980) The teaching of concepts: a review of instructional design research literature. *Review of Educational Research* **50**: 55–70.

Tennyson, R. D., Chao, J. N. and Youngers, J. (1981) Concept learning effectiveness using prototype and skill development presentation forms. *Journal of Educational Psychology* **73**: 326–34.

Tennyson, R. D., Youngers, J. and Suebsonthi, P. (1983) Concept learning by children using instructional presentation forms for prototype formation and classification-skill development. *Journal of Educational Psychology* **75**: 280–91.

Thorndyke, P. W. (1977) Cognitive structures in comprehension and memory in narrative discourse. *Cognitive Psychology* **9**: 77–110.

Thorndyke, P. W. and Yekovich, F. R. (1980) A critique of schemata as a theory of human story memory. *Poetics* **9**: 25–50.

Tulving, E. (1972) Episodic and semantic memory. In E. Tulving and W. Donaldson (Eds) *Organisation of memory.* New York: Academic Press.

———— (1985) How many memory systems are there? *American Psychologist* **40**: 385–98.

Tumblin, A. and Gholson, B. (1981) Hypothesis theory and the development of conceptual learning. *Psychological Review* **90**: 102–4.

Tversky, B. (1985) Development of taxonomic organisation of named and pictured categories. *Developmental Psychology* **21**: 1111–19.

Tversky, B. and Hemenway, K. (1983) Categories of environmental scenes. *Cognitive Psychology* **15**: 121–49.

Vygotsky, L. S. (1962) *Thought and language.* Cambridge, Mass.: MIT Press.

Wang, M. C. and Lindvall, C. M. (1984) Individual differences and school learning environments. *Review of Research in Education* **11**: 161–225.

Watts, D. M. and Zylbersztajn, A. (1981) A survey of some children's ideas about force. *Physics Education* **15**: 360–65.

Werner, H. and Kaplan, E. (1950) The acquisition of word meanings: a developmental study. *Monographs of the Society for Research in Child Development* **15**: number 51.

Wessells, M. G. (1982) *Cognitive psychology.* New York: Harper and Row.

Wicklegren, W. A. (1976) Network strength theory of storage and retrieval dynamics. *Psychological Review*, 1976, **83**: 466–78.

———— (1979) *Cognitive psychology.* Englewood Cliffs, N. J.: Prentice-Hall.

Wittgenstein, L. (1953) *Philosophical investigations.* New York: Macmillan.

Woolfolk, A. E. and McCune-Nicolich, L. (1984) *Educational psychology for teachers.* Englewood Cliffs, N. J.: Prentice-Hall.

Zadeh, L. S. (1965) Fuzzy sets. *Information and control* **8**: 338–75.

# Name Index

Anderson, C. W.  137, 187, 193
Anderson, J. R.  9, 47, 48, 82, 90, 104, 112, 134, 165, 168
Anderson, R. C.  38, 39, 114, 130, 199
Anglin, J. M.  4, 5, 6, 16, 55, 91, 92, 106, 125, 131
Armstrong, S. E.  59, 92, 104
Attneave, F.  93, 112
Ausubel, D. P.  13, 16, 57, 76, 108, 113, 130, 131, 134, 145, 156, 171, 177, 178, 199

Barnett, F. C.  184
Barsalou, L. W.  6, 58, 60, 62
Bartlett, F. C.  31, 47
Beck, A. T.  7
Beeson, G. W.  165
Bell, B.  123, 125, 190
Berlin, B.  13, 59, 63, 96, 99
Bierce, A.  68, 186
Blewitt, P.  132
Bolton, N.  16, 109
Bomba, P. C.  130
Borges, J. L.  14
Bornstein, M. H.  130
Bower, G. H.  173
Bowerman, M.  112, 131
Bransford, J. D.  40, 41
Brooks, L.  100, 101, 105, 106
Brooks, L. W.  182
Brown, R.  53, 75
Brumby, M. N.  187, 189, 190
Bruner, J. S.  16, 29, 39, 108, 110, 118, 135, 154
Burnes, D.  185

Calfee, R.  177
Cantor, N.  54, 98, 112, 158
Carraher, R. G.  38
Carella, J.  3
Carey, S.  19, 111, 120
Carmichael, L. L.  44
Carroll, J. B.  17, 18, 21, 23, 29, 71, 108, 121, 137, 138

Carter, Jimmy  68–9
Chaffin, R.  80
Champagne, A. B.  128
Chi, M. T. H.  12, 26
Chiesi, H. L.  45
Chomsky, N.  28
Clark, D. C.  136, 137, 140, 143, 146
Clark, E. V.  6, 17, 19, 124, 130, 131, 132
Clark, H. H.  19
Clarke, Arthur C.  42
Cohen, B.  85
Cohen, G.  14, 23, 24, 25, 29, 76
Cohen, J. B.  130
Collins, A. M.  78, 79, 80, 82, 84
Conrad, C.  80

Dahlgren, L. O.  187
De Groot, A. D.  45
De Silva, W. A.  113, 115
Deno, S. L.  113
Dickerson, M. O.  161
Dimsdale, J. E.  195
Dougherty, J. W. D.  57
Driver, R.  172, 186, 187, 199
Duffelmeyer, F. A.  114
Dunn, C. S.  160

Eggen, P. D.  136, 144–5
Einstein, A.  165
Elio, R.  104
Ellis, H. C.  21, 29, 111
Engelkamp, J.  19
Entwhistle, N. J.  183

Farah, M. J.  3, 6, 89, 90, 100, 103, 126
Fehr, B.  112
Fenker, R. M.  170
Fensham, P. J.  158
Fisher, K. M.  186, 191
Fitzgerald, J.  183
Flavell, J. H.  5, 47

Freyberg, P.  123, 125, 186, 190, 191, 199

Gagné, E. D.  81, 165, 168, 169, 172, 173
Gagné, R. M.  140
Gardner, R. W.  117
Garis, L.  57
Geeslin, W. E.  170
Gibbons, H.  115
Gilbert, J. K.  187, 190
Glass, A. L.  21, 86, 95, 103, 106, 113, 176
Goldman, D.  112
Golikoff, R. M.  130
Gordon, W. J. J.  164, 165, 174
Gorman, R. M.  153, 154
Greenberg, J.  112, 124
Griffiths, A. K.  190
Gunstone, R. F.  189

Halford, G. H.  6
Hampton, J. A.  92, 98
Hartley, J.  3
Hastie, R.  45, 47
Heinlein, Robert  41
Herrnstein, R. J.  3, 21
Herron, J. D.  142, 145
Hewson, P. W.  182, 188, 193
Homa, D.  3, 16, 107, 112, 121, 124, 125, 128
Honeck, R. P.  24
Horowitz, L. M.  98
Howe, M. J. A.  172, 174
Hull, C. L.  28, 109

James, W.  141
Janis, I. L.  42
Johnson, D. D.  114, 115, 121
Johnson, D. M.  114, 115, 116
Johnson, P. E.  12

Kafka, Franz  48
Kagan, J.  141

Kant, I.　31
Keil, F. C.　126
Kemler-Nelson, D. G.　103, 104
Kempa, R. F.　125
Klausmeier, H. J.　20, 91, 105, 109, 113, 115, 121, 122, 135, 136, 142, 146, 148, 149, 151, 154
Koestler, A.　18–19
Kossan, N.　102, 103
Kreyenberg, L.　188
Kubler-Ross, Elisabeth　158–9
Kuhn, T. S.　13, 51, 193

Labov, W.　21, 63, 64, 65
Lachman, J. L.　71, 76, 80, 82, 84
Lacquer, W.　158
Lakoff, G.　66, 68, 71, 72–3, 167
Landau, B.　104
Langer, E. J.　51
Leinhardt, G.　12
Levin, J. R.　174
Levine, M.　109, 110
Loftus, E. F.　44, 80, 82, 84
Lubow, R. E.　3
Luria, A. R.　173

McClelland, J. A. G.　190
McCloskey, M. E.　63
McDonald, Garry　35
Macnamara, J.　19, 29
Mager, R.　139
Malott, R. W.　3
Mandl, H.　183, 185, 199
Mandler, J. M.　15, 45, 46, 48, 49, 51, 52, 86, 130, 131, 134, 135, 192
Markle, S. M.　136, 140, 142, 143
Markman, E. M.　34, 130, 131–2
Martin, R. C.　110
Mayer, R. E.　37, 135, 154, 165, 178, 199
Medin, D. L.　8, 23, 85, 86, 91, 93, 99, 100, 102, 103, 104, 106, 112
Merrill, M. D.　91, 136, 145, 147, 154
Mervis, C. B.　4, 16, 59, 62, 73, 99, 125, 156, 157, 174
Messick, S.　116, 117, 121
Meyer, B. J. F.　185
Meyer, D. E.　82
Millward, R. B.　85, 90

Minstrell, J.　194
Muensterberg, H.　44
Murphy, G. L.　56, 85, 128

Nebelkopf, E. B.　117
Neisser, U.　63
Norman, D. A.　48, 50, 69, 83, 167, 168
Novak, J. D.　169
Nussbaum, J.　26, 42–3, 51, 123, 186, 188, 192, 193, 195, 196–7

Olson, D.　57
Ortony, A.　31, 67, 68, 69, 73
Orwell, George　97
Osborne, R.　179, 187, 190, 199
Osherson, D. N.　13

Palermo, D. S.　120
Palmer, S. E.　15, 86, 87, 90, 106
Park, O.　136, 141, 143, 144, 151, 160
Pavlov, I.　51
Petrie, H. G.　164, 165, 174, 194
Piaget, J.　16, 26, 47, 124, 125, 129, 130, 132–4, 189, 193
Pichert, J. W.　38
Pines, A. L.　8
Pohl, Frederik　42
Posner, G. J.　182, 191, 193, 195
Posner, M. I.　89, 93, 95, 112, 128
Preece, P. F. W.　120, 169, 192
Pressley, M.　172, 173
Pulman, S. G.　59

Quine, W. V. O.　119, 120, 121

Reagan, Ronald　69
Reder, L. M.　172
Reed, S. K.　96
Rey, G.　66
Reynolds, R. E.　165
Riley, D. A.　19, 100
Rips, L. J.　21
Rosch, E.　4, 13, 16, 54, 56, 57, 59, 62, 73, 80, 91, 93, 99, 121
Rose, P. L.　161
Rowell, J. A.　193, 194–5
Rumelhart, D. E.　31, 34, 37, 39, 41, 42, 44, 52, 69, 83, 167, 168
Russell, Bertrand　191

Schaefer, G.　138, 192
Schank, R. C.　47
Scholnick, E. F.　132
Schwartz, B.　118, 119, 120
Schwartz, R. M.　165, 180, 181
Seligman, M. E. P.　119
Serra, M. C.　116, 138
Shoben, E. J.　74
Shustack, M. W.　165, 168
Sigel, I. E.　5, 65, 124, 130, 131
Silver, R. L.　159
Skemp, R. R.　8, 19, 24, 40, 51, 52, 65, 108, 114, 125, 137, 138, 142, 168, 176, 199
Skinner, B. F.　154
Smith, E. E.　8, 13, 23, 56, 78, 80, 84, 85, 86, 91, 93, 99, 100, 102, 103, 104, 106
Sokal, R. R.　10
Sowder, L.　136
Spiker, C. C.　130
Spiro, R. J.　44
Stasz, C.　117
Stavy, R.　194
Stokes, T. F.　20
Stones, E.　16, 57, 113, 123
Strauss, M. S.　130
Stuart, H. A.　169, 172
Sutton, C. R.　26, 169, 192
Sweeny, C. A.　174
Szasz, T. S.　71

Tamir, P.　189
Tasker, R.　178–9
Taylor, S. E.　36, 45, 50, 52
Tennyson, R. D.　91, 136, 141, 143, 144, 145, 147, 151, 154, 159, 174
Thorndyke, P. W.　45, 48, 49
Tulving, E.　74, 77
Tumblin, A.　109
Tversky, B.　55, 112, 132

Vygotsky, L. S.　92, 124, 125, 137

Wang, M. C.　116
Watts, D. M.　187, 189, 190
Weber, Max　161
Werner, H.　115
Wessells, M. G.　44, 65, 78
Wicklegren, W. A.　25, 58, 64, 75, 82, 84, 107, 114
Wittgenstein, L.　60
Woolfolk, A. E.　145, 153

Zadeh, L. S.　64

# Subject Index

'(T)' after a page number indicates a table, '(F)' a figure

Abstract concepts, 24, 103
  and cognitive development, 134
  school taught, 137
Abstract schemata, 84
  teaching, 179–85
Abstraction
  and concept learning, 3–4, 5(F), 92, 108–9
Accommodation, 129–30
  changing misconceptions by, 193
  and cognitive development, 133
Action schemata, 47
Advance-organisers
  and abstract schemata, 180
  and schemata teaching, 177–8
Analog formats, 88–9
Analogical reasoning, 100
Analogies
  as advance-organisers, 177
  effectiveness of, 165–7(F)
  teaching concepts with, 163–9(F)
Analysis of concepts, 141–2(T)
  evaluation of, 149
Analytic formats, 88–9
Anaphoric references, 156–7
Anomalies
  changing misconceptions by, 193–5
  in schemata, 129
Archetypes, 98
Artificial concepts, 24–5
Assimilation
  and cognitive development, 133

Basic-level concepts, 53–7, 118
  educational applications, 156–7
Best-example procedures, 159–60, 162–3
  metaphors and analogies in, 164

Categories
  and concepts, 4–5
  moveable boundaries, 65–6
  unclear boundaries, 62–7(F), 92, 93, 99–100,
    102–3, 158, 162–3

Category representation, 85–106
  circumstantial differences, 105–6
  classical view of, 86, 90–3, 136, 140, 158
  exemplar view of, 86, 100–3, 125
  individual differences in, 104–5
  levels of, 105
  in memory, 15
  prototype view of, 86, 93–100(F), 102, 125,
    158
  teaching, 159–63
  types of, 86(T)
Change, schema for, 182–3(F)
Children
  concept development in, 130–2
  theories of cognitive development, 132–5
Chunking, 173
Classificatory level
  in concept learning, 105
Classroom interaction
  in schemata teaching, 178–9
Cognitive conflict
  and changing misconceptions, 193
Cognitive development
  Bruner's theory of, 135
  Piaget's theory of, 132–4
Cognitive economy, 9
  and basic-level concepts, 56
  and semantic memory, 80, 82
Cognitive structure, 11, 74
Cognitive styles, 116–18
  and learning styles, 183
Composites, 97–8
Comprehension
  and schemata, 39–43(F)
Compressed conflict
  in metaphors, 165
Concept analysis, 141–2(T)
  evaluation of, 149
Concept development, 122–35
  in children, 130–2
  and traditional teaching, 155
Concept learning, 107–21
  evaluation of, 147–50
  from instances, 108–13
  individual differences in, 116–18
  levels of, 105

Concept learning—*contd.*
    reasons for concept acquisition, 118–21
    through language, 113–16
    *see also* Teaching concepts
Concept mapping, 169–72(F)
    as advance-organisers, 178
    and misconceptions, 192
Concepts
    and abstraction, 3–4, 5(F)
    basic terms, 17–23
    basic-level, 53–7, 118, 156
    category boundaries, 62–7(F)
        extension of, 125
        unclear cases, 63–5, 92, 93, 99–100, 102–3, 158, 162–3
    characteristics of, 53–73
    as constructions, 158–9
    definition, 2, 4–6, 17–18
    and exemplar typicality, 58–62(F), 157–8
    learning new, 13
    levels of, 54, 57, 151
    and metaphors, 67–73
    methods of studying, 25–9
    need for, 1–3
    questions about, 13–16
    schema for, 180–1(F)
    and schemata, 51–2
    in semantic memory, 74–84
    and stimuli, 6
    teaching of, 14–15
    types of, 23–5, 71–2
    uses of, 6–13
    value of naming, 19
Conceptual differentiation, 117
Conceptual structures, 74, 119
    development of, 15–16, 126–30(F)
    in children, 130–1
Concrete concepts, 23–4, 103
Concrete level
    in concept learning, 105
Conjunctive concepts, 25
Conservative focusing, 110
Coordinate concepts
    as idealisations, 161
    teaching, 151–3(F)
Courses, planning and organising
    schemata teaching, 176–7
Cultural differences
    in basic-level concepts, 57
    in category boundaries, 65
    in concept acquisition, 121

Declarative representation, 15
Defining features, 21
    and category representation, 92, 93, 94, 99, 102, 103–4
    of coordinate concepts, 151
    shift from prototype to, 125–6
Definitions
    and concept learning, 114, 141
Dimensions of concepts, 23
Direct analogy, 164

Discovery learning
    and concept teaching, 145–6, 153–4
Discrimination, 19, 20, 124
Disjunctive concepts, 25

Education
    importance of concepts in, 8
Educational applications
    basic-level concepts, 57, 156–7
    models of semantic memory, 84
    typicality of concepts, 157
    vague category boundaries, 157–9
Educational implications
    of category representation, 106
    of schemata, 42–3(F)
    of story schemata, 50
    of typicality, 66–7
    of unclear boundaries, 66–7
Elaboration
    as memory strategy, 172
Elinor model
    and change schema, 182–3(F)
    and semantic memory, 83–4(F)
Enactive representation, 118, 135
Evaluation
    and concept learning, 147–50
    and concept mapping, 171
Event concepts, 23
Event schemata, 47
Evolutionary factors
    in concept learning, 119–20
Exemplar representation, 86, 100–3, 125
    teaching of, 159–63
Exemplars, 21
    of basic-level concepts, 55–6
    and concept learning, 108, 113, 115
    in concept teaching, 142–3, 145, 146–7
    of coordinate concepts, 151–2
    matched pairs of, 143–4(F), 146, 147
    typicality of, 58–62(F), 157–8
Experiential concepts, 71–2
Expository method
    of concept teaching, 145
    and discovery learning, 153

Family resemblance structures
    and exemplar typicality, 60–2(F), 158
Features of concepts, 21–2(F)
    characteristic, 92, 94, 126
    relations between, 92–3
    *see also* Defining features
Field-dependence and independence, 117
Focus gambling, 110
Formal level
    in concept learning, 105
Free-sort tasks, 117
    studies of concept learning, 26
Functional features, 21

Generalisation, 19–20, 124
Guided discovery, 154

Habituation techniques, 27–8, 130, 134
Holist learning styles, 183
Hypothesis-testing
  and concept learning, 109–11

Iconic representation, 135
Idealisations
  teaching, 160–2
Identity concepts, 6
Identity level
  in concept learning, 105
Imagery
  as memory strategy, 173–4
Individual differences
  in category representation, 104–5
  in concept learning, 116–18
Inferences
  and concepts, 8–9
Instances, 20–1
  and concept learning, 108–13
Instantiations of schemata, 32–3
Instructional text
  teaching schemata for, 185
Interviews
  studies of concept learning, 26

Keyword technique
  as memory strategy, 174
Kind concepts, 6

Language
  and concept development, 131–2
  and concept learning, 113–16
Learning
  and schemata, 44–5, 46(F)
Learning styles, 183

Macropropositions, 185
Matched pairs
  in concept teaching, 143–4(F), 146, 147
Meaningful recall, 44
Medical information
  schema for, 180
Memory
  and category representation, 15
  episodic, 77
  long-term, 77
  and schemata, 44–5, 46(F)
  strategies in concept teaching, 172–4
  working, 77
  *see also* Semantic memory
Metaphorical concepts, 71–2
Metaphors
  as advance-organisers, 177
  and concepts, 67–73
  definition, 67–9
  drawbacks of, 70–1
  effectiveness of, 165
  problems with, 168
  teaching concepts with, 163–9(F)
  using a cluster of, 167

Misconceptions, 186–99
  changing, 193–9(F)
  characteristics of, 186–7
  examples of, 187–90
  reasons for, 190–2
  ways of determining, 192
Motivation
  and concept learning, 138
Multi-dimensional scaling
  studies of concept learning, 26–7(F)

Narratives
  as memory strategy, 173
Natural concepts, 24–5
News reports
  teaching schemata for, 184

Object concepts, 23
Ontological concepts, 71, 72
Organisation of material
  and memory, 173

Partonomies
  definition, 11
  development in children, 130
  and schemata, 33–4(F)
Parts of speech, 23
Perception
  and schemata, 37–9(F)
Perceptual features, 21, 137
Person schemata, 47–8
Personal analogy, 164–5
Problem-solving
  and concepts, 12
Procedural representation, 15
Processes, and representations, 89
Propositions, 12, 75
Prototype representation, 86, 93–100(F), 102, 158
  teaching of, 159–63
Prototypes
  and concept learning, 111–12
  definition, 93
  development of, 124

Reception method
  of concept learning, 29
Reification of metaphors, 168
Relational features, 21, 137
Reports
  teaching schemata for, 184–5(T)
Representation
  changes in format and content, 125–6
  enactive, 118, 135
  formats in concept teaching, 144–5
  iconic, 135
  nature of, 86–90(F)
  *see also* Category representation

Scanning, 118
  in hypothesis-testing, 110

Scene schemata, 45–6
Schemata, 30–52
  characteristics of, 32–4, 176
  and comprehension, 39–43(F)
  and concepts, 51–2
  definition of, 31–2(F)
  development of, 122–35
  disadvantages of using, 50–1
  educational implications, 42–3(F)
  evolution of, 190
  memory and learning, 44–5, 46(F)
  selection, 36–7
  in semantic memory, 74–84
  teaching of, 175–99
  types of, 45–50
  uses of, 37–45
School-taught concepts, 137
Science
  and metaphors, 70
Scientific concepts
  and hypothesis-testing, 111
  misconceptions regarding, 187–9
Scientific reports
  teaching schemata for, 184–5(T)
Scientific theories
  schema for, 181–2(T)
Selection method
  of concept learning, 29
Selective looking, 27
Semantic feature hypothesis, 132
Semantic memory
  characteristics of, 75–7
  concept and schemata organisation, 74–84
  Elinor model, 83–4(F)
  spreading activation model, 80–2(F)
  theories of, 77–84
  TLC model of, 78–80(F)
Semantic priming, 82–3
Serialist learning styles, 183
Spatial concepts, 71, 72
Spreading activation model, 80–3
  and semantic memory, 80–3(F)
Stereotypes, 9, 97
Stimuli
  and concepts, 6
Stimulus domains, 25
Story schemata, 48–50(F,T)
  teaching, 183
Structural concepts, 71, 72
Students
  and change schema, 182–3
  changing existing schemata, 185–99
  and concept mapping, 171
  and schemata teaching, 178–9
Subordinate concepts, 54, 151
Superordinate concepts, 54, 57, 151

Synonyms
  and concept learning, 114–15

Taxonomies, 9–11(F)
  and basic-level concepts, 14, 53–5(F)
  and concept mapping, 169
  development of, 126–30(F)
    in children, 130–1, 132
Teachable language comprehender (TLC)
  and semantic memory, 78–80(F)
Teachers
  and concept mapping, 170–1
  and schemata teaching, 178–9
Teaching concepts, 14–15
  analogies in, 163–9(F)
  and concept development, 123
  concept mapping, 169–72(F)
  coordinate concepts, 151–3, 161–2
  discovery learning, 153–4
  exemplars and non-exemplars, 142–3, 145, 146–7
  memory strategies in, 172–4
  metaphors in, 69–70, 163–9(F)
  need for, 139(T)
  objectives, 139–41, 139–41(T)
  prototype and exemplar representations, 159–63
  subject disciplines, 139(T)
  traditional methods, 136–54
  *see also* Concept learning
Teaching schemata, 175–99
  abstract schemata, 179–85
  changing existing schemata, 185–99
  sample lessons, 196–9(F)
Text, schemata for, 183–5(F)
  schemata for, 183–5(F)
Textbooks
  schemata teaching, 176–7
Typicality of concepts, 58–62(F)
  in category representation, 92, 93, 99, 102
  educational applications, 157

Verbatim recall, 44

Word and concept systems
  in semantic memory, 75
  in the spreading activation model, 80–3(F)
  in the TLC model, 78–80(F)
Word association
  and misconceptions, 192
Word definitions
  schema for, 180–1(F)
Words
  and concept development, 131–2
  and concept learning, 138
  and concepts, 18–19
  meanings of, 19
    and concept learning, 115, 132